D1739068

A Two-Way Street

*The Institutional Dynamics of the
Modern Administrative State*

A Two-Way Street

*The Institutional Dynamics of the
Modern Administrative State*

George A. Krause

University of Pittsburgh Press

Published by the University of Pittsburgh Press, Pittsburgh, Pa. 15261

Copyright © 1999, University of Pittsburgh Press

Manufactured in the United States of America

Printed on acid-free paper

10 9 8 7 6 5 4 3 2 1

LIBRARY OF CONGRESS CATALOGING-IN-PUBLICATION DATA

Krause, George A., 1965–

   A two-way street : the institutional dynamics of the modern administrative state /   George A. Krause.

     p. cm.

   Originally presented as the author's thesis (Ph. D.—West Virginia University, 1992)

   Includes bibliographical references and index.

   ISBN 0-8229-4102-3 (cloth : perm. paper)

    1. Administrative agencies—United States.   2. Administrative agencies—United   States

Case studies. 3. Bureaucracy—United States.   4. Bureaucracy—United States   Case stud-

ies.   I. Title.

   JK421 .K72 1999

   351.73—dc21   99-6440

                                                         CIP

A CIP catalog record for this book is available from the British Library.

This book is dedicated to three generations of Western Pennsylvania women: Beatrice, Leona, Candida, Sherry Ann, and LeeAnne

Contents

Figures and Tables

Figures

Tables

Acknowledgments

This book began in the late fall of 1992 as the beginnings of my doctoral dissertation thesis while I was a doctoral student in Political Science at West Virginia University. During the course of the next twenty-one months, my dissertation committee prodded me to work hard in improving this product. I owe a considerable debt to Neil Berch, Robert DiClerico, Robert Duval, Allan Hammock, David Williams, and John Kilwein for their time and assistance in allowing me to pursue this endeavor. In addition, I wish to thank the Academic Research Office at West Virginia University and the Gerald R. Ford Presidential Library for providing generous research support during the dissertation phase of this project. Their financial support funded both my research travel and my initial statistical software needs.

Besides my dissertation committee at West Virginia University, there are a number of individuals who provided invaluable advice and insights on earlier versions of various portions of this book. I am extremely grateful for having colleagues such as Peri Arnold, Dan Carpenter, John Freeman, Scott Furlong, Tom Hammond, Anne Khademian, Ken Meier, Chris Plein, and Bert Rockman. Each of these individuals provided me with thoughtful suggestions and criticisms of my work in its earlier stages. I am also very appreciative for the time and effort of both the anonymous readers who reviewed this manuscript for the University of Pittsburgh Press. Their insightful comments have been extremely beneficial in improving both the substance and the style of this manuscript. Although not every piece of advice appears in the final draft of this book, almost all of their suggestions were either incorporated or addressed in some manner. A portion of this book manuscript draws upon an earlier journal article on the subject, entitled "The Institutional Dynamics of Policy Administration: Bureaucratic Influence over Securities Regulation," that was published in the *American Journal of Political Science* (November 1996, 1083–121).

Besides the critical inspection of my work conducted by the aforementioned political scientists, there were many other people who were generous in sharing their time, talents, and expertise with me. Individuals in the Securities and Exchange Commission (SEC), Antitrust Division (AD) of the Department of Justice, the Congressional Budget Office, the Office of Management and Budget, and the House Committee staffs offered insights that informed my research in a substantive manner during various interviews conducted in June 1993. Finally, Niels Aaboe, Eileen Kiley, Kathy Meyer, Hope Kurtz, and their colleagues at the University of Pittsburgh Press deserve a special debt of gratitude for assisting me in transforming a dissertation into a publishable manuscript. This book is a direct reflection of their unlimited patience and clear direction. Of course, none of the individuals acknowledged for their assistance bear responsibility for any shortcomings found in this book since these lie solely with the author.

As I get older, I have greater appreciation for the lively political, economic, and social issue discussions that I engaged in with my mother, Leona, and sisters, Candy and Sherry, while I was growing up. Thank you for allowing your son and younger brother to express his opinion on these subjects at a young age, even when they differed from yours in some instances. Whether it was critically assessing the arguments contained in this book or being patient when I needed to work late into the evening (and often early into the morning) my wife, LeeAnne, has been a constant source of love, encouragement, support, and good humor. Finally, I would like to thank God for making the entire process over the past six years an enriching journey.

A Two-Way Street

The Institutional Dynamics of the
Modern Administrative State

Chapter 1

Introduction

An Overview of Administrative Politics

Policy administration is the central role of public bureaucracy. Arguably, the most important research question at the nexus of public administration and political institutions is whether politicians control the bureaucracy or the bureaucracy possesses independent authority from democratic institutions of governance. The answer has varied during the intellectual evolution of thought on the role of politics in policy administration over the past century.

Scholars at the turn of the twentieth century made the normative assertion that politics must not encroach on the business of public administration (Wilson 1887; Goodnow 1900). These progressive reformers were responding to political conditions of the late nineteenth century. During this era, bureaucratic positions in the federal government were dispensed to those with connections to the political party bosses, mostly from the state level. This procedure, in turn, had ramifications for the direction and content of public policy in two meaningful ways. First, public administrators of the 1800s came under much greater political influence since their positions were often obtained through cronyism. Second, these bureaucrats did not have expertise in policy administration. In response to both conditions and the rapid rise in the size and scope of the federal government, the progressive reformers and many others in government began to call for greater expertise and political neutrality in policy administration. Such changes would provide a more effective means to carry out the policy intentions of institutions of democratic governance (Knott and Miller 1987; Skowronek 1982).

Beginning with the writings of Dwight Waldo (1948), Paul Appleby (1949), David Truman (1951), and Norton Long (1952), those studying public administration within political science began to examine the positive aspects of agency-political relationships in American government. This strand of research argues that, because of the immense size and scope of bureaucratic institutions, politicians in essence could not easily manipulate or influence administrative behavior. These scholars maintain that policy administration is largely unimpeded by electoral institutions because of the increasing fragmentation of American political institutions, and the greater delegation of responsibility to the bureaucracy. Thus, bureaucratic organizations are seen not only as being insensitive to influence emanating from political institutions but also as containing their own policy preferences. Extensions concerning "bureaucratic dominance" produced specific instances or cases where bureaucratic agencies are either impervious to the desires of politicians, or able to alter the original intentions of elected officials during implementation of public policy (Aberbach and Rockman 1976; Crozier 1964; Downs 1967; Freeman 1965; Lowi 1969; Wilson 1980). Political institutions did not display much interest in matters of policy administration (Dodd and Schott 1979; Ogul 1976; Scher 1963), thereby further strengthening the role of bureaucratic institutions in policy implementation.

Beginning in the early 1980s, Barry Mitnick (1980), Barry Weingast (Weingast and Moran 1982, 1983; Weingast 1981, 1984), and Terry Moe (1982, 1985a) collectively asserted that bureaucratic institutions were in fact influenced (or possibly even controlled) by elected officials. This assertion spawned a host of works espousing political control over the bureaucracy employing the principal-agent paradigm. The main tenet of this framework was that politicians not only take a keen interest in policy administration but are also successfully able to exert influence over the bureaucracy because of their constitutional position as superior to bureaucracy. A vast amount of empirical evidence has lent credence to these theoretical assertions (Hedge and Scicchitano 1994; Rothenberg 1994; Thompson and Scicchitano 1985; Scholz and Wei 1986; Scholz, Twombly, and Headrick 1991; Wood 1988, 1990, 1991, 1992; Wood and Anderson 1993; Wood and Waterman 1991, 1993, 1994).

Concurrently, however, there has also been a backlash to the political control thesis by various students of public bureaucracy whose epistemological approaches range from formal methods (Bendor, Taylor, and Van Gaalen 1985,

1987; Hammond and Knott 1996) to quantitative-empirical analyses (Eisner and Meier 1990; Ringquist 1995) to descriptive inquiries (Eisner 1991; Khademian 1992; Knott and Miller 1987). This literature reasserts the position of earlier scholars from various traditions within public administration and stresses that there are intrinsic limits to politicians' attempts to control the bureaucracy.

The extensive body of research has produced conflicting findings concerning the nature of agency-political relations. Part of this controversy may be attributed to studies examining different administrative organizations/policy areas, theoretical models that are oversimplified, and various discordant empirical model specifications. A potential problem with research on this subject lies with its narrow focus on the determinants of agency behavior as a procedure to test hypotheses concerning bureaucratic autonomy and political control.[1] The problem is especially disconcerting given that existing research arrives at different conceptual (theoretical) models of what determines administrative behavior. Although the bureaucratic politics perspective, for instance, does recognize that bureaucracy is subject to external controls by politicians and environmental factors outside the scope of agency influence (Eisner and Meier 1990; Eisner 1991; Meier 1987; Rourke 1984), it mostly accentuates the role played by bureaucratic and organizational factors in affecting agency performance. Principal-agent models assert, on a theoretical level, that information advantages on the part of administrative agencies are negatively related to the level of political control they experience. These effects may range from ineffectual (Niskanen perspective) to unabridged political control (congressional dominance perspective of Weingast and associates).[2] Moreover, these models suggest that the use of monitoring devices and incentive structures can reduce this information advantage (asymmetry) to varying degrees.[3]

The theoretical models used to describe administrative politics are naive, since they fail to consider agency-political relations as a system. Existing studies are not capable of arriving at the general structure of behavioral relations between the president, Congress, and the bureaucracy, because of their simplifying assumptions (for exceptions, see Hammond and Knott 1993, 1996). Research does not provide an adequate treatment of how the administrative behavior of political principals is shaped by administrative institutions as well by the larger policy environment.

A more general and unified theoretical apparatus must be set forth to allow for the vast continuum of agency-political relationships ranging from bureaucratic influence to political influence (control). Recouching these theoretical arguments in broader terms as a system can provide us with a more realistic portrayal of administrative politics. The bureaucratic autonomy view implies that there are substantial limitations associated with external (political) controls over the bureaucracy, while the political control outlook maintains that external (political) controls serve as the dominant force driving agency behavior. *Most scholars infer that agency-political relations fall somewhere between the polar opposite positions on the bureaucratic autonomy/political domination continuum; however, there is great disagreement over the actual point on the continuum that accurately describes the nature of political-bureaucratic relations.*[4] The model presented in this study allows for a variety of agency-political relations expressed in existing theories. The subsequent empirical findings generated in this study are less subject to criticism than results from previous studies since this model is less restrictive in its behavioral assumptions, thus lending a more accurate and balanced portrayal of agency-political relations.[5]

A major objective of this study is to show that previous formulations for arriving at a point along this continuum have been too simplistic. Both the theoretical framework and the research design proposed in this study will give us a more general account of political-bureaucratic relations. Furthermore, the theoretical model presented in the next chapter can be utilized for different types of administrative agencies that exhibit various types of characteristics and relationships with political principals.[6] At the heart of the thesis proposed in this study is the view that agency-political relationships are interactively complex and evolve dynamically over time. What follows in the next section is a detailed discussion and critique of two competing perspectives on administrative behavior in a democracy: (1) *bureaucratic autonomy theories,* which posit that administrative institutions are able to behave in a manner that reflects considerable discretion or leeway from elected officials; and (2) *political control theories,* which reflect the notion of an overhead theory of democracy (Redford 1969) in which administrative agencies faithfully respond to the wishes of democratic institutions.

Bureaucratic Autonomy Versus Political Control Theories of the Administrative State

Bureaucratic Autonomy Theories of Administrative Politics

The bureaucratic autonomy perspective maintains that administrative agencies possess a significant amount of discretion because of various factors such as the vagueness of legislative statutes, constituent ties, administrative values, and bureaucratic incentives (Eisner and Meier 1990). Discretion provides agencies the opportunity to alter original policy intentions during the implementation stage (Aberbach and Rockman 1976; Appleby 1949; Crozier 1964; Downs 1967; Lowi 1969; Meier 1987; Rourke 1984). The fragmented nature of the American political system diffuses power to the subunits of government (Freeman 1965; Ogul 1976; Rourke 1984), thus granting administrative agencies even greater discretion. There are four general sources of bureaucratic autonomy (or discretion) that can occur.

First, there may be *indifference on the part of political principals* regarding matters of policy administration. For instance, some scholars claim that congressional oversight efforts over agency activities are generally both sporadic and ineffective (for an opposing viewpoint, see Aberbach 1990), since specific oversight activities such as formal hearings and investigations are undertaken infrequently and often with very little impact on agency behavior (Dodd and Schott 1979; Ogul 1976; Scher 1963; Wilson 1980; for a different perspective regarding congressional oversight activity and its impact on agency behavior see McCubbins and Schwartz 1984). Likewise, presidents will not find it in their best interests to expend large amounts of precious political capital engaging in bureaucratic policy making when the expected net payoff of involvement with respect to regulatory policy is low (Cary 1967; Kohlmeier 1969; Noll 1971; Ripley and Franklin 1991; Weingast 1981).

The second major source of bureaucratic autonomy pertains to the discretion-enhancing effects of *bureaucratic professionalization.* This originates from agencies' level and utilization of specialized knowledge, that is, policy expertise. To be specific, agency professionalization is a source of administra tive strength that results in bureaucratic autonomy/discretion (Eisner and Meier 1990; Eisner 1991, 1992; Kelman 1980; Katzmann 1980; Meier 1987; Mosher 1968; Rourke 1984; Worsham, Eisner, and Ringquist 1997). This is attributable to the creation of an environment where the predominant skills and outlook of agency members—based on occupational and/or academic categories—invariably shape the organization's behavior. A unique professional/occupational ethos may exist for members within a profession (Wilson 1989). Also, individuals within any given profession will view both problems and their solutions differently than others will, based upon their occupational training and/or educational experiences (Eisner 1991).[7] This topic has received special attention, given the executive managerial changes in the federal government (via the Office of Management and Budget [OMB]) that began to take hold during the late 1970s and early 1980s in order to advance economic modes of analysis in policy administration (Derthick and Quirk 1985a, 1985b; Eads and Fix 1984; Eisner and Meier 1990; Eisner 1991, 1993; Marcus 1980).[8]

Third, the joint effects of *decentralized decision making* and *increased political competition* among elected officials is another source of autonomy for administrative agencies. This is garnered by the joint product of increased decentralized decision making and greater competition among political principals. During the past century, decision making has become increasingly decentralized, for both presidents and Congress. For the presidency, decentralized decision making has been the product of the growth in the size of the executive branch, making control of the bureaucracy a more difficult task. Institutional development, in turn, has created obstacles for presidential administration attempts to control the bureaucracy. This complex environment may lead to instances where agencies will be able to play competing political principals against one another to gain greater autonomy (Bryner 1987; Dahl and Lindblom 1953; Hammond and Knott 1993, 1996; Wilson 1989).

Finally, *information asymmetries between agencies and political principals* are the final source of bureaucratic autonomy. This perspective is heavily steeped in the principal-agent paradigm's claim that a significant portion of an agency's power (to varying degrees of effectiveness) is derived from information asymmetries (Banks and Weingast 1992; Bendor, Taylor, and Van Gaalen 1985, 1987; Miller and Moe 1983; Moe 1984; Niskanen 1971, 1975; Woolley 1993).[9] Information regarding the agency's intentions (e.g., honesty, personal goals, policy positions) and its actual performance cannot be perfectly foreseen by politicians because of (1) politicians' limited expertise, and (2) the high transaction costs associated with obtaining this information.[10]

Although these major sources of bureaucratic autonomy all contain substantive merit, they are presented in such a manner that they understate agency power in one way, while overstating it in another. On one hand, advocates of the bureaucratic politics perspective base their theories on concepts of political indifference, administrative professionalization, and decentralized decision making within democratic institutions. Thus, agencies are viewed as possessing insulated autonomy from outside political forces in terms of the bottom line—administrative policy outputs.[11] This line of reasoning implies that agencies operate in an environment where political principals (such as the president and Congress) are not able to respond systematically to variations in agency behavior. As a result, systematic empirical findings consistent with the bureaucratic politics perspective are not based upon the direct behavior of administrative agencies but instead reflect an indirect focus on agency behavior via internal administrative-based factors (Eisner and Meier 1990; Eisner 1991, 1992; Ringquist 1995).

On the other hand, principal-agent (i.e., information asymmetry) explanations of bureaucratic autonomy fail to consider the importance of politics and institutions. For instance, these models fail to acknowledge the distinct possibility that Congress could be the agency's superior in the hierarchy of governmental authority (Moe 1984).[12] Niskanen's view of agency-political relationships deems politicians unable to reduce information asymmetries via adaptation.[13] The shortcomings associated with bureaucratic autonomy theories do not mean that this perspective is erroneous. Rather, these explanations of agency behavior have not been adequately investigated with respect to macro political-bureaucratic relations in a modern administrative state that embodies dynamic interaction among government institutions.

Political Control Theories of Administrative Politics

The past decade or so has seen many convincing arguments that significant political control is exerted over administrative agencies by democratic institutions. Many of these recent arguments have been cast within the principal-agent paradigm originally developed in the areas of both law and financial economics. Principal-agent based models of political control (or influence) state that the preferences of elected officials (principals) are imposed on administrative organizations (agents) through a variety of dependent relationships (Moe 1984; Weingast 1984; Weingast and Moran 1983).[14] Terry Moe (1984) adds that politicians seek control, while agencies have discretion. According to Moe, bureaucratic activity (measured in terms of policy outputs) will generally conform to the policy preferences of both the president and the relevant congressional committees because of monitoring devices and incentive structures employed by these principals (Breton and Wintrobe 1975; McCubbins and Schwartz 1984).[15] In other words, principal-agent models espousing political control generally presume that bureaucratic autonomy/discretion is severely constrained because the agency is held accountable to political institutions. Therefore, external controls over the bureaucracy are perceived as the dominant force motivating agency behavior. These external democratic controls may take the form of congressional dominance, presidential control, and multiple (political) principal control.

Scholars espousing a "congressional dominance" perspective of agency-legislative relations have focused on congressional-bureaucratic relations most-ly within the principal-agent paradigm. They contend that a congressional-electoral imperative is the key force underlying bureaucratic policy making and implementation since members of Congress (MCs) provide a flow of policy benefits. In return for their services, MCs will receive electoral support from both constituency groups and voters (Mayhew 1974; Fiorina 1977, 1981, 1982; Weingast and Moran 1982, 1983; Weingast 1981, 1984).[16] Constituent groups specialize in monitoring agency behavior under this arrangement. These groups use monitoring as a device to inform MCs of agency behavior. McCubbins and Schwartz (1984) contend that MCs are effectively able to respond to this constituent sentiment (termed a "decibel meter"). Agency responsiveness to congressional wishes is also reinforced by forms of retribution such as sanctions and incentives. Bureaucratic discretion is not much of a concern within the congressional dominance framework since (1) Congress sets up specialized bodies (i.e., subcommittees) to mitigate shirking, and (2) it creates only the number of agencies that it can reasonably handle.[17] Much of this research claims that Congress can elicit bureaucratic responsiveness via *ex post* controls such as the appropriations process, legislative statutes, influence over appointment selections, and congressional oversight activity; or through *ex ante* techniques of control that are employed by political principals as a means of structuring agency choices before agency action takes place—for example, procedural requirements[18] and original legislative hearings.[19] Empirical support has been found for congressional influence over bureaucratic behavior through various *ex post* mechanisms (Faith, Leavens, and Tollison 1982; Grier 1991; Moe 1985a; Miller and Moe 1983; Scholz and Wei 1986; Scholz, Twombly, and Headrick 1991; Weingast 1984; Weingast and Moran 1983; Wood and Anderson 1993; Wood and Waterman 1994).

A second form of political control over the bureaucracy manifests itself through presidential behavior. There are a number of ways in which presidents can attempt to influence agency behavior. First, persuasion—in the form of presidential rhetoric (Wood and Waterman 1993) or symbolic politics (Twombly 1992)—can be effective in directing bureaucratic agency behavior. Second, presidents can attempt to control agency behavior through executive reorganization efforts. These actions do not generally either result in significant savings or alter agency behavior in a desired way (Arnold 1986; Gormley 1989; Meier 1980; March and Olsen 1984, 1989; Pfiffner 1988; Seidman and Gilmour 1986—but see Hult 1987). Finally, most studies conclude that blunt *ex post* instruments of presidential control—in the form of appointments and budgets/resources—across a wide range of administrative agencies and structures can play a potent role in shaping agency behavior (Bendor and Moe 1985; Carpenter 1996; Chappell, Havrilesky, and McGregor 1993; Cohen 1985; Moe 1982, 1985a, 1985b; Padgett 1980, 1981; Scholz and Wei 1986; Scholz, Twombly, and Headrick 1991; Stewart and Cromartie 1982; Wood 1988, 1990; Wood and Waterman 1991, 1993; Wood and Anderson 1993). There is ample empirical evidence that presidents play the main role in staffing the top levels of the bureaucracy (Meier 1987; Moe 1987a, 1987b; Nathan 1983; Waterman 1989).[20]

West and Cooper (1989–1990) assert that the president has been more powerful vis-à-vis Congress in recent years. This is not surprising for a number of reasons. First, the Civil Service Reform Act of 1978 created the Senior Executive Service, which enhanced presidential control over top administrators. Second, the creation of the OMB in 1971 (replacing the Bureau of the Budget) has served to expand the presidential sphere of influence over the administration of policy. OMB has been used increasingly as an instrument of presidential control and influence (Nathan 1983; Waterman 1989; Wood and Waterman 1994). Many bureaucratic agencies and their programs have been created (and administered) under the auspices of the president via various means such as executive orders and administration-drafted legislative proposals.[21] Recent presidents have been more concerned with the administration of policies than their predecessors (Cooper and West 1988; Durant 1992; Moe 1985b; Nathan 1983; Pfiffner 1988; Waterman 1989; West and Cooper 1989–1990).

The most fruitful research on the subject incorporates multiple political principals in both their theoretical frameworks and empirical model specifications. This refinement has generated a more comprehensive view of the concept of political control of administrative institutions. The empirical evidence corroborates this approach by showing that multiple political principals—consisting of some combination of Congress, president, and/or the courts—control (or influence) agency behavior (Meier 1993a; Moe 1985a; Ringquist 1995; Rothenberg 1994; Scholz and Wei 1986; Scholz, Twombly, and Headrick 1991; Wood 1990; Wood and Anderson 1993; Wood and Waterman 1991, 1993). A general representation of these models (including Congress and the president as political principals) is depicted in figure 1.1. This figure shows that the president, Congress, and environmental factors independently exert an effect on the behavior of administrative agencies. Such a model implies that these causal factors are not affected by one another, nor are they influenced by agency behavior since causation can only flow in one direction. Unfortunately, the formulations of this model provide limited and narrow insights into the various intricacies related to the multiple principal arguments. For instance, which principals are generally more dominant? Does this vary according to agency and/or institutional design? Under which conditions will each principal dominate?[22] Multiple political control theories are an improvement over earlier attempts to describe the involvement of primary governmental actors/institutions, yet fail to provide a number of disparate pieces to solving this puzzle.

There are, however, three main conceptual problems with most of the current principal-agent models of political control over the bureaucracy.[23] First, this paradigm fails to recognize the role of internal organizational factors such as expertise, leadership, cohesion, political support, administrative capabilities and administrative values (in terms of training or education of agency personnel)[24] that influence agency behavior.[25] By ignoring these internal bureaucratic factors that have been brought to our attention by a host of public administration scholars (Eisner 1991, 1992; Eisner and Meier 1990; March and Olsen 1984, 1989; Meier 1987; Mosher 1968; Rourke 1984), the results obtained from principal-agent models of political control over the bureaucracy appear incomplete. The second and more important problem relating to the present conceptualizations of political control models pertains to behavioral organizational theory and the conduct of public administration in the American political system. Past research within the principal-agent based political control paradigm implies that political authority is characterized by command or fiat, as classical organization theory posits (Weber 1946). In other words, one key assumption of such models is that elected officials impose a natural hierarchy on bureaucratic agencies. In reality, the nature and degree of success of these authoritative relations will rest upon some level of agreement between relevant political and bureaucratic actors (Barnard 1938; Simon 1947).[26] Thus, principal-agent (and political-bureaucratic) relationships are most likely to fall somewhere between a strict hierarchical relationship and a market-oriented structure (Williamson 1975, 1985). The study undertaken here attempts to test the hierarchy assumption found in the existing treatments of the political control of the bureaucracy literature. Finally, the fundamental basis of the principal-agency problem subsumes that there exists both a strategic principal as well as a strategic agent, interacting in a dynamic manner (Mitnick 1980; Perrow 1986). Thus, existing treatments of the principal-agent model of politi-

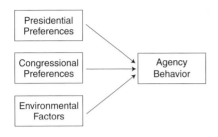

FIGURE 1.1 A General Representation of Multiple Political Principal Models (President and Congress)

cal control over bureaucratic agencies do not allow the latter institutions to behave in the manner originally proscribed according to this theory. This project, however, does test for principal-agent relations in a manner consistent with the original intent of these theories.

Agency-political relationships are both dynamic and interactively complex, with political principals often affecting each other's policy preferences, and the agency helping to shape the policy behavior of their political principals in certain instances.[27] Existing theoretical and empirical characterizations of the relationship between political and bureaucratic institutions are both incomplete and misleading. The next section sheds light on the nature of institutional interaction within a dynamic systems framework.

A Dynamic Systems Model of Administrative Politics

The controversy surrounding both the political control and bureaucratic autonomy theories of administrative politics has been at center stage for those studying public bureaucracy within political science. Because administration often determines whether policy has its intended impact (Mazmanian and Sabatier 1983; Meier 1987; Rourke 1984), it has taken on considerable theoretical and substantive importance. Therefore, the manner in which policy is administered by bureaucratic institutions will have a sizable effect on the content and outcomes of public policy.

Existing studies of administrative politics focus on the determinants of agency behavior to demonstrate whether political control of bureaucratic institutions or bureaucratic autonomy exists. However, this approach to the issue has three notable flaws. First, policy administration is strictly equated with agency performance or behavior. Prior theoretical and empirical research has treated agency behavior as a dependent concept that is able to respond to political stimuli only in the form of preferences or behavior (Carpenter 1996; Eisner and Meier 1990; Moe 1982, 1985a; Scholz, Twombly, and Headrick 1991; Weingast and Moran 1983; Wood 1988; Wood and Anderson 1992; Wood and Waterman 1991, 1993, 1994). Even research that espouses the bureaucratic autonomy thesis places its trust in finding this condition *indirectly* either through internal administrative factors that result in policy change (most notably administrative professionalization [Eisner and Meier 1990; Eisner 1991]) or through static formal models used to analyze the limitations of political control (Bendor, Taylor, and Van Gaalen 1985, 1987; Hammond and Knott 1993, 1996). Nonetheless, the current body of research presumes that politicians can shape administrative behavior, while the opposite does not hold true.

Those studying agency-political relationships ignore the importance of understanding how the behavior of political principals can be influenced by administrative agencies. Existing models of bureaucratic performance tacitly assume that political preferences may influence agency activity, but that the opposite possibility does not exist. Such an assumption, even if it is implicit and unintentional, is tenuous at best given what has been established about how public policy is created. Policy administration is the product of joint (endogenous) interaction between governmental organizations and political institutions, subject to environmental considerations (Anderson 1990; Dye 1966; Jones 1984; Meier 1987; Rourke 1984; Truman 1951). If one agrees with this widely held belief, then it is necessary to analyze not only which factors determine or shape administrative behavior but also what considerations affect the behavior of political principals. A preferable (and more direct) course of action in attempting to address this question is to examine the dynamic behavior of administrative agencies interacting with other political institutions. By doing so, one can explore not just whether agency behavior is responsive to the desires of elected officials, but also whether the agencies can influence the behavior of political principals. Therefore, instead of being able to determine only whether a bureaucratic agency is autonomous, one can also find out if it exhibits power in policy administration (or the policy process) that extends beyond its own organizational apparatus.

The second shortcoming of existing models of bureaucratic behavior is their restrictive (in some instances nonexistent) view of causal relations among democratic institutions involved in policy administration. This study deals with this issue by relaxing the assumption of independence of the president and Congress (with respect to its relationship with the bureaucracy) by allowing for dynamic interaction between political institutions. The framework presented here acknowledges interaction between political institutions. Research on budgetary politics (Cox, Hager, and Lowery 1993; Kiewiet and McCubbins 1985, 1988, 1991) and research on legislative politics (Bond and Fleisher 1990; Light 1991; Peterson 1991) note that there exists a strong relationship between the president and Congress. Quite remarkably, past research on administrative politics has generally implied that elected officials have *separate, independent* (from one another) impacts on agency behavior. This implicit assumption precludes the possibility that these democratic institutions' behavior toward an agency may also partly be a reflection of each other's behavior or preferences.

Strong reliance on the independence assumption between political actors has severe consequences that may lead to faulty inferences and conclusions. For instance, if presidential behavior is being influenced by congressional behavior, then the decision-making calculus of the former institution will partly reflect not only its preferences (and possibly the behavior and/or preferences of the agency) but also congressional desires—this is especially true with regard to agency budgets. It is well documented elsewhere that presidents (via the OMB) play a large agenda-setting role for congressional deliberations regarding appropriations (Davis, Dempster, and Wildavsky 1966, 1971, 1974). In fact, Kiewiet and McCubbins (1988, 1991) contend that final appropriations for domestic agencies and programs are heavily influenced by president/OMB budget estimates submitted to Congress. If this is true, then it is apparent that the institutional behavior for these political principals may well be dynamically interrelated. The framework proposed in this study can directly test these assertions in an empirical manner.

The final shortcoming of existing models of agency behavior suggests that agency response to political stimulus occurs in an immediate (same period) or manner. Recent studies, such as Wood and Waterman (1993, 1994) and Carpenter (1996) aptly note that this conceptualization is not consistent with classic works on organizational theory, which claim that administrative entities cannot change behavior instantaneously because they do not have perfect information-processing capabilities (Simon 1947, 1955; March and Simon 1958). Thus, bureaucratic agencies will exhibit tendencies toward inertia concerning adaptation to their larger environment (Crozier 1964; Downs 1967). Some of this inertia may come from previous commitments made by the agency (Kaufman 1981). The recent investigations take this inertia into account by constructing models of the bureaucracy's lagged adaptation to its larger policy environment.

At the same time, however, research on the bureaucracy in political science has not addressed the possibility of sophisticated response. This form of behavior is distinct from past studies on this subject since the focus is on how unexpected deviations in behavior or preferences (such as *innovations* or *shocks*) affect the behavior of institutions within the governmental system. Relations that reflect this type of behavior have been left unexplored by existing research. Although agencies and elected officials use previous years' information as a means to gauge behavior in a deterministic fashion, there may be instances where agencies and/or political institutions respond to unanticipated changes within the larger institutional environment. For example, an agency's current regulatory enforcement effort may not only respond to past budgetary signals, as the concept of dynamic adaptation inferred by bounded rationality would indicate, but also respond to policy perturbations among these institutions, thus reflecting sophisticated behavior. This perspective is consistent with, yet distinct from, formal research on public policy that views individuals and/or institutions as operating in a strategic manner by behaving rationally (Austen-Smith 1987; Bendor and Moe 1985, 1986; Bendor, Taylor, and Van Gaalen 1985, 1987; Hammond and Knott 1993, 1996; Miller and Moe 1983). The empirical findings of a recent study investigating the policy subsystem dynamics of commercial bank regulation in the United States demonstrate that sophisticated and strategic behavior among institutional participants exists beyond lagged adaptation that reflects bounded rationality (Krause 1997).[28]

The framework of analysis proposed in this study attempts to extend our knowledge of how administrative agencies and democratic institutions are related to one another when it comes to policy administration. To reiterate, the three cornerstones of the dynamic systems model of administrative politics proposed in this study are as follows:

1. Mutual adaptation (endogeneity) between elected officials and bureaucratic institutions may exist. Simply, the preferences of political principals may affect the behavior of the administrative agency in question; but the opposite may also hold. This aspect implies that relations between the president, Congress, and the bureaucracy are dynamically interrelated.

2. Elected officials (i.e., president and Congress) do not necessarily behave or form preferences in isolation from one another. Instead, the behavior of political institutions may be influenced by one another in an endogenous fashion.

3. Each institution will operate in a sophisticated manner on one level by behaving strategically through (a) initiating unanticipated changes in behavior (often referred to as *policy innovations* or *shocks* or *perturbations*), and (b) re-

sponding to such behavior in some manner. Sophisticated behavior between any set of institutions is distinct from expected or anticipated forms postulated in prior research.

Each of these three components suggests that administrative politics is best understood when conceptualized as a dynamic system of interdependent institutions, which respond to one another, and also to events and conditions within each institution and in the larger policy environment. This study attempts to uncover the complexity and actual dynamics inherent in administrative politics, findings that are not considered in existing studies.

The theoretical framework presented in this book involves the quantitative analysis of both budgetary and enforcement data. The budgetary data represents the budgetary preferences of political principals (president and Congress) with respect to the amount of vigor they wish to see in agencies that are enforcing laws. These concepts are represented by presidential/OMB budget requests and congressional appropriations for any given administrative entity. The regulatory enforcement data is captured through the use of aggregate policy-output measures that usually dominate studies of administrative politics and policy implementation. These measures not only contain merit for political scientists but are also verified by interviews with relevant government actors.[29] The main advantage of employing these types of measures is that they can generate a portrait of institutional behavior by the president, Congress, and the bureaucracy in a historical context. Another benefit of employing these type of measures is that they make possible the testing of this framework in nonregulatory policy environments, since budgets and policy outputs tend to reflect the behavior of political principals and bureaucratic agencies in most, if not all, areas of policy administration.[30] This model is utilized to analyze the "two-way street" of contractual authority inherent when considering the institutional dynamics of the modern administrative state that has been noted in classic public bureaucracy works by both Barnard (1938) and Simon (1947).[31]

Outline of This Study and Concluding Remarks

Chapter 2 presents the dynamic systems model of administrative politics. It not only presents a more detailed discussion of the finer aspects of this theoretical framework but also lends some substantive examples and demonstrates why the dynamic systems model proposed in this investigation is a more appropriate and realistic way of examining the relationships between elected officials and bureaucrats. Chapter 3 involves a brief, historical, background overview of the two agencies to be investigated in this study—the Securities and Exchange Commission (SEC) and the Antitrust Division of the Department of Justice—and of the discordant findings of past research examining these policy areas. Chapter 4 briefly explores the limitations of past research and then presents the empirical testing of the dynamic systems model of administrative politics using data from both case studies. Chapter 5 addresses the larger significance of the dynamic systems model of administrative politics for the study of agency-political relationships as the model relates to democratic governance in the modern administrative state. This concluding chapter summarizes the portrait drawn from this analysis, explores the implications for the administration of public policy in a democratic system of government such as the United States, and discusses how this framework can help facilitate future research investigating the politics of the modern administrative state.

There have been great strides made within political science over the past fifteen years to enhance our knowledge of agency-political relationships. The lack of theoretical unity displayed in administrative politics research reflects the disparate findings often encountered. This shortcoming has led some scholars to suggest that a general theory of administrative behavior for federal agencies is not attainable (Wilson 1989). Kenneth Meier (1993b: 6) contends that public administration/administrative politics research needs to address this dilemma and states:

We need to encourage some macro-empirical theorists with broad views of public administration to integrate the mid-range public administration theories into a mega theory. My suspicion is that such an integrating framework will come from blending current work in democratic theory with the realities of the modern administrative state. (For similar views see Waldo 1990; Gaus 1950.)

A theoretical framework that is comprehensive and less restrictive than current theories of administrative politics is set forth in this manuscript. Such a framework can be applied to other policy areas where bureaucratic institutions are engaged in distributive and redistributive policies. The dynamic systems model presented here is designed to create a common theoretical ground for future research efforts investigating the study of macro-level relationships among the president, Congress, and administrative agencies. Through additional empirical inquiry based on this endeavor, students of public bureaucracy can begin to develop more detailed theories of both responsive bureaucratic and political institutions.

Chapter 2

A Dynamic Systems Model of
Administrative Politics

The Case for a Unified Model of Administrative Politics

In the previous chapter I discussed the various arguments underlying the different theories and the arguments used to understand political-bureaucratic relations in the U.S. democratic system. Scholars have conceptualized this relationship as exhibiting "congressional dominance," "presidential control," "shared political control," or "bureaucratic autonomy," just to name a few examples. This body of work has generally conceded the narrowness in its approaches. Moe (1987a: 480–82), for example, argues that the principal-agent framework recognizes the conflict of interest present not only between principal and agent but also in the existence of hidden information and/or actions embedded within these relations (Arrow 1985). Moe adds that this will lead to imperfect political control of the agent by the principal.[1]

Previous research has made a valuable contribution to our understanding of institutional politics. Analyzing the effects of congressional subcommittee policy liberalism (see Weingast and Moran 1983; Moe 1985a), presidential appointments (Nathan 1983; Waterman 1989; Wood 1988; Wood and Anderson 1993; Wood and Waterman 1991, 1993), or the role of a newly created bureaucratic evaluation committee or similar internal change (Eisner and Meier 1990; Eisner 1992; Ringquist 1995) on agency behavior are interesting and worthwhile scholarly endeavors.[2] This line of inquiry, however, does not explain the general institutional roles of Congress, the president, and the agency, since these models are both incomplete and limited in a dynamic sense.[3]

A more complete manner in which to gauge the nature of these relations is to reconceptualize agency, Congress, and presidents as separately representing unique institutional behaviors. In the tradition of the "new institutionalism" found in political science (Calvert, McCubbins, and Weingast 1989; Hammond and Knott 1996; March and Olsen 1984, 1989; McCubbins, Noll, and Weingast 1987, 1989; Knott and Miller 1987; Moe 1984, 1988, 1989, 1990; Rockman and Weaver 1993; Woolley 1993), which utilizes institutions as the units of analysis (as opposed to individuals), the thesis set forth in this study maintains that the macro-politics of the administrative state can be best analyzed by focusing on the behavior of these institutions through time.[4] Budgetary signals emanating from elected officials (commonly termed political principals) and the regulatory performance for the administrative agency in question reflect institutional behavior.[5] This does not mean that other institutional-based factors such as legislative oversight, legislation, key appointments, and agency professionalization are neglected in this approach. Rather, these factors will possibly affect the behavior for each of the respective governmental institutions in a purely deterministic manner. Focusing on budgetary behavior is well founded; past research demonstrates that agency resources are both strongly related to variations in agency output and closely related to the value placed by political principals upon an agency, either in the form of substantive resource changes (Wood and Anderson 1993; Wood and Waterman 1991, 1993) or as a latent political signal intended to affect agency behavior (Bendor and Moe 1985; Carpenter 1996; Padgett 1980, 1981; Weingast and Moran 1983).[6]

Although a systems perspective has been used elsewhere to study administrative behavior, it has captured only the agency decision-making process (Moe 1985a) and mutual interdependence of national and subnational policy outputs (Wood 1992), not the interrelatedness of political and administrative institutions. These studies do not treat the president, Congress, and the bureaucracy as an *endogenous* system of institutions whose behavior may be interdependent. In his pathbreaking investigation of policy decision making on the National Labor Relations Board, Terry Moe (1985a: 1100, n. 7) acknowledges that his model is not a complete system representing both political institutions and the agency:

Obviously, a more complete specification of the system would recognize the likelihood of mutually adaptive adjustment between each political actor and the NLRB, and indeed among the political actors themselves. As a first step, however, it is reasonable to assume that the political authorities are exogenous. This assumption greatly simplifies what is already a complex task, and it should not bias the current estimation.

Moe's model contains strong restrictions based on the assumption "that the regulatory context is a two-tiered, strictly hierarchic system" (1985a: 1100). This "hierarchical" assumption is the basis of principal-agent models used to analyze political control over administrative agencies.

The dynamic systems perspective of governmental institutions proposed in this study is distinct from these works because it does not make restrictive assumptions about behavioral relations among elected officials and administrative agencies. *Therefore, assumptions about hierarchy and the nature of institutional influence are not assumed but, instead, are empirically tested.* As a result, this framework is a more general approach to characterizing the politics of the modern administrative state since it does not easily allow one to make casual a priori statements of "political control," "congressional dominance," "bureaucratic autonomy," and the like. In other words, existing research narrows the scope of causal and responsive mechanisms of these actors and institutions by limiting discourse to certain aspects of these behavioral relationships. Both the complexity of behavioral relations and disagreement over what factors influence agency behavior require that we step back and view the broader policy landscape in order to understand the general nature of agency-political relationships. This framework acknowledges both the general validity of competing theories and the complexity surrounding political-bureaucratic relations by examining the most broad and fundamental elements of this debate via theoretically informed induction.

Put simply, the goal of this study is to investigate dynamic relations among political institutions and administrative agencies. The general nature of this framework recognizes that different agency environments will result in the development of different types of relationships with political institutions because of varying levels of political support, policy expertise, organizational vitality, and leadership (Meier 1993a, 1993b; Rourke 1984; Wood and Waterman 1991). Thus, this conceptual model is applicable to other administrative settings involving agencies that are involved in non-regulatory policy areas (i.e., distributive and redistributive).[7]

The dynamic systems model of administrative politics integrates the insights from various theories of administrative politics to arrive at a unified model of agency-political relationships pertaining to policy administration. The approach undertaken in this book attempts to provide a much richer picture of what is transpiring among governmental institutions involved in policy administration without ignoring other exogenous factors that impinge on the behavior of these institutional actors from both environmental conditions outside the system as well as factors within each institution. In addition, this framework has the added flexibility of allowing for intra-institutional causal factors to have an impact on the broader institutional preferences analyzed here. The thematic explanation and justification of this theoretical model is set forth in the next section.

A Dynamic Systems Model of Politics in the Modern Administrative State

The dynamic systems model of administrative politics is a macro-level perspective of agency-political relations focusing on general, aggregate institutional behavior across time. At the same time, this model is informed by micro-level behavior since it allows for endogenous institutions and strategic response. This unified framework is intended to lend a more realistic (and comprehensive) account of policy administration in a complex democratic system such as the one in the United States by encompassing competing explanations of administrative behavior into a single model. A need for such a construct has arisen over the past decade or so. For instance, Moe (1987a: 481–82) argues that one cannot determine a priori just how imperfect control is going to be.[8] Moe adds that only a careful empirical investigation of each agency-congressional relationship can reveal the true extent of political control. In a similar vein, congressional dominance scholars such as Calvert, Moran, and Weingast (1987: 494) admit the need to disentangle the subtle forms of influence of various institutional participants.

This study addresses these concerns by offering a framework for analyzing agency-political relationships as a dynamic system of institutional behavior. The core of agency-political relations necessitates an exploration of the dynamic interactions between key institutional participants. The central argument proposed here is that students of American bureaucracy and political institutions must embrace a broader view of agency-political relations, a view that encompasses different aspects of existing theories. One must understand administrative as well as political behavior—and how these factors are interrelated in a dynamic manner—for research on the politics of the modern administrative state to progress.

The dynamic systems model of administrative politics is portrayed diagrammatically in figure 2.1. This approach involves inspecting the president, Congress, and administrative agencies as a dynamic system in which governmental institutions interact with one another in the implementation of public policy.[9] The courts, however, are not included in the dynamic systems model of administrative politics, as applied to aggregate enforcement activity, since they generally play a *discrete, sporadic* role in policy administration with respect to aggregate bureaucratic outputs. The judiciary is often viewed as the weakest of external institutions, with respect to the overall level of regulatory enforcement control exercised by administrative agencies. Courts are capable of playing an important role in determining specific agency (individual) actions/cases or the types of actions/cases that are undertaken. "Courts, despite their function in dispute resolution, are not designed to be bureaucratic monitors. . . . Courts interact with bureaucracies only in specific cases or controversies" (Meier 1993a: 167). Unlike the legislature (Congress), which has oversight activity and the appropriations process, and the chief executive (president), who possesses the budget request process, policy planning, and formal appointment powers over top-level agency administrators, the courts are not capable of routine monitoring of a continuous nature. Rather, the courts' interest or involvement with the bureaucracy lies with only specific cases or controversies, thus the courts do not enjoy a *continuous* form of communication with the agency, as is the case with presidents and Congress. Furthermore, empirical studies typically conclude that presidents and Congress are most prominent in affecting the volume of regulatory enforcement outputs. This is not to suggest that courts do not have any influence, just that their influence is sporadic and less apt to deal with bureaucratic monitoring that is commonly associated with aggregate enforcement vigor or activity of administrative agencies measured via policy outputs. This is consistent with the notion of *sporadic accountability* (O'Loughlin 1990: 288–89), indicative of the best case scenario in which the courts may significantly influence bureaucratic behavior for the type of administrative behavior being examined in most studies of agency enforcement (including this study).[10]

Unlike previous systematic studies, this diagram clearly shows that these institutions are truly interdependent, as reflected by the two-way causal linkages running between each set of institutions. At the same time, this method does

FIGURE 2.1. A General Representation of the Dynamic Systems Model of Administrative Politics (President and Congress)

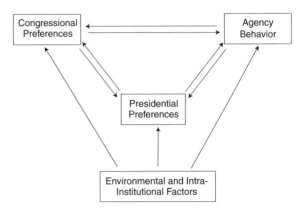

not treat governmental behavior as solely operating in a "black box" environment. Rather, the model acknowledges that both environmental conditions (such as economic conditions) and intra-institutional factors (such as oversight-subcommittee policy preferences, presidential appointments, and the internal creation of a policy office within an administrative agency) will also shape the aggregate institutional behavior of these participants. Although these intra-institutional factors are important in explaining the behavior of administrative agencies and political institutions, they are too often characterized as being the leading causal mechanism in explaining agency performance.

There are two main problems associated with the overemphasis of these factors. First, many of these events are discrete stimuli that do not represent the institutional strength of relevant actors for a lengthy period of time. This limitation hampers one's ability to make strong causal and inferential claims about the general institutional nature of political-bureaucratic relations. For example, if the Reagan administration appoints an individual as an agency head, and a drop in bureaucratic outputs ensues, this does not necessarily mean that all presidents possess the same general level of institutional strength over bureaucratic agencies and/or willingness to exercise it so vigorously. Second, oversight-subcommittee policy liberalism will often play an important role in affecting the amount of vigor with which the agency pursues its mandate. At the same time, however, oversight committees cannot determine the level of resources appropriated to agencies in any given year, nor can these subchamber bodies reflect Congress's behavior as a whole institution.[11]

One plausible solution to this dilemma is to treat the most noted items that drive behavior (resources and agency performance) as representing behavior for each of the relevant institutions. Although there are many different instruments that elected officials can use to influence bureaucratic behavior (such as oversight activity, executive orders, administrative design, and so on), agency budgets are analyzed for the purposes of this study. It can also be said that bureaucratic outputs serve as one indicator of agency policy and, therefore, cannot completely describe all facets of administrative behavior.[12] Some question the veracity of such bureaucratic output measures, given that not all enforcements are necessarily equal.[13]

The decision to employ budgets and bureaucratic outputs, however, is justifiable on four counts.[14] First, budgetary resources and agency enforcement outputs are accurate reflections of institutional behavior, whether they appear in the form of signals (Bendor and Moe 1985; Carpenter 1996; Weingast and Moran 1983) or as substantive behavior of these institutions (Downs 1967; Lewis-Beck 1979; Meier 1985; Quirk 1981; Seidman and Gilmour 1986; Redford 1969; Weingast 1984; Wilson 1989; Yates 1982).[15] Second, these factors are continuous; thus they shed light on the general causal and responsive nature of institutional relations among administrative agencies, the president, and Congress—as opposed to just single-case discrete occurrences, events, or static snapshots of agency-political relations. Third, this model allows for the analysis of sophisticated behavior (i.e., policy innovations or perturbations) displayed by these institutions, which, in turn, can supply us with information on whether unexpected deviations from predictable behavior result in policy congruence or divergence between any pair of institutional actors. Fourth, and most important, this study views budgetary requests and appropriations as being an accurate reflection of distinct institutional behavior for both president and Congress (Carpenter 1992, 1996). This perspective differs from many studies that view resources as being a shared tool of political influence between the president and Congress (Moe 1985a; Wood 1988; Wood and Waterman 1991, 1993, 1994; Wood and Anderson 1993).

Implicit in both this framework and the past research discussed in the preceding chapter is the notion that agency-political relationships will rest on some level of agreement between political principals and bureaucratic agencies.[16] This agreement between elected officials and bureaucratic agencies may reflect behavioral relations that are more complex than previously implied. These relationships may vary depending upon numerous factors such as the institutional design/proximity of the agency (Moe 1988, 1989, 1990; Seidman and Gilmour 1986), the amount of information asymmetry benefiting the administrative agency (which may be related to the technical complexity of the agency mission), and personal interest/salience on the part of the politicians (in terms of the amount of time and effort they are willing to expend) for any given policy area.[17] The stronger the agency from an institutional perspective, the more capable it will be to (1) respond in a negative (antagonistic) fashion to perturbations in behavior on the part of political principals; (2) elicit a positive response from its political principal(s) in reaction to an unexpected deviation from their own (agency) behavior; (3) directly affect the behavior of the political principals in a predictable (direct) causal manner; and (4) remain unresponsive to predictable (direct) variations in behavior emanating from political principals.

The institutional proximity of the agency to political principals may play an important role in describing the nature of behavioral relations. In this sense, politicians and interest groups define the playing field for agency-political relations via administrative design (Moe 1988, 1989, 1990). Controlling for all else, agencies will be more responsive to the political principal closest to them since they generally possess closer long-term historical relations.[18] For example, an independent regulatory commission, ceteris paribus, will be relatively more responsive to signals and the institutional behavior of Congress vis-à-vis presidential administrations since these bureaucratic institutions are better designed to mitigate executive influence vis-à-vis congressional pressure.[19] Conversely, in the case of executive agencies, these bureaucratic organizations will be more responsive to the institutional behavior of presidents vis-à-vis Congress, ceteris paribus, since they are designed to enhance executive influence.[20]

Information asymmetries may also affect agency-political outcomes. The larger the asymmetry between agency and political principals, the easier it is for any given agency to affect the behavior of its political principals in the manner stated above. The size of this information asymmetry will be positively related to the complexity associated with the agency's policy mission. As the size of the information asymmetry (in favor of the agency) increases, it will be more difficult for political principals to affect agency activity in a predictable or unpredictable manner. Also, a greater interest displayed by elected officials toward the mission of the agency will increase the likelihood that (1) political institutions can directly affect bureaucratic performance in a gradual, lagged adaptive fashion consistent with notions of bounded rationality and incrementalism, and/or (2) political principals will systematically respond to unanticipated deviations from expected behavior (such as policy innovations) on the part of the agency. Finally, bureaucratic agencies should generally be unresponsive to attempts at control by political institutions when (1) the latter, through their past behavior, are not able to directly affect the former's activity in a lagged adaptive manner, and (2) agency performance either responds to unanticipated behavior emanating from political principals in a negative manner or does not respond at all.

The preceding discussion implies that politicians (employer or principal) and the agency (subordinate or agent) will have a "zone of acceptable behavior" (based upon the contractual agreement) where they are relatively free to operate in an equilibrium state.[21] Outside this zone, a temporary shock will transpire and create a short-run disequilibrium between administrative agencies and political institutions. As a result, a governmental institution (including the agency) will try to affect the behavior of other relevant governmental institutions by responding to the appropriate entity in a strategic manner. For example, if political principal(s) step outside this "zone," thus resulting in a disequilibrium state, the agency has the ability to respond through its regulatory performance (i.e., policy outputs).[22]

If the agency response is potent enough, political principals may respond in some manner. One example of this pattern is the Reagan administration's relationship with the Environmental Protection Agency (EPA). During the initial years of the Reagan presidency, EPA resources (budgets) were drastically cut, thus upsetting the political-bureaucratic equilibrium. In response to the events of the first two years of the Reagan administration, EPA morale and performance levels sank to very low levels. Observing the dissatisfaction on the part of the EPA and the ensuing congressional pressure to stem the antiregulatory tide of the Burford era, the Reagan administration responded by accepting the resignation of the controversial EPA chief Ann Burford and appointing the moderate William Ruckleshaus while simultaneously reversing EPA budget cuts.[23] This in turn led to an increase in EPA enforcement activity, resulting in a move toward an equilibrium state among these institutions.

Finally, changes in agency behavior because of internal organization factors (such as agency professionalization) may not upset the political institution bureaucratic agency equilibrium in those instances where the preferences of political principals are not in conflict with the behavior of the agency. An example of such a case occurs in antitrust regulation. According to Eisner and Meier (1990) and Eisner (1991, 1992), changes in antitrust enforcement activity could be attributed to the emergence (or "triumph") of economics within the Antitrust Division of the Department of Justice and the Federal Trade Commission, respectively. In these isolated cases, the activity of these bureaucracies was not in conflict with the Reagan administration or with congressional oversight subcommittees. Therefore, neither administrative organization had the need to emit stimuli that would lead to a call for policy change on behalf of the president.[24]

Although these illustrations are *incident specific,* they do indicate that agency-political relations are both dynamic and behaviorally complex. There now follow three broad principles of this theoretical model. These tenets sharply differ from past research because this framework involves the relaxation of assumptions that are either explicitly or implicitly inferred by such models.

Politicians, Bureaucrats, and Mutual Adaptation

The formal and empirical literature on bureaucratic politics focuses on the bureaucratic agency as being responsive to political actors, not vice versa. This is incongruent with the basic understanding of principal-agency relationships as viewed by organizational theorists. A principal-agent relationship must allow for dynamic interaction as well as strategic behavior on the part of each actor (Perrow 1986; Mitnick 1980). Furthermore, classic treatises on the bureaucracy maintain that the federal bureaucracy plays a formidable independent role which cannot be simply thought of as a component of democratic institutions. In his classic book *American Bureaucracy,* Peter Woll (1963: 3) notes: "[Bureaucracy] is a powerful and viable branch of government, playing a political game to advance its own interest in legislative and judicial, as well as executive matters." Woll, among others, view the bureaucracy as playing a vital *pro-active* role in shaping policy administration (see also Meier 1993a; Rourke 1984; Simon, Smithburg, and Thompson 1950). Whether political control or bureaucratic autonomy actually exists, past systematic research has assumed that administrative agencies (via policy outputs and budgets) are passive receptors to either political forces or internal bureaucratic factors. This assumption is tenuous since administrative organizations (via regulatory performance and/or budgetary requests) are quite capable of sending signals that affect the behavior of political principals—that is, political institutions and bureaucratic agencies may be endogenous to one another.

Because existing studies treat political institutions as being exogenous to bureaucratic agencies, agency-political relationships exhibit *non-mutual adap-*

tation. Although non-mutual adaptation may exist in some instances, to assume that such a pattern always holds is unwise. For example, to suggest that Ronald Reagan's deregulatory movement early in his first term was completely independent of the recent past agency behavior before his administration took office is clearly a flimsy assertion at best. Reagan's call for devolving financial and administrative programs, in fact, was a testament to his distaste for the increasing size and scope of government that had transpired during the 1970s as well as an extension of the Carter administration's deregulatory initiatives.

Formal models of agency-political interaction suggest that politicians anticipate and adapt to agency behavior (Banks and Weingast 1992; Bendor, Taylor, and Van Gaalen 1985, 1987). These works maintain that politicians are able to anticipate and adapt to bureaucratic behavior given the informational advantages enjoyed by administrative agencies. If this is true, bureaucratic organizations and democratic institutions can possibly be considered *mutually adaptive* or *endogenous* to one another in such instances. (Chapter 4 will document the quantitative testing of the general propositions set forth by these formal models.) Two notable illustrations of this were Executive Orders No. 12291 (mandating that executive branch agencies undertake cost-benefit analysis of proposed major regulations) and No. 12498 (establishing a regulatory planning process based upon the precedent of the Carter administration), which were both issued by the Reagan administration. In these instances, the regulatory behavior of the Reagan administration was responding to the recent past behavior of administrative agencies.

By not placing restrictive assumptions on the behavioral relations of these actors, the concept of mutual adaptation among institutional actors can be explicitly tested within this theoretical model. Although the strength of the model is its treatment of agency-political relations as a dynamic endogenous (i.e., interrelated) system of participants, relationships between sets of institutions can be analyzed in a dyadic manner within a multivariate framework.

There are four possible types of agency-political relationships (see figure 2.2). The first two instances reveal situations where administrative agencies are not subject to political influence (or control). The *bureaucratic influence hypothesis* describes those situations in which agency behavior can significantly influence the institutional behavior of political principals, but not vice versa. This will not only reflect a sense of independence from the elected officials but also exhibit bureaucratic power in affecting the behavior of elected officials. In such instances, agencies exhibit influence by shaping the behavior of political institutions. For the purposes of this study, such a pattern of behavior suggests that an agency is able to affect the budgetary signals it receives from political principals (president and/or Congress) based on its regulatory performance. The *bureaucratic autonomy hypothesis* occurs when agency behavior does not respond to the institutional behavior of its political principals, and vice versa. In these situations, agencies behave independently yet do not affect the institutional behavior of elected officials since the former's regulatory performance is independent of the latter's budgetary signals and vice versa.

The third type of hypothesis reflects *mutual adaptation* or *dynamic feedback.* In these circumstances, agency behavior will influence the behavior of political principals and the opposite will also hold true. This type of relationship reflects the dynamic adaptive process of feedback between administrative agencies and elected officials whereby agency outputs influence budgetary signals from political institutions, and vice versa. Finally, if agency behavior is influenced by the institutional behavior of political principal(s), and not vice versa, one can infer that *political influence (or control)* exists. This final category is consonant with the claim of various political control theories of the bureaucracy, which conclude that democratic institutions are the primary force in determining administrative behavior.[25] Put in simple terms, an agency's regulato-

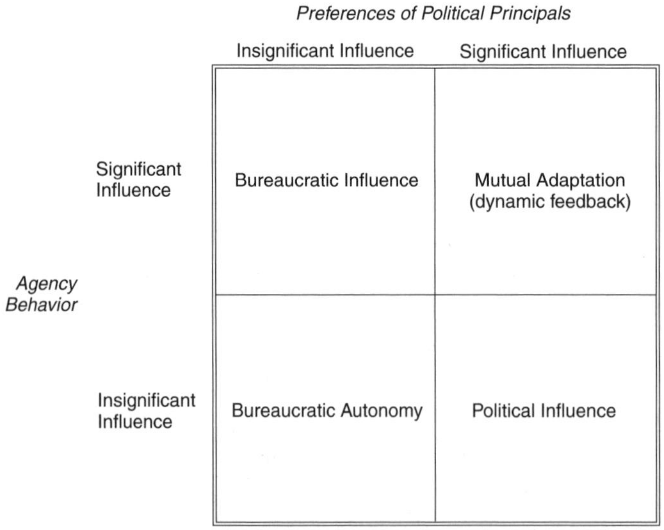

Preferences of Political Principals

	Insignificant Influence	Significant Influence
Significant Influence	Bureaucratic Influence	Mutual Adaptation (dynamic feedback)
Insignificant Influence	Bureaucratic Autonomy	Political Influence

Agency Behavior

FIGURE 2.2. A Classification Scheme for Agency-Political Dyadic Relationships

ry performance will respond to budgetary signals emanating from political institutions.

Analogous to Miller and Moe's (1983: 308–09) formal investigation into the budgetary and bureaucratic output aspects of agency-political interaction, that claims a *theoretical* range of agency-political outcomes between bureaucratic manipulation and political domination, this study claims that agency-political relations will range from bureaucratic influence to political influence. The point on this continuum may vary by the case being analyzed since all agency-presidential-congressional relationships will not yield identical outcomes. However, a general model, which can classify such behavior in an empirical setting that can be tested with quantitative data, is set forth in this study.

The Interaction of Politicians in Policy Administration

The existing empirical research on agency-political relations assumes that the behavior of elected officials is shaped independently of one another. To presume that political actors or institutions are insulated from one another when formulating their policy views or actions is questionable. For example, it is quite reasonable to conceive that the Reagan administration's regulatory behavior in 1986 could be related to the recent past behavior of its own administration and/or Congress. By examining political principals' behavior without utilizing information from the recent past, one not only receives an incomplete picture of which forces drive agency behavior but also completely ignores a key component of what may actually motivate the current institutional behavior of political principals.

Strong reliance on the implicit assumption of independence between political actors has serious consequences that may result in faulty inferences and erroneous conclusions. For instance, if presidential behavior is influenced by congressional behavior, then the decision-making calculus of presidents in matters of policy administration will partly reflect not only their behavior (and possibly the agency's behavior) but also congressional wishes in a reciprocal (policy congruence) or antagonistic (policy divergence) manner. This is especially true when examining the construction of agency budgets. It is well known that presidents (via the OMB) play a large agenda-setting role for congressional deliberations regarding appropriations (Davis, Dempster, and Wildavsky 1966, 1971, 1974). In fact, Kiewiet and McCubbins (1988, 1991) contend that final congressional appropriations for domestic agencies and programs are heavily influenced by president/OMB budget estimates submitted to Con-

gress. Thus it is apparent that the institutional behavior of these political principals is interrelated (i.e., endogenous to one another) in a dynamic manner.
Conversely, it will be possible that legislative institutions have an impact on
the budgetary behavior of the president for any given agency. An example of
such behavior was the Reagan administration's attempt to drastically cut regulatory resources earmarked for the SEC's policing of securities and commodities markets during the mid 1980s, which was mitigated by bipartisan support
in Congress (Khademian 1992).

The assumption of independence between the president and Congress concerning their relationship with the bureaucracy is relaxed, thus allowing for dynamic interaction between political institutions. This perspective is consistent
with the tradition of political scientists who view public policy as consisting of
the endogenous interaction between administrative organizations and between political institutions subject to environmental conditions (Anderson
1990; Dye 1966; Jones 1984; Meier 1987; Rourke 1984; Truman 1951).

Politicians, Bureaucrats, and Sophisticated Behavior

Existing research on administrative politics generally assumes that bureaucratic organizations adapt to elected officials' behavior. This adaptation has
been described as either instantaneous (Moe 1985a; Scholz and Wei 1986;
Scholz, Twombly, and Headrick 1991; Wood and Anderson 1993) or gradual
(Carpenter 1996; Wood 1988; Wood and Waterman 1991, 1993). In either instance, both administrative agencies and external political institutions in the
policy environment are incapable of dealing with unanticipated behavior on
the part of the other. This existing portrait of public bureaucracy is grounded
in the concepts of incrementalism, inertia, and adaptive (gradual) learning or
adjustment, which serve as a behavioral foundation for the modern study of
such organizations. These theories, however, fail to recognize that institutional
participants may alter their future behavior as a result of a deviation from expected behavior in the form of shocks or innovations on the part of some other
institutional actor. However, political institutions (administrative agencies) do
have the capability of responding to innovations emanating from administrative agencies (political institutions). An illustration of this point deals with the
changing of the general attitude of the Reagan administration toward administrative agencies for the period from 1984 to the end of his presidency. The Reagan administration moderated its policy views regarding many executive
branch agencies following a tempestuous first two years of conflict, criticism,
and internal bureaucratic dissension.[26]

By transcending the *"anticipated"* (or predictable) component of behavior that is the sole focus of past research on agency-political relations, the analysis of sophisticated institutional behavior has three implications for the study of administrative politics. First, it recognizes that the behavior of political and bureaucratic institutions may be *adaptive* to each other as well as to the environmental constraints placed exogenously upon them. This adaptation, however, will not be constrained to past or current anticipated behavior, as existing theoretical and empirical studies maintain. Rather, policy actors/institutions may also possess *"sophisticated reaction"* mechanisms,[27] which allow them to respond to unanticipated behavior (i.e., policy shocks) emanating from other actors/institutions.[28] This line of argument is consistent with the assertion that "sophisticated maneuvering" is part and parcel of the realities associated with budgetary decision making (Miller and Moe 1983: 308). Second, there are circumstances in which the behavior of a government institution will appear to rely on its own past institutional position or be completely independently determined, when in fact it is not. For instance, the president and an administrative agency may not base their behaviors respectively on the past but might instead focus on responding to *unanticipated* changes (i.e., policy shocks) in the current environment, because of the abundance of information and/or institutional sophistication. Under such conditions, it is possible that these institutions exhibit *"rational expectations"* regarding the behavior of other institutions.

Finally, the analysis of innovations (also termed "perturbations" or "shocks") implies that both political and agency behaviors will be incomplete at any given point in time since these unanticipated deviations from expected behaviors reflect new information made available. The process is consistent with the premise that these institutions do not have perfect information regarding policy administration in any given setting. Rational expectations theory is based upon the premise that the use of information is a valuable tool that can help an actor (or sets of actors working together) achieve economic and/or political objectives (Hansen and Sargent 1980; Lucas and Sargent 1981; Mishkin 1983; Muth 1961; Sargent 1984; Shaw 1984). For the purposes of this research, both the agency and its political principals will utilize *all* relevant and available information at their disposal, up to and including the previous period t-1, in order to make a forecast or prediction on the future behavior of other institutions responsible for policy administration. In other words, institutional participants do not simply rely upon past experiences in formulating their expectations (Shaw 1984: 47). Thus, governmental institutions responsible for the administration of public policy are thought of as being "forward-looking optimizers" who have a sound knowledge of the true structure of the social system in which they participate. Rational expectations, however, do not imply that these institutions either will have perfect information or are capable of conducting a full evaluation of competing alternatives (Shaw 1984: 47). Instead, each institution is able to efficiently process information given its limited capabilities (Goldstein and Freeman 1990, 1991; Williams and McGinnis 1988, 1992).[29] For purposes of this study, the concept of rational expectations can be mathematically represented in the following general notation:

$$_{t-1}P^e_t = E(P_t|\Omega_{t-1}) + \nu_t \tag{1}$$

where the expected values for any given policy variable P^e (e.g., agency regulatory performance, presidential/OMB budget requests, and congressional budgetary appropriations) during the current period $_t$ subject to last period's expectations $_{t-1}$, is a function of the conditional mathematical expectation (i.e., mean) of the policy variable given the information available up to and including the previous period $E(P_t|\Omega_{t-1})$,[30] plus any new information ("innovations") that become available during the current period ν_t. In lay terms, the current behaviors of political and bureaucratic institutions are subject to last year's policy expectations and will be a function of the current year's policy expectations, given information acquired up to and including last year, plus any new information that becomes available during the current year. Thus, deviations from expected behavior during the current period reflect newly acquired information. For an institution to possibly exhibit rational expectations, it must be able to react to unanticipated events by contemporaneously modifying expectations and yet not use past information to formulate its current behavior based on this particular formulation of the rational expectations hypothesis test.[31]

The definition of rational expectations employed in this research is consistent with a significant portion of the agency-political relations body of research suggesting that perfect information does not exist (Banks and Weingast 1992; Moe 1984; Niskanen 1971, 1975), while also acknowledging that organizations (as well as political institutions) have limited cognitive abilities in the processing of information (Allison 1971; Bendor and Moe 1985, 1986; Carpenter 1996; March and Olsen 1984, 1989; March and Simon 1958; Simon 1947; Wood and Waterman 1993). What distinguishes rational expectations from the concepts of dynamic adaptation/bounded rationality is that whereas the former states that decisions are made with all relevant and available information, the latter posits that decision making is generally made in a gradual manner through a purely retrospective, extrapolative exercise.

The dynamic systems model proposed in this study allows for the competing possibilities that these institutional participants may be viewed (1) as forward-looking optimizers who may have strong insight into the "true" structure of the social system in which they participate, or (2) as poorly informed "backward-looking" adaptive learners who revise their actions based only upon their past experiences with any given actors.[32] In the past, theories of administrative politics either implicitly or explicitly suggested that the agency cannot adapt to unanticipated behavior as a result of these sudden deviations/perturbations from expected behavior (termed "shocks" or "innovations"). Consistent with both the "new economics of organization" and institutional choice theories of administrative politics, however, the conditions where imperfect information exists may be addressed in a systematic manner through anticipation and strategic behavior (Bendor and Moe 1985; Knott and Miller 1987; Moe 1984, 1988, 1989). The approach taken here accounts for varying, and sometimes conflicting, possibilities of these different theories as it relates to the study of administrative politics.

Most of the research does not address the issues of strategic interaction and sophisticated behavior.[33] Some complex models of agency-political relationships suggest that the concept of shocks or innovations on the part of the agency is impossible regarding new policy initiatives because of reporting requirements such as the notice-and-comment procedures that force agencies to publish rule changes in *The Federal Register* and hold public hearings on proposed rules (Hammond and Knott 1993; McCubbins, Noll, and Weingast 1987, 1989). Although this appears to be true for an actual policy directive, agency output (i.e., regulatory performance) and budgetary signals may often take on an uncertain nature that may "surprise" political principals since these latter concepts are not necessarily listed in such an open manner before they actually are made available or occur. These types of phenomena are also inherently more difficult in ascertaining changes compared to discrete administrative policy or rule changes.[34]

The nature of this sophisticated behavior will also give insight into whether policy congruence or divergence exists between any two sets of institutional actors. If the policy innovations emanating from one institution are *negatively* correlated with another institution, one can infer that a certain amount of institutional policy divergence (or conflict) exists between these relevant parties. If policy innovations emanating from one institution are *positively* correlated with another institution, however, one can infer that a certain degree of policy congruence/agreement exists between these relevant participants. This aspect of the dynamic systems model is novel because past research has only been able to address questions concerning the existence or absence of political influence. The concepts of adaptation, sophisticated reaction, and rational expectations will be operationalized and empirically assessed in chapter 4.

Hypotheses Examined from the Dynamic Systems Model of Administrative Politics

Constructing hypotheses in this setting is rather difficult since many of the competing theories make different assertions; and the framework proposed here is a broad approach to investigating theoretical issues surrounding agency-political relationships. Some generalizable hypotheses can be made, however, regarding the institutional interactions among these dynamic government institutions. These hypotheses deal with issues of administrative design, hence institutional proximity. The responsiveness of political and bureaucratic institutions will be closely related to their proximity with each other. This has important implications for the study of agency-political relationships within a democratic system. For example, by having information on the administrative design/institutional proximity of bureaucratic and political institutions, one acquires a better sense not only of differences in responsiveness but also of the *nature* of responsiveness (i.e., reciprocal/policy congruence or antagonistic/policy conflict), as well as of the *type* of responsiveness (i.e., lagged adaptation and/or sophisticated responses). In addition, agencies created independent of the chief executive (e.g., independent regulatory commissions, government corporations) should be expected to have a greater impact on the institutional behavior of elected officials than other types of bureaucratic institutions (i.e., executive departments and bureaus). This is because such agencies typically do not have a "filter" on their behavior because of their independent nature; therefore, they will be more prone to elicit responses from political institutions.

However, institutional proximity will also play a role in affecting the impact of agency behavior on the behavior of political principals. The closer an agency is to a specific political institution, the easier it will be for the institution to affect the agency's behavior. For example, one would expect that an agency that is independent from the chief executive—such as an independent regulatory commission—should be more responsive to congressional stimuli relative to the president, the reason being that many agencies outside the purview of the chief executive have legislative bypass authority which allows them to testify in congressional hearings without first consulting the president or administration officials. These types of agencies also have greater freedom and greater budgetary (and resource) freedom from presidential administrations. For instance, the Antitrust Division budgetary requests and policy programs must first be coordinated with the Department of Justice before they can be sent to the White House for consideration. On the other hand, an independent regulatory commission such as the SEC does not have to coordinate its resource requests or policy plans with another executive branch agency. Conversely, an executive branch agency such as the Antitrust Division should be more responsive to presidential signals than to congressional signals because of the former's closer institutional proximity.

Some hypotheses can be formulated concerning sophisticated response to policy innovations emanating from within the system. First, the costs associated with information acquisition will be less for those institutions who are comparatively closer to one another.[35] Therefore, sophisticated behavior will be more likely for institutions that are (controlling for other relevant factors) in relatively close proximity to one another. Alternatively stated, an institution will find it easier to respond to policy innovations/perturbations coming from another institution when information costs are relatively low (i.e., size of the information asymmetry becomes smaller). Based upon differences relating to agency design, one may be more likely to observe sophisticated behavior occurring between the president and an executive branch agency than between the president and an independent regulatory commission because the former relationship is much closer from an institutional position perspective than the latter one. Conversely, one should also be more apt to see sophisticated behavior between Congress and an independent regulatory commission than between Congress and an executive branch agency, ceteris paribus. The likelihood of sophisticated behavior may be negatively related to the technical complexity of the agency's policy mission, while being positively related to the salience surrounding the agency's policy mission. Many contend that the budgetary process between agency and president (via the OMB)[36] is a long protracted process of negotiation and fine-tuning (Carpenter 1992, 1996; Kamlet and Mowery 1980; Wildavsky 1979), especially compared to agency-congressional appropriations relations; thus, one should expect to see a greater likelihood of sophisticated behavior on the part of political institutions, holding all else constant.

Concluding Remarks

This chapter has attempted to encompass the many alternative (and often competing) arguments found in the existing research on agency-political relations by setting forth a dynamic systems model of administrative politics consisting of agency-congressional-presidential interaction. Unlike prior studies, the model presented here does not presume the following: (1) that only politicians can directly influence agency behavior, not vice versa; (2) that, with respect to policy administration, political institutions do not interact with one another (i.e., cannot affect each other's behavior regarding the agency in question); or (3) that behavior on the part of these institutional actors can only involve conceptual variants of lagged adaptation (Carpenter 1996; Wood and Waterman 1993, 1994), bounded rationality, and adaptive learning (Cyert and March 1963; March and Olsen 1976, 1984, 1989; March and Simon 1958; Simon 1947). This latter point is consistent with the principal-agent models that describe the existence of information asymmetries between political institutions and administrative agencies (Mitnick 1980; Moe 1984; Niskanen 1971).

Hammond and Knott's (1993, 1996) contention that different conditions and situations will result in varying degrees of political control or bureaucratic autonomy contains a great deal of merit; however, their assertion that the institutional strength possessed by each actor cannot be determined is unfounded from a macro viewpoint. This view is a reflection of their models' static microanalytic nature.[37] Through a dynamic analysis over a sufficiently extended period of time, however, one can make relatively confident inferential statements regarding the general nature of agency-political relations. The framework presented here allows one to make *general* statements regarding the causal and responsive nature for each institution pertaining not only to their behavior but also to the behavior of others within the system across time.

This method of examining agency-political relationships is consistent with the new institutionalism and its attempts at assessing behavioral relations between American governmental institutions. The dynamic systems model of administrative politics views institutions as continuous organisms that learn, adapt, and evolve across time in an interdependent manner (Cyert and March 1963; Lindblom 1959; Cohen and Axelrod 1984; Feldman 1989; March and Olsen 1976, 1984, 1989; March and Simon 1958). These institutions take preeminence over individual policy actors (i.e., different presidential administrations, political appointees) or events (legislation, court decisions) since the latter are not only transient but are also constrained by the historical arrangements, rules, and design of their positions.

The framework presented here is an extension of previous research in that it asserts that bureaucratic performance is a product of a pluralist outcome involving the dynamic interrelated relationships between agencies, Congress, and the president, subject to environmental conditions.[38] Unlike past investigation, which often focuses on one-shot episodic discrete occurrences and their subsequent impact on behavior, each institutional participant is examined—since (1) individuals and their impact on policy are often transient, and (2) single discrete events may tell us that actor X can influence the behavior of actor Y but cannot help us assess the nature and degree of institutional strength associated with the position or office these individuals hold.[39] The model of administrative politics set forth in this study captures the essence of fluidity that is inherent in policy implementation.

Most important, this study allows for the possibility that agency behavior (in terms of its regulatory performance) can influence the behavior of political institutions (bureaucratic influence) or be independent of them in a bidirectional manner (bureaucratic autonomy). Not only does this possibility relax the strong a priori assumption of hierarchy that is inherent in political control models (Moe 1982, 1985a; Weingast and Moran 1983; Wood 1988, 1990, 1992; Wood and Waterman 1991, 1993, 1994), but it also differs sharply from recent studies claiming that internal factors within the agency—such as professionalization—serve as the basis for agency autonomy (Eisner and Meier 1990; Eisner 1991, 1992; Eisner, Worsham, and Ringquist 1993). Thus, an agency may not only affect the behavior of its political principals via indirect means (Meier 1987: 43–45) but may also affect them directly through its own unique regulatory performance signals.

The main implication of this approach is that it allows for complete and diverse forms of institutional interaction in administrative agency-political institution relationships. Rather than ask the conventional questions "Do elected officials control the bureaucracy?" or "Do internal (bureaucratic) factors determine agency behavior?" as past research has done, the purpose here is to go further and ask a broader, more fundamental question: "What is the general nature of behavioral relations among political institutions and administrative agencies?"[40] If we wish to acquire a deeper understanding of the modern administrative state, the main thrust driving research should be concerned not only with which factors influence agency behavior but, rather, must also focus on the causal and responsive mechanisms of governmental institutions that are relevant to policy administration. I do not mean to state that this study will find evidence for every possible type of behavior or relationship noted in this chapter, since there are only two administrative agencies examined in this book: the Securities and Exchange Commission (SEC) and Antitrust Division of the Department of Justice (DOJ). What is vital to remember is that the hypotheses and ideas generated in this book should be theoretically instructive for any future research that applies this framework to other policy settings in assessing relationships between administrative agencies and political institutions.

Chapter 3

The Institutional Dynamics of Policy Administration in Practice

The Cases of Securities and Antitrust Regulatory Enforcement

Introduction

Two important areas of regulatory enforcement are investigated in this book—the Securities and Exchange Commission (SEC) and the Antitrust Division (AD) of the Department of Justice (DOJ). These agencies are responsible for enforcing regulatory statutes in the area of securities and commodities industry and antitrust activities, respectively. Numerous studies of the administrative and political aspects of these policy areas and corresponding agencies provide disparate findings on what motivates each agency in its enforcement of these private sector activities. A brief background of each agency and its policy mission is in order.

The Securities and Exchange Commission was created under the 1934 act in order to implement and oversee these regulations. The SEC is given responsibility to eliminate certain types of abuses that are prevalent in the securities industry, such as fraud, price discrimination, illegal exchange practices, and the sale and acquisition of illegal information (Moe 1982). The SEC's power base lies in its five commissioners, who are appointed to five-year terms by the president of the United States. To assuage the effects of partisan politics, there can be no more than three members serving on the commission at any one time from the same political party as the current president (Khademian 1992: 36; Schwartz 1973: 2684). SEC commissioners play a vital role in agency affairs through selecting cases, prioritizing regulatory activities, constructing resource (i.e., budgetary and staffing) requests, and providing general policy direction for the agency. Both Khademian (1992) and Moe (1982) note that the SEC receives broad support from the industry it regulates. In addition, the SEC receives political support both from presidents and Congress in terms of resource allocations and the appointment of skilled political executives (Cary 1967; Kohlmeier 1969).

The Antitrust Division of the Department of Justice was created in 1933 as an executive bureau housed under the aegis of the Department of Justice. This agency is responsible for enforcing criminal matters under the Sherman Act of 1890 (including its various amendments) that involve any activities resulting in restraint of trade in foreign and interstate commerce through monopolization and mergers. It also shares (with the Federal Trade Commission [FTC]) administrative responsibilities for Sections 2 (prohibition of price discrimination), 3 (prohibition of exclusive dealing and tying contracts), 7 (prohibition of corporate mergers that may substantially reduce competition), and 8 (prohibition of interlocking directorates that could reduce competition) of the Clayton Act of 1914 (Katzmann 1980: 192).[1] Unlike the FTC, the Antitrust Division has no adjudicative powers; therefore, it must appeal to the courts for authority to enforce antitrust laws against persons or firms against which allegations are brought up (Shugart 1990: 128). The Antitrust Division is generally viewed as being much more effective at regulatory enforcement than the FTC (Shepherd 1985; Shugart 1990; but see Katzmann 1980 for a different viewpoint). What is clear, however, is that the motivations underlying the intensity of enforcement vigor are molded jointly by the behavior of elected officials and the administrative behavior of bureaucrats.[2]

Why Securities and Antitrust Regulatory Enforcement?

Both enforcement of securities and enforcement of antitrust regulations are selected because previous analyses of securities and antitrust regulation do not unequivocally determine the nature of agency-president-congressional relations.[3] Studies have yielded different findings and drawn disparate conclusions. It is essential, however, to select cases and base subsequent findings upon instances that do not appear anomalous. Because the aim of this project is to examine agency-political relationships from a more general framework, the selection of cases that have already been investigated by others contain the benefits of (1) settling the discordant findings generated from commonly accepted research and (2) revealing the complexity of political-bureaucratic relations previously left unaccounted for by those employing restrictive theoretical models and empirical specifications. Data and methodological requirements associated with the theoretical portion of this study also make it vital that agencies with sufficiently long histories be selected. For both case studies, annual data for the 1949–1992 period has been collected and analyzed.[4]

The cases selected here are similar in three important ways. First, both agencies deal with the popular and highly salient area of economic regulation. The areas of securities and antitrust regulation play a pivotal role in the operation of the American economy. Economic decision making and behavior is greatly affected by the regulations that govern the market system, a fact not just reflected by the popular creation and enactment of laws used to regulate these activities but also reinforced by research by scholars in the fields of political science, economics, law, and public policy. Second, both bureaucratic institutions have historically been perceived as very competent and professional administrative organizations. One reason is that they are staffed by skilled professionals whose technical policy expertise in law and economics supersedes that of many MCs. On a theoretical level, such a case selection is consistent with past studies of public bureaucracy, which acknowledge that bureaucratic agencies possess information advantages over political overseers (Banks and Weingast 1992; Bendor, Taylor, and Van Gaalen 1985, 1987; Miller and Moe 1983; Moe 1984; Niskanen 1971, 1975; Woolley 1993). Another similarity between these two regulatory policy areas is that securities and antitrust regulation are both viewed as essential to maintaining a capitalist economic system, since each agency's purpose is to provide fairness in markets, as well as to create conditions that lead to a vibrant macroeconomy. As a result, it is not surprising that these administrative agencies generally receive stronger bipartisan political support for their policy missions than do many other federal agencies.

These case studies, however, differ in three meaningful ways: (1) administrative design,[5] (2) policy jurisdiction, and (3) the type of target groups their actions are intended to alter. The administrative design of the SEC is as an independent regulatory commission that contains a partisan-balanced set of commissioners. The SEC also enjoys relative autonomy from the president and cabinet officials because of its institutional design.[6] For instance, unlike many executive bureaus, the SEC does not have to meet with administration officials for "clearance" when they testify before Congress. Budgetary matters are dealt with directly by OMB officials, whereas executive bureaus often need to coordinate their budget requests with a larger executive department (and the White House in certain instances) before dealing with OMB and congressional actors. The Antitrust Division, on the other hand, is an executive bureau that must operate under the auspices of presidents via the DOJ. The policy direction of the Antitrust Division is subject to greater presidential influence than that of an independent regulatory commission because, from an institutional perspective, it is more closely aligned with the White House.

The different administrative design is one way to examine whether there is significant variation in political-bureaucratic relations between the two cases. The following general questions are just some examples of the issues that can be addressed within the theoretical framework and empirical analysis set forth in this study. (1) Is the SEC less responsive to presidential signals than the Antitrust Division? (2) Is the SEC more responsive to congressional budgetary signals than the Antitrust Division, which can be protected by the White House? (3) Since the SEC appears more autonomous by administrative design, will it have a greater ability to affect political preferences (via regulatory performance) vis-à-vis the Antitrust Division?

The second difference is that these two administrative agencies have different clientele relationships with those they regulate. The SEC regulates an entire industry (for the most part) all by itself whereas the Antitrust Division shares regulatory responsibilities with the FTC. This may mean that the SEC has greater independence from political interference relative to the Antitrust Division since the former has sole administrative jurisdiction over its policy area. On the other hand, the Antitrust Division may be less likely to succumb to politicians' desires than the SEC. The Antitrust Division is more difficult to control because it can share blame for overall antitrust policy with the FTC, while the SEC has no other agency to pass the buck to if under political pressure.

The final difference is that the SEC's regulations affect a single industry: the securities and commodities brokers. The regulatory reach of the Antitrust Division, on the other hand, stretches across a multitude of industries in the American economy. The SEC's relatively concentrated regulatory authority—

compared to the more diffuse targeted group under scrutiny of the Antitrust Division—should result in the former having greater institutional strength (i.e., bureaucratic autonomy or power) in relation to the latter because it will likely have greater concentrated authority in its policy area.

The Politics of Securities Regulation:
Policy Background and History

The history of securities regulation in the United States is a rather lengthy and complex one that can be addressed here only in summary form. The central focus here is on the theoretical aspects of macro agency-political relations, not the unique policy history of a regulatory area.[7] Securities regulation came about in 1933–1934 as a response to New Deal efforts and public demand for an increase in general regulatory activity in economic affairs, due in large part to economic hardships resulting from the Great Depression. Before 1933, the securities industry was self-regulated by the New York Stock Exchange (NYSE) and the New York Curb Exchange (today known as the American Stock Exchange [AMEX]). After the stock market crash of 1929 and the ensuing economic depression, there was a move by the federal government toward regulating securities markets. Burgeoning efforts at government regulation of this industry entailed engaging legal and industry expertise to help draft, implement, and oversee both the legislative and the administrative aspects of this regulation (Khademian 1992: 23; McCraw 1984). The balance of interests among industry, regulators, and democratic institutions was instrumental in producing the Securities Act of 1933 and the Securities Exchange Act of 1934. According to Anne Khademian, much of the responsibility for writing this legislation was delegated by Congress to lawyers sympathetic to New Deal programs (1992: 24). Both legislative acts gave the federal government the broad authority not only to regulate the issue, purchase, and sale of securities in the best interest of the general public but also to prosecute fraud and other abuses of the stock market.

A Period of Regulatory Expansion: The Early Years of
Securities Regulation

Nearly the first twenty years of formal securities regulation involving the SEC saw this agency initiate and embrace the disclosure-enforcement strategy. This approach consisted of cooperative rule-making authority with the industry, and aggressive enforcement of both securities laws and disclosure (Khademian 1992: 37). This regulatory apparatus was the compromise of competing political interests (43). During the 1930s, the SEC's power was further enhanced in three ways. First, the Roosevelt administration supported the Public Utilities and Holding Company Act (PUHCA) of 1935. This legislative act required public utility holding companies to register with the SEC and to disclose their financial activities and securities-related dealings (47). This meant that the disclosure-enforcement regulatory strategy was extended to holding companies. Furthermore, the SEC was given the authority to break up and reorganize companies that did not meet PUHCA's legal stipulations. Second, Congress expanded the agency's jurisdictive authority by establishing SEC oversight of affairs involving over-the-counter market activities via the Maloney Act of 1938 (49). This latter delegation of regulatory power to the SEC was in response to the highly publicized Wall Street embezzlement scandal involving NYSE president Richard Whitney (Khademian 1992: 57; Ritchie 1980: 78). Third, the Investment Company Advisors Act of 1940 further extended the SEC's policy mandate by requiring registration, regulation of practices, and disclosure of any possible situations where a conflict of interest might exist for an advisor dealing with public transactions (Gujarati 1984: 359–60; Khademian 1992: 54). This legislative act was intended to deter mutual fund embezzlement and fraud. These three actions significantly enhanced the enforcement powers of the SEC. Moreover, each of these discrete specific cases exhibited congressional-president-agency interaction.

Policy Retrenchment, Expansion, and Regulatory Reform

During much of the 1950s, securities regulation was scaled back through budget cuts and a precipitous decline in enforcement activity. Much of this was attributed to the fiscal conservatism associated with the Eisenhower administration (Khademian 1992: 58–59). Ralph Demmler, the first SEC chair during the Eisenhower administration, embraced and advocated this frugal approach. Demmler's three-year tenure as SEC chair could be viewed as one exemplifying regulatory retrenchment of the agency's original policy mandate as a strong-arm enforcer of securities markets. Resources allotted to the agency during this period were reduced.[8] During this retrenchment phase, MCs—including Democrats—did not exhibit strong opposition since policy change was initiated by the legal securities experts at the SEC, who had earned a great deal of respect and authority (via congressional delegation) during the first twenty years of federal securities regulation (Khademian 1992: 60).[9]

This situation, however, began to change dramatically in the early 1960s for three reasons. First, industry growth—measured via market volume and industry employment—placed a greater strain on SEC enforcement mechanisms, and a dramatic rise in illegal securities activities ensued (e.g., the AMEX scandal and market crash). Second, the Kennedy administration wanted to alter the direction of securities regulation by placing a stronger emphasis and greater responsibility for enforcement activity on the SEC in order to handle the burgeoning growth of this industry. To carry out these formidable policy plans, in 1961 the administration appointed Columbia law professor Manuel Cary as SEC chair. During Cary's six-year term, the agency became more active by expanding its policy mission of regulating securities and commodities markets. Third, the 1964 amendments to the Securities Act of 1934 imposed strong disclosure requirements for a vast majority of the firms (those with more than $1 million in assets and 750 shareholders) involved in securities market transactions (Cary 1967: 91–92; Khademian 1992: 63). In conjunction, these three events resulted in greater policy expansion for the SEC regulation of securities and commodity markets.

Attempts at stringent regulatory enforcement by the SEC during the early 1970s was disrupted because of political scandals involving top-level appointees in the Nixon administration. The first low point came in 1971 when Nixon's SEC chair William Casey, in response to an open investigation, tried to obtain favorable treatment for International Telephone and Telegraph (IT&T) from the DOJ. IT&T had promised to become a major financial contributor to the 1971 Republican National Convention if the firm received beneficial treatment (Khademian 1992: 123). Casey's replacement the following year, Bradford Cook, was forced out ten weeks into his term as a result of his interference in another SEC investigation involving a company headed by Robert Vesco, which contributed to Nixon's 1972 reelection campaign. These political scandals had the net impact of restoring the credibility of the career staff at the SEC as an enforcer of securities markets. The Nixon administration's reputation in the area of securities regulation was tarnished as a result of these appointment fiascos, however. In order to restore confidence in the top echelon at the SEC, the administration was forced to make two key appointments. The well-respected, moderate Ray Garrett was appointed SEC chairman in 1973. The following year, Irving Pollock was appointed a commissioner to the SEC. Pollock's reputation as a tough yet fair-minded regulator made his appointment very important for restoring credibility for the agency at the commissioner level (Khademian 1992: 142–43).

During this period the SEC's enforcement vigor and budgetary resources were dampened to some extent by efforts from the Nixon White House (Khademian 1992: 135). The agency offset the lack of support from the Nixon administration by seeking congressional aid (Khademian 1992: 138). During this turbulent time, for example, the 1970 amendments to the Investment Company Act modestly reformed mutual fund practices by allowing the SEC to take actions against excessive fees or to sue for breach of fiduciary duty. Khademian (1992: 67) contends that these amendments were largely obtained through both the SEC's strong efforts and its reputation in Congress as being staffed by policy experts. These amendments, however, did limit the SEC's power to impose "fair" fees or set standards. Furthermore, this legislation placed the burden of proof concerning these types of abuses with the SEC or harmed shareholders (*CQ Almanac* 1970: 890–94; Khademian 1992: 65).

Important legislative change came about in the form of the 1975 amendments to the Securities Acts. These amendments were in response to the meteoric rise in the volume of trade that eventually resulted in the "back-office" crisis of 1968 (Baruch 1971).[10] The 1975 amendments contained three components that greatly augmented the amount of power Congress delegated to the SEC. First, this piece of legislation enhanced the SEC's role in enforcement and market oversight activities related to the Securities Exchange Act. This was done by giving the SEC preemptive rule-making authority over members of industry who were not previously subject to SEC control—such as clearing houses and financial data suppliers (Khademian 1992: 71). These amendments also attempted to promote greater competition by removing intermarket barriers to trade and by replacing the fixed-rate broker rate system with competitive (variable) rates. Finally, Congress delegated the implementation of these structural reform initiatives to the securities and legal expertise of the SEC.[11]

In the end, a combination of rapid growth in the securities industry, executive branch scandals under the Nixon administration, and congressional committee support led to a significant rise of regulatory enforcement powers at the SEC's disposal. The alteration of securities regulation was then not given much attention during the Ford and Carter administrations.[12] The only change in securities regulation during this era came from the 1975 amendments, which were pushed onto the agenda and largely formulated by Congress without much presidential leadership. Instead, the Ford and Carter administrations maintained the status quo disclosure-enforcement framework (Khademian 1992; but see Moe 1982). Enforcement activity picked up in a gradual fashion during the 1975–1980 period, but it did not last for very long as the Reagan administration tried to pull the teeth out of SEC enforcement through both budget cuts and the appointment of Mike Shad as SEC chair.

The Assault on Securities Regulation During the Reagan Years

The strong enforcement powers and regulatory vigor acquired by the SEC during the mid and late 1970s was met with a terrible backlash from the securities industry. The industry believed that the strong regulatory apparatus was a hindrance to the nation's economic growth (Khademian 1992: 154). The election of Ronald Reagan as president in 1980 signaled yet another twist in the regulatory cycle for the securities industry. In Reagan's first year in office, he appointed Mike Shad to the SEC chair. Shad was an individual with extensive private sector experience in the securities and commodities industry, and he shared the Reagan administration's general proclivity for deregulating the American economy, largely through administrative means. This was borne out clearly before his appointment when he supported limiting disclosure and enforcement growth during the 1970s (159). During his tenure as SEC chair, from 1981–1986, Shad promoted the most widespread regulatory retrenchment—in terms of SEC enforcement and resource levels—of any chair since Ralph Demmler in the mid-1950s. Both the Reagan administration and Chairman Shad had a very different view of securities regulation than that of their predecessors. They felt the agency's main function was to encourage capital formation as a means of spurring economic growth (155). Although Shad kept enforcement activity at moderate levels for a very brief one-year period, the policy views of both the Reagan administration and Shad were soon reflected by the decline in SEC enforcement activity in subsequent years (175).[13]

At the heart of the Reagan deregulatory agenda was the use of economic analysis as a means to make regulatory decisions (Eads and Fix 1984; Reagan 1987). This method of analysis was emphasized by Shad during his tenure as SEC chair. During the 1980s, economics played an increasingly important role in securities regulation under the auspices of the newly created Office of the Chief Economist (OCE) within the SEC chair's office. Unlike antitrust regulation, attempts to employ economic modes of analysis in case selection and enforcement activity were not very successful because legal doctrine reigned supreme for two reasons. First, economic modes of analysis were viewed with disdain by many both at the SEC and in Congress because they were perceived as a means to justify political purposes (i.e., less stringent regulatory enforcement). Second, from the very beginning securities regulation was dominated by lawyers.[14] This was still the case in the 1980s, when economists began to take on a more prominent role within the agency.

The administrative tactics of the Reagan administration and Chairman Shad were viewed unfavorably by others. Many at both the SEC (including commissioners and career staff) and in Congress (especially the House Democrats on the Energy and Commerce Committee) strongly opposed these deregulatory efforts. The SEC budgetary cuts proposed by the Reagan administration were not only opposed by a majority of SEC commissioners (Shad notwithstanding) and House Democrats, but also by Senate Republicans such as Alfonse D'Amato (R-NY). The general feeling of those opposed to the cuts was that the agency's ability to faithfully and adequately address its regulatory duties would be put in jeopardy (Khademian 1992: 172–75). Both presidential and congressional behaviors were consistent with the commonly held view that budgetary resources not only play a vital role in affecting the lifeblood of an agency's mission (Downs 1967; Lewis-Beck 1979; Meier 1985; Quirk 1981; Seidman and Gilmour 1986; Redford 1969; Weingast 1984; Wilson 1989; Yates 1982) but can also serve as a means to signal approval or disapproval of agency activities (Bendor and Moe 1985; Carpenter 1992, 1996; Khademian 1992: 174; Padgett 1980, 1981; Weingast and Moran 1983).[15]

The securities industry supported SEC budgetary increases for the purpose of maintaining fair securities and commodity markets. The net policy effect in the area of securities regulation and enforcement during the early 1980s was that enforcement became much less stringent than in the preceding two presidential administrations. During the late 1980s through the early 1990s, however, the pendulum swung back in favor of more stringent securities regulation and enforcement. This was because of coalitional support among the SEC, the securities and commodity industry, and MCs from both political parties. Also, the salience of securities regulation rose dramatically during this period, as highly publicized cases involving insider trading and other fraudulent market practices resulted in greater pressure from the public for tougher enforcement of securities laws and regulations.

The Politics of Antitrust Regulation: Policy Background and History

The roots of antitrust regulation in the United States reach back to the late nineteenth century. During the industrial revolution, gross disparities and inequities in private business practices became clearly evident. During the 1880s, for instance, mergers and price agreements between firms left workers, farmers, consumers, and independent businesses worse off at the expense of large business interests. In response to this situation, this latter set of actors formed a coalition to resist the domination and further proliferation of these arrangements termed *"trusts."* The need for market restraint led to a call for antitrust laws and regulations. Historian Richard Hofstadter (1991: 23–24) noted in 1965 that this form of regulation had three thematic goals or purposes—economic, political, and social/moral:

The goals of antitrust were of three kinds. The first were economic; the classical model of competition confirmed the belief that the maximum economic efficiency would be produced by competition, and at least some members of Congress must have been under the spell of this intellectually elegant model, insofar as they were able to formulate their economic intentions in abstract terms. The second class of goal was political; the antitrust principle was intended to block private accumulations of power and protect democratic government. The third was social and moral; the competitive process was believed to be a kind of disciplinary machinery for the development of character, and the competitiveness of the people—the fundamental stimulus to the national morale—was believed to need protection.

Out of this general concern came the adoption of the Sherman Act of 1890. The technical purpose of this legislation was to bring about the optimal degree of competition in individual economic markets (Shepherd 1985), but the new legislative act did not have any substantive force in its early years.

Learning to Crawl: The Formative Years of Antitrust Regulation, 1890–1938

Although antitrust enforcement efforts were modest during this period, there were three noticeable events that would have implications for years to come. First, two antitrust principles were instituted via court decisions. The significant *Addlyston Pipe and Steel Company v. United States (1899)* decision concluded that cartel agreements to divide markets or fix processes were to be illegal. Five years later, the federal government obtained the power of corporate divestiture in the *Northern Securities Company v. United States (1904)* decision. This "trust-busting" authority was placed with the federal government because of a phrase in the Sherman Act that permitted the Attorney General of the United States to seek enforcement through judicial proceedings. Finally, in 1911 Chief Justice White issued the "rule of reason" edict within the context of the Sherman Act. This decree had the net effect of limiting the power of antitrust enforcement for several decades, because it reversed the burden of proof onto the agencies to jointly demonstrate (1) that a monopoly or restraint existed, and (2) that it had "unreasonable" origins or effects.[16] These measures, in conjunction, created a situation where the Sherman Act had no real effect on the structure and performance of American industry.

The political climate surrounding antitrust regulation began to change during the 1906–1920 period, when antitrust activism was most visible in the White House. Presidents Roosevelt, Taft, and Wilson tapped into the populist notion of "trust-busting" in the name of competitive fairness for U.S. industries and macroeconomic expansion. With the exception of the "rule of reason" doctrine, the judicial branch began to play an important role in shaping the broad contours of antitrust policy. Three landmark judicial decisions coming from the classic cases of *Standard Oil v. United States (1911)*, *American Tobacco Corporation v. United States (1911)*, and *U.S. Steel Corporation v. United States (1920)* showed that the winds of policy change were in full force. The federal government (via the Antitrust Division) was granted the right to use divesture decrees as a means to halt anticompetitive business practices. On the legislative side, Congress passed the Clayton Act in 1914. This piece of legislation outlawed specific acts broadly defined in the Sherman Act.

The 1920–1938 period saw an era of malaise in antitrust regulatory efforts. In this era, a "good" trust was one that did not exceed a market share of 50 percent. These "reputable" trusts were safe from government action (Dewey 1990: 6–7). The net result of this "rule of thumb" for antitrust regulation was that there were very few perpetrators of this guideline. Moreover, presidents displayed little policy interest in matters relating to antitrust enforcement. For these reasons, it came as no surprise that the enforcement activity of the Antitrust Division came to a halt during this period (Shepherd 1985: 131).

A Revival in Antitrust Regulation: The Evolution and Fall of Structuralism Philosophy, 1938–1976

The advent of the structure-conduct-performance antitrust regulatory philosophy began in 1937, four years after the creation of the agency in 1933. Marc Eisner (1991: 77) notes in referring to the task forces put together by FDR to study the troubled economy in 1937 that, at this time, "The economic arguments that informed the policy debates can be conveniently referred to as economic structuralism. The central insight was that market structure was causally linked with corporate conduct and economic performance." The next year, President Franklin D. Roosevelt appointed Yale University law professor Thurman Arnold to head the Antitrust Division to mount a highly publicized campaign against monopolistic business practices. What began was active use of the Structure-Conduct-Performance (SCP) paradigm in antitrust regulation. This philosophical approach remained the consensus position in industrial organization for most of the postwar period until the 1970s when the Chicago school began to challenge the structuralist consensus (Eisner 1991: 107).

The Truman administration also pursued vigorous enforcement of antitrust laws, especially in the area of monopoly trusts, as being a necessary component for national economic recovery (Dewey 1990: 9). The emphasis of this regulatory strategy for the next thirty-five years was clearly dominated by a structure-conduct-performance philosophy. This approach to regulatory enforcement placed a tremendous emphasis on vertical activities involving mergers, monopolies, and exclusive dealing arrangements. The accent of this anticompetitive strategy was on creating economic markets where firms had fair opportunities to produce and sell a good or service. The passage of the Celler-Kefauver Act served to specifically amend Section 7 of the Clayton Act (i.e., prohibit corporate mergers that risked drastically reducing competition). The net result was that this piece of legislation was designed to further prevent anticompetitive mergers.

The pace of antitrust regulatory advancement slowed considerably during most of the 1950s. During the Eisenhower administration, the Antitrust Division pulled back from pursuing cases against corporate giants such as IBM and AT&T (Shepherd 1985: 132). However, antitrust regulatory efforts expanded moderately under the leadership of Donald Turner during the 1965–1968 period. A sizable portion of AD enforcement activities under Assistant Attorney General–Head of the Antitrust Division Turner's era were centered around regulating electric and other utility-based companies (Eisner 1991). There was very little renowned action, however, taken toward issues pertaining to oligopoly and monopoly during this time. The number of conglomerate mergers increased dramatically in the mid to late 1960s (Shepherd 1985: 132).

The Antitrust Division during both the Nixon and Ford administrations pursued a vigorous enforcement agenda. Much of this effort was reflected in major cases against AT&T, Xerox, oil companies, and cereal firms. The regulatory effort during this period was geared toward combating both vertical and horizontal activities. With regard to the latter, the Antitrust Division promoted new competition in industries via merger administrative procedures, which focused on levying penalties for firms involved in price-fixing. The Hart-Scott-Rodino Antitrust Improvements Act of 1976 assisted regulatory enforcement of merger activities by creating a premerger notification system that provided the Antitrust Division with adequate material to appraise the competitive and legal implications of any such activity (Eisner 1991). Premerger screening augmented the advisory role of the Antitrust Division since the agency could alter the proposed arrangement, instead of having divestiture as the only tool to shape market structure.

The Struggle Between Legal and Economic Approaches to Antitrust Regulation

Domination of antitrust regulation by agency attorneys within the Antitrust Division was no longer the case with the birth of the Economic Policy Office (EPO) in 1972. This office was instituted by Assistant Attorney General Thomas Kauper and it operated under the leadership of his assistant, George Hay. Before the early 1970s, lawyers had determined which cases would be pursued and/or brought to court. The creation of the EPO meant that economic analysis was used initially as a litmus test of sorts to determine the efficacy of a case, and then eventually as a way to judge whether antitrust violations had occurred (Eisner and Meier 1990; Eisner 1991). Eisner (1991: 137) notes that the purpose behind the creation of the EPO was to form an economic staff rich in quality and size in order to assign an economist to every case at an early stage. The shifting of power from lawyers to economists within the agency had major policy implications since each group of professionals within the agency used different analytical tools and approaches in tackling antitrust issues. For example, based on their educational and professional experiences, lawyers placed a premium on advocating and interpreting the rules and laws of antitrust regulation, whereas economists used relatively well defined economic theories to arrive at policy decisions. From an organizational perspective, the economists and their brand of analysis assisted the Antitrust Division to operate in a more efficient and ordered manner.

During this same period of time, the field of industrial organization in economics and law was undergoing a major intellectual transformation of its own. Scholars at the Chicago School of Economics (as well as others at various institutions who shared their views) during the 1960s began to criticize the structure-conduct-performance framework of antitrust analysis. Two influential books—written almost a decade later by Robert Bork (1978) and Richard Posner (1976)—articulated the Chicago School philosophy, which espoused the belief that vertical activities within an industry (e.g., monopoly and certain types of mergers) should not be of concern to the enforcement of antitrust laws; rather, the emphasis should be on horizontal market activities, most notably price-fixing. Bork (1978) staked out an extreme position by insisting that conventional price theory (i.e., price-fixing) should be the sole method of evaluating the efficacy of antitrust issues. The logic underlying Bork's argument was that this form of antitrust is the only one that affects social welfare through a reduction in the benefits enjoyed by consumers.

This intellectual approach had relevance in the enforcement of antitrust laws as the role of economics began to infiltrate the Antitrust Division— through the creation of the EPO as well as through the increasing proportion of economists to attorneys within the Antitrust Division during the 1970s (Eisner and Meier 1990; Eisner 1991).[17] The death knell of the structure-conduct-performance philosophy did not come from within the agency but from the outside, with two famous cases—*United States v. General Dynamics (1974)* and *United States v. Marine Bancorporation (1974)*—that employed the analytic thinking of these new economic approaches in dealing with antitrust issues. In both cases, the courts ruled in favor of the private company, which sent a strong message to those enforcing antitrust laws: economic modes of analyses would be utilized in arriving at judicial decisions on matters of antitrust regulation.

The predominance of the Chicago School's emphasis on horizontal market activities rose concurrently with the importance of economic analysis, in that such analytic means were used to decide upon which cases to pursue, and that they shaped the content of antitrust regulatory policy. Even though Jimmy Carter had appointed John Shennenfield, a proponent of the structure-conduct-performance framework, Eisner (1991: 149) maintains that this selection had no significant impact because of the power enjoyed by economists in case selection.[18] Because of his desire to see government regulations subject to economic litmus tests, the emphasis on economic modes of analysis in antitrust regulation would also prove beneficial to Ronald Reagan when he assumed office in January 1981. Thus, the Reagan administration did not have to invest the same amount of human energy to "convert" agency personnel as they would do in many other areas of regulatory policy (Nathan 1986).

Accordingly, some scholars contend that significant policy change from the structure-conduct-performance to the Chicago School of economics did not transpire until the Reagan administration assumed office in 1981 (Anderson 1986; Dewey 1990; Mueller 1986; Wood and Anderson 1993). These individuals claim that conglomerate, vertical, and horizontal mergers (involving small market shares) were abandoned for the sake of emphasizing price-fixing agreements that reduced consumer welfare within the Antitrust Division as a policy objective (Dewey 1990: 39; Shugart 1990: 189). This approach focused on allocative efficiency, not fairness and equity, as the defining litmus test for antitrust regulation (Eisner 1991: 190; Wood and Anderson 1993). While it is true that Reagan administration appointments to leadership positions within the Antitrust Division were "Chicago School"–trained lawyers and economists, Eisner claims that this was a continuation of an intra-organizational trend that placed a premium on economic modes of analysis that predated Reagan's arrival to Washington in 1981 (Eisner and Meier 1990; Eisner 1991: 185; but see Wood and Anderson 1993 for an opposing viewpoint). It is argued by some (Eisner 1991: 206; Sullivan 1986) that the Reagan antitrust philosophy was predicated upon advocating competition, even at the expense of enforcing the existing antitrust laws.

The Reagan administration's antitrust record clearly demonstrates that most of the reforms it supported were administrative-oriented strategies, as opposed to legislative action (Shugart 1990: 190). For example, the Antitrust Division was reorganized under the leadership of Assistant Attorney General Douglas Ginsburg in 1984. This reorganization effort was designed to streamline the organizational apparatus within the Antitrust Division through the creation of two analogous units reflecting the agency's interest in litigation activities and regulatory intervention (Eisner 1991: 193; Gorinson 1985). The reorganization also had the effect of granting additional legitimacy for economics within the Antitrust Division by renaming the director of the EPO as Deputy Assistant Attorney General for Economic Analysis (Eisner 1991: 194). Eisner (1991: 189) notes that all AD heads under Reagan (from William Baxter to Richard Rule) were activists of the "Chicago School" economic approach to antitrust issues. Moreover, he argues that during this time the policy goals of political executives within the Antitrust Division were converging with the policy goals of the careerists within the agency.

Besides the predominant "administrative" strategy that transpired during the Reagan presidency, a less pervasive assault was launched on the legislative front. The purpose of these various legislative proposals was to update existing statutes to embody economic modes of analysis and decision making. One notable proposal was the Merger Modernization Act of 1986. This legislation was designed to modify the language of the Clayton Act so as to make antitrust laws more lax by focusing on probabilistic outcomes as opposed to structure and processes (Cohodas 1986; Eisner 1991: 208; Shugart 1987, 1990: 177). In the final analysis, since many of the reforms associated with the Reagan revolution in antitrust were implemented administratively and not legislatively, these policy intentions have been all but dismantled.[19] Shugart (1990: 190) echoes this perspective by stating that history will view antitrust regulatory policy during the 1980s as a temporary aberration.

Coming Full Circle: Conflicting Views of Agency-Political Relations in Securities and Antitrust Regulation

Past research on administrative behavior in the areas of securities and antitrust regulation has been abundant yet has yielded precious little clarity regarding the nature of agency-political relations. This is troubling since each study comes from a distinct theoretical perspective, which produces empirical tests of hypotheses that ignore issues of endogenous institutions and dynamic behavior across time. For example, Kohlmeier (1969) charges that regulatory enforcement has been more stringent under Democratic presidential administrations than under Republican administrations—for the obvious reason that the latter are more *"business friendly"* than the former.

Terry Moe's (1982) classic article, however, finds surprising results that run contrary to Kohlmeier's assertion. Moe found that regulatory enforcement varies across presidential administrations, and that it was significantly lower for both the Kennedy and Johnson (Democratic) presidential administrations than in the Truman years. This same study also reveals that regulatory enforcement was significantly higher for both Eisenhower and Nixon-Ford (Republican) presidential administrations than during the Truman years.

Around the same time, Weingast (1984) asserts that congressional involvement in securities regulation was dormant in the 1940s and 1950s but was activated in 1960 when the SEC became an active policy maker. According to Weingast, congressional involvement in SEC affairs is directly tied to the greater political payoffs associated with the agency's more vibrant policy-making function. Weingast contends that increases in the federal budget have been associated with even larger SEC budgets in the post-1959 period. Alternatively stated, congressional investment in the SEC (reflected by resource allocations) significantly rose in the post-1959 period. Based on his investigation, Weingast concludes that congressional dominance over SEC activities has occurred during the 1960s and 1970s.

None of the aforementioned works gives the bureaucracy an active role as a policy maker. Instead they treat it as a passive instrument of politicians. Rather than extend the "political control" thesis, Khademian (1992) argues that the SEC has a *politically independent* and *significant* role to play in the formulation of securities policy, because of the highly technical nature of the SEC policy mission and the respect it receives from politicians and industry alike. Through its policy and technical expertise, the SEC must cooperate with congressional committees to have the power to alter agency behavior (Khademian 1992: 185–96).[20] Thus, Khademian concludes that the SEC does have some degree of independent power.

In the area of antitrust regulatory enforcement, scholars differ on the nature of behavioral relations between the Antitrust Division (DOJ), the president, and Congress.[21] Both the bureaucratic autonomy and the power perspectives receive considerable support. Eisner and Meier (1990) argue that the main explanation for the changing substantive nature of antitrust regulation lies with the creation of the EPO in 1972 under Assistant Attorney General Thomas Kauper. According to Eisner and Meier, this office was a bastion for conservative "Chicago" economic philosophy. This change to a different antitrust philosophy resulted in an internal change within the Antitrust Division from attorneys to economists as major players in regulatory enforcement activity. Eisner and Meier's empirical findings suggest that neither the Reagan administration nor Congress played a significant role in shaping U.S. antitrust policy. Rather, internal bureaucratic policy change (as a result of agency professionalization) is the main factor explaining variations in the substance of antitrust policy. Katzmann (1980) states that the Antitrust Division is perceived to be generally free from political pressures since it is buffered from the administration. Katzmann, however, does acknowledge that bureaucratic discretion does not hold in all instances.[22] In a similar vein, Suzanne Weaver's (1977) analysis of the Antitrust Division also concludes that antitrust enforcement behavior is not related to the behavior of elected officials but rather reflects a desire on the part of lawyers within the Antitrust Division to acquire litigation experience (especially in areas pertaining to some sort of collusive practice) for purposes of advancing their own individual careers. These works strongly suggest that the Antitrust Division customarily enforces antitrust regulations largely independent from political influence.

Wood and Anderson (1993), however, argue that agency professionalization in the AD case is determined in a "top-down" manner—in accordance with Redford's (1969) theory of overhead democracy, whereby antitrust policy is a product of various combinations of factors such as presidential administrations, appointments, budgets, congressional-oversight-policy liberalism (measured by annual mean ADA scores), legislation, landmark judicial decisions, issue salience, and macroeconomic conditions. Contrary to Eisner and Meier (1990), their findings also reveal that the mix of economists to attorneys did not affect the substance of antitrust regulation during the 1970s and 1980s. Wood and Anderson are not alone in their views that politicians do influence antitrust regulation. Donald Dewey (1990: 10) also concurs with the political control view by arguing that the Reagan administration changed the course of antitrust regulation in the United States by applying Richard Posner's (1979) "lens of price theory" to important antitrust issues. Others have also found that political influence, in one shape or another, has had a significant impact on the volume of antitrust enforcement activity conducted by the Antitrust Division (Lewis-Beck 1979; Moe 1982).

One thing is apparent. There is much disagreement regarding whether bureaucratic agencies—which are responsible for enforcing securities and antitrust regulation—behave in an autonomous manner, or if they are simply responding to political pressures from democratic institutions. Given the behavioral complexity among bureaucratic agencies and political institutions, it is hardly surprising to see disparate findings. Each study makes logically intuitive claims backed by solid empirical evidence of some sort. Since these types of relationships are intricate to begin with, and there is also no clear consensus on whether bureaucrats behave in an independent fashion, it is essential that a general unified model of agency-political relations be used to test these theoretical notions. The bottom line is that the body of existing research does not consider the administration of securities or antitrust regulation as a dynamic interrelated system of government institutions; therefore, one can only store limited faith in the insights acquired from existing studies. The next chapter presents the empirical application of the dynamic systems model, as a way of obtaining both a more general and a more realistic portrait of administrative politics in a democratic system such as the United States.

Chapter 4

An Empirical Investigation into the Institutional Dynamics of Regulatory Enforcement in a Democratic System

Introduction

The lack of theoretical unity within the research on administrative politics reflects the often disparate findings one encounters when studying institutional relationships. The dynamic systems model of administrative politics is designed in a manner that allows one to empirically test competing theoretical notions of agency-political relationships: bureaucratic influence, bureaucratic autonomy, mutual adaptation, or political control. This framework also affords an opportunity to make distinctions between gradual adaptive behavior and sophisticated behavior by institutions.

For instance, securities regulation in the United States has been the subject of many studies in the area of administrative politics, where evidence has been contradictory regarding which institution or institutions are the sources of administrative behavior. One study shows that Congress is the dominant force behind securities regulation, policy, and agency (SEC) behavior (Weingast 1984); another alleges presidential control over regulatory enforcement by the SEC (Moe 1982); another claims that the power of policy expertise exhibited by SEC staffers is subsequently parlayed into bureaucratic autonomy for the agency (Khademian 1992). Obviously, the findings and conclusions drawn from each study appear in direct conflict with the others.

Similarly, a host of studies by political scientists has explored antitrust regulation in the United States. Some claim that bureaucratic politics (via administrative professionalization) has led to changes in regulatory priorities on behalf of the Antitrust Division (Eisner and Meier 1990; Eisner 1991).[1] Both Anderson (1986) and Mueller (1986) contend that major changes in antitrust policy and enforcement reflected the Reagan administration's desire to substantially alter antitrust regulation. Others allege that antitrust policy falls along partisan lines within the White House (Moe 1982; but see Posner 1970; Lewis-Beck 1979; Wood and Anderson 1993 for evidence to the contrary). Perhaps the most comprehensive study to date is by B. Dan Wood and James Anderson (1993), who view antitrust regulation as a product of a larger institutional framework, reflected by presidential and congressional behavior and subject to macroeconomic conditions and key judicial decisions within the context of a pluralist version of Redford's (1969) overhead theory of democracy, where both the president and Congress play an important role in shaping administrative behavior.

Each of these studies exhibits some major shortcomings. First, they all utilize static theoretical models that inhibit discussion of the dynamic complexity and heterogeneity that characterize administrative politics.[2] Second, each of these studies attempts to explain antitrust regulation by focusing solely on agency behavior. In doing so, they provide an incomplete picture not only of how governmental institutions interact with one another, but also of the manner in which antitrust enforcement efforts are determined. Rather, the dynamic systems model of administrative politics is premised on the notion that, in order to understand relationships between bureaucratic organizations and political institutions, it is necessary not only to explain the behavior of the agency under investigation but also to comprehend the behavior of the political principals. Finally, those espousing the bureaucratic politics/administrative professionalization thesis claim that internal bureaucratic factors—and not political considerations—are essential in determining whether a given agency behaves in an autonomous manner. This may not be the case. These approaches ignore the longer historical thread running throughout institutional relationships among governmental organizations. Furthermore, they do not serve as a direct or conclusive means to demonstrate agency autonomy because they do not examine the way in which agency behavior (measured as its policy output) is interrelated to the behavior of democratic institutions. The utilization of the dynamic systems framework presented earlier can surmount the inherent conceptual problems contained in this previous body of research. This theoretical framework is most helpful in determining the nature of behavioral relations between the president, Congress, and administrative agencies in the areas of securities and antitrust regulatory enforcement from an aggregate, institutional perspective.

The purpose of this chapter is simple: to discover the general pattern of behavioral relations that exists among the SEC, president, and Congress across time. Budgetary signaling behavior and regulatory enforcement vigor serve as the vehicle to analyze these behavioral relationships (the justification for employing these variables in this framework is discussed at length in chapter 2 and appendix B). Through the empirical application of the dynamic systems model proposed earlier, insights can be obtained into the complex causal and responsive mechanisms between these institutions. For instance, agencies may emit potent signals of their own to elected officials. Past formal studies of bureaucratic politics suggest that politicians and agencies send signals to one another (Banks and Weingast 1992; Bendor and Moe 1985; Niskanen 1971).[3]

The dynamic systems model proposed here, because of its relative theoretical neutrality, encompasses various competing explanations of administrative politics found in previous research. Therefore, one can have a higher level of confidence in the empirical findings and subsequent inferences generated here, since the portrayal of the political environment under study is more comprehensive than any existing treatment on this topic. There follows an empirical application of the dynamic systems model of administrative politics to securities regulatory enforcement by the Securities and Exchange Commission (SEC). The next section applies the dynamic systems model to antitrust regulatory enforcement by the Antitrust Division (AD) of the Department of Justice (DOJ). The final section of this chapter summarizes the importance of the empirical findings for students of bureaucratic politics.

Applying the Dynamic Systems Model of Administrative Politics to Securities Regulation

This section applies the dynamic systems model of administrative politics to the case of securities regulation in the United States. The aim here is not simply to determine which of the past studies are correct regarding the driving forces underlying securities regulation in the United States. Instead, the larger focus is on *to what extent* and *in which ways* is each of these theories accurate? The relaxing of three key oversimplifying assumptions of past studies—that is, one-way interaction from elected officials to the agency; absence of interaction between elected officials; and the preclusion of sophisticated response—is assessed empirically in this chapter.

The Dynamic Systems Model of Administrative Politics and Its Application to Securities Regulation

The dynamic systems model of administrative politics has three unique components. The first component deals with mutual adaptation between elected officials and the agency. This form of behavior appears true in the case of securities regulation where Khademian (1992: 185) notes that the SEC and Congress seem to be interdependent, which in turn suggests that elected officials (i.e., Congress and president) may possibly react to the behavior of administrative institutions. This idea is consistent with Anne Khademian's (1992) research on securities regulation. Khademian contends that the bureaucracy is not given an independent role in political-control-based models of principal-agent relations (207). The dynamic systems model treats the agency as an *"active player"*[4] in policy administration by allowing us to examine whether and how the agency responds to political forces, and also how its regulatory enforcement behavior may affect the behavior of any political principals attempting to influence (or control) the agency.[5] This method of examining the *bureaucratic influence hypothesis* (or lack of influence) is much more direct than other proxies used to create the same concept (most notably internal sources of agency professionalization and/or innovation—e.g., Eisner and Meier 1990; Eisner 1992).[6]

The first component of this framework deals with the dual possibilities (1) that the SEC has the ability to exhibit its dependence or independence through its regulatory performance, and (2) that agency-political relationships reveal mutual adaptation (i.e., interaction/interrelatedness). Some support for the initial claim (also purported by Khademian) suggests that agency enforcement behavior is a method to gauge the SEC's independence as an agency. This was corroborated during the course of my interviews with relevant policy actors. A high-ranking SEC career official acknowledges that bureaucratic discretion exists. He adds, however, that agency expertise serves as a double-edged sword, which not only grants the agency discretion but also "actually makes it more difficult to communicate with Congress and the White House" (interview with author, June 1993). As a result of this policy expertise (i.e., information asymmetry), political principals tend to be suspicious of agency activities. This same official also claims that the SEC can help shape the behavior of its political principals by emitting signals of its own through enforcement activity. In the same interview, he states that "both the president and Congress exhibit sensitivity to the number of enforcement cases since it measures productivity in their eyes."

Also, many of the individuals interviewed for this study feel that the relationship between agency and democratic institutions is an interrelated one. For example, an OMB budget/policy analyst dealing with securities regulation states that a "very interactive relationship" exists between the OMB and the SEC (interview with author, June 1993). A top-level congressional committee staff member who deals with securities regulation states that "members of Congress are responsive to agency performance" (interview with author, June 1993). At the same time, individuals interviewed for this study also profess that bureaucratic agency-political institution relationships are a "two-way street"—with the SEC being sensitive to the behavior of its political principals—as is maintained by scholars adopting an "Overhead Democracy" perspective (Moe 1982, 1985a; Redford 1969; Weingast and Moran 1983; Wood and Waterman 1991, 1993, 1994; Wood and Anderson 1993). For instance, a senior official at the SEC admits that "the agency is sensitive to presidential and congressional wishes to some extent," a sentiment echoed by an assistant director of regulatory enforcement who states that "the SEC is sensitive to budgetary signals coming from both the president and White House" (interviews with author, June 1993).

The second component of this framework acknowledges interaction between the regulatory behavior of both the president and Congress. Research on budgetary politics (Cox, Hager, and Lowery, 1993; Kiewiet and McCubbins 1985, 1988, 1991) and legislative politics (Bond and Fleisher 1990; Light 1991; Peterson 1991) note an interrelated relationship between the president and Congress. Quite remarkably, past research on administrative politics generally implies that elected officials have *separate, independent* (from one another) impacts on agency behavior. This implicit assumption precludes the possibility that the behavior of these democratic institutions toward an agency may also partly be a reflection of each other's behavior. This substantive point is clearly consistent with Khademian's (1992) well-documented case study concerning the politics of securities regulation. To be more specific, the tension between the congressional committees and the president (via the OMB and the White House staff) can be quite strong. The interviews conducted with these relevant policy actors lend support for this linkage between democratic institutions. For example, a Congressional Budget Office (CBO) budget and policy analyst who deals with issues relating to securities regulation does admit that there is a certain degree of periodic tension regarding the SEC between the OMB and Congress. These relations, however, generally tend to be cooperative (interview with author, June 1993). The most tense periods of presidential-congressional relations transpired during the Nixon and Reagan administrations when there was active pursuit of policy change, which resulted in conflict with Democrats in Congress (especially in the House). In both cases, congressional Republicans came to the defense of their Democratic colleagues to oppose White House plans for the agency. This bipartisan congressional support is not surprising since MCs on both sides of the aisle generally desire vigorous regulatory enforcement of securities laws (Khademian 1992). Moreover, the lack of a partisan cleavage for this policy environment within Congress suggests that the effects of divided government will not be quite as pervasive compared to many other regulatory environments.

In sum, the general pattern of behavior between the democratic institutions of the presidency and Congress can provide us with a great deal of information and insight into how they interact with one another when it comes to securities regulation. Even more important, this interaction will shape the behaviors these institutions exhibit directly toward the agency. The general argument here is an extension of the first novel component of this framework listed above: in order for one to understand or explain agency behavior across time, one must examine the interactive linkages between the president, Congress, and the agency. Failing to look at this system in a complete manner not only creates an unrealistic portrait of administrative politics but also misses much of the behavior that is instrumental in shaping agency-political relationships and policy administration.

The final component of this dynamic systems framework allows for the possibility of sophisticated behavior and reaction on the part of these institutions. Sophisticated behavior appears to be customary in the case of the SEC. In the course of the interviews with those involved in securities regulation, similar sentiments were echoed repeatedly. For instance, the assistant director of enforcement at the SEC declared that the SEC, White House/OMB, and congressional participants have an idea of what is going on in terms of current behavior on the part of others within the system as a result of numerous meetings held and requests made throughout the year (interview with author, June

1993). A senior SEC official states that informal communications among governmental institutions are strong. This individual's experiences at the SEC lead him to view informal contacts, such as impromptu telephone discussions, as being more important than formal lines of communication (e.g., agency reports, hearings, and official documents). He adds that each institution looks out for its own interests. These comments would lead one to believe that these institutions behave in strategic and subtle ways that do not fit the prevailing conception—of a "lumbering," sluggish adjustment process—that is found in most of the administrative politics literature. This same senior SEC official stated that "There is a free flow of information between the president, Congress, and the agency. Political actors acquire their knowledge from constituents that have problems with the industry,[7] issue salience via the media, and press releases issued by companies" (interview with author, June 1993). An OMB policy analyst in the area of securities regulation reinforced this point by stating that the OMB and the SEC have fairly sound knowledge regarding what the other is currently doing. A congressional committee staff member involved with securities regulation also claims that the individuals and their institutions "do not play games with one another" (interview with author, June 1993). A CBO policy and budget analyst adds to this by suggesting that these various institutions do have knowledge of current policy and use this information to formulate their expectations about institutional behavior; however, perfect information does not exist (interview with author, June 1993). This point is consistent with our theoretical framework as well as with the longstanding view in administrative politics that information is not perfect, nor costless; thus bureaucratic inertia may exist to some extent (Crozier 1964; Downs 1967; Tullock 1965; Wilson 1989) as well as gradual adaptation (Bendor and Moe 1985; Carpenter 1992, 1996; Simon 1947; March and Simon 1958; Wood and Waterman 1993).

This portrait of securities regulation contradicts the conventional theories of administrative politics, which postulate that these actors (especially the administrative agency) can form their behavior *solely* in response to known changes in certain key factors (such as budgetary and appropriation figures, enforcement behavior, economic conditions, and so on). The conventional theories suggest that these institutions do not respond to unanticipated movements (shocks) in the behavior of other actors. Instead, sophisticated behavior reveals that these institutions are aware of the current larger policy environment and operate in an information-abundant environment. From such a perspective, it is not difficult to deduce that sophisticated behavior (and possibly rational expectations) may take place within the system of institutions responsible for policy administration. At any rate, this dynamic systems model is novel in that it allows us to test the assumption of sophisticated behavior (and possibly rational expectations as a special case) often found in formal models between political institutions and the bureaucracy that is typically eschewed in both the qualitative and quantitative empirical literature on this topic.

Operationalization of the Dynamic Systems Model: The Case of Securities Regulation

The application of the dynamic systems theoretical model to the case of securities regulation allows for dynamic interaction among the president, Congress, and the SEC (in terms of their budgetary and enforcement behavior). These relations allow for the possibility of bidirectional causality running between each pair of institutional participants. In total, there are six possible causal linkages between these institutions, comprising the following dyadic relationships: SEC-president, SEC-Congress, president-SEC, president-Congress, Congress-SEC, Congress-president. As a result, one can test hypotheses relating to the causal and responsive mechanisms that underlie these relationships (discussed at greater length in chapter 2). This section attempts to explore whether past congressional appropriations and/or presidential budget requests (via the OMB) have any effect on current agency behavior (in terms of budgetary requests or regulatory enforcement).[8] This portion of the model will capture the *lagged adaptive* aspects of administrative politics and behavior—implied by the notion of bounded rationality—which have been widely documented in past research on administrative behavior (Carpenter 1992, 1996; March and Simon 1958; Moe 1985a; Simon 1947, 1955; Wood and Waterman 1993, 1994).

In addition, one can further test the responsiveness of these institutions by exploring the notion of sophisticated behavior. This can be accomplished by investigating the dynamic historical movements of each institution's policy innovations/shocks (i.e., unexpected deviations in behavior). The analysis of policy innovations on behalf of these governmental institutions reflects the importance of imperfect information and uncertainty that abound in administrative agency-political institution relationships (Epstein and O'Halloran 1994; Calvert, McCubbins, and Weingast 1989; Niskanen 1971; Miller and Moe 1983; Moe 1984). Although this theoretical model acknowledges these conditions, it does not assume in any explicit a priori fashion that institutional behavior is limited by only past observations or realizations of relevant factors, as would be posited by more traditional behavioral approaches of public administration (Bendor and Moe 1985; Carpenter 1992, 1996; Simon 1947; March and Simon 1958; Wood and Waterman 1993). Rather, sophisticated behavior may exist within the context of this analysis, thus implying that administrative and political institutions will rely on new information above and beyond past experiences. Furthermore, such empirical findings will lend credence to rational choice–based models' assumptions of policy actors who behave in an informed and strategic manner by using relevant information available to them in order to help facilitate their decision making.

The variables in the endogenous portion of the model representing the political institutions are constant-dollar presidential (OMB) budgetary requests and congressional appropriations for the SEC. These variables reflect the budgetary-preference signals that emanate from the president and Congress. The agency component of the model is captured as bureaucratic policy outputs, entailing three measures of SEC regulatory enforcement: (1) the total annual number of administrative proceedings (consisting of [a] administrative proceedings initiated under the SEC Act of 1934, [b] administrative proceedings under the Investment Advisers Act of 1940, [c] stop-order administrative proceedings initiated, and [d] temporary suspensions); (2) the total annual number of investigations; and (3) the total annual number of injunctive actions issued. Each of the variables is analyzed separately to assess whether there are differences in bureaucratic agency-political institution relations across different types of agency enforcement output.[9]

The current framework also encompasses factors that are external to these relations by treating them as exogenous (in a strictly deterministic sense) to the behavior of the president, Congress, and SEC. The *"deterministic"* component for each model specification represents the environmental and intra-institutional factors that not only shape agency behavior but also impact the institutional behavior for both the president and Congress. The ideological behavior of the relevant congressional oversight committees and subcommittees for both the House and Senate chambers are incorporated in each model.[10] These measures are operationalized as the relative median Americans for Democratic Action (ADA) score for each relevant sub(committee) located in each chamber. These variables should have a positive effect on agency behavior, congressional appropriations, and presidential budgetary requests.[11] Substantively, relatively more liberal committees vis-à-vis the floor in each chamber are hypothesized to generally result in higher rates of enforcement and spur greater regulatory support from the president and Congress, separately.

Previous studies of securities regulation claim that presidential partisanship is an important factor in explaining variations in regulatory behavior (Khademian 1992; Kohlmeier 1969; Moe 1982). This variable is assigned a value of one during years in which Democrats control the White House, and zero for Republican administrations. The relationship of this variable with political and agency behavior is uncertain. For example, Moe's (1982) findings reveal that Republican administrations support stricter enforcement of securities laws and regulations relative to Democratic administrations. Both Khademian (1992) and Kohlmeier (1969) insist the opposite is true, with Democratic administrations generally supporting greater regulatory enforcement of the securities industry than Republican administrations. These assertions suggest that partisanship of a presidential administration will have a differential effect on the SEC's (political institutions) regulatory (budgetary) behavior. The sign of the relationship between this variable and congressional behavior is unclear. On one hand, if any given partisan administration (e.g., Democratic) exhibits a higher level of budgetary signaling than its partisan counterpart (e.g., Republican administration) and also has a positive impact on congressional behavior relative to the other partisan administration, then one could infer that to some extent congressional budgetary signals move together with presidential budgetary signals along a presidential partisan dimension. If, however, any given partisan administration (e.g., Democratic) displays a higher level of budgetary signals than its partisan counterpart (e.g., Republican administration) but also exerts a negative impact on congressional budgetary signals relative to the other partisan administration, then one can infer that to some extent congressional budgetary signals should move in an opposite direction than presidential budgetary signals. This, in turn, may suggest that—at least along lines of presidential partisanship—congressional behavior will substantively differ (in terms of direction) from that of the current administration.

General macroeconomic conditions may also play a role in affecting not only the enforcement behavior of the agency but also the budgetary behavior of political principals. For this reason they are included in each model specification. Economic growth (measured as the annual percentage change in real GNP) from the previous year should be positively related both to the politicians' desire for more vigorous enforcement as well as to the strengthening of the agency's pursuit of this objective. The simple intuition underlying these relationships implies that governmental institutions will be more lax in the area of regulatory enforcement during periods of low economic growth, from the fear that it will inhibit economic expansion (or further exacerbate economic contraction). Conversely, periods of robust economic growth will lead governmental institutions to pursue regulatory enforcement of the securities industry with enhanced zeal, since these entities do not have to contend with or fear a sluggish economy.[12] Also, SEC enforcement activity is somewhat positively related to the size of the securities industry (Khademian 1992: 70), a prominent example being the rise in regulatory enforcement during the late 1960s and early 1970s, which could be attributed to the industry's rapid growth (in terms of the number of brokers and dealers). Therefore, the size of the securities industry is utilized as a control variable to account for variations in political and agency behavior that can be attributed to the potential size and scope of regulating the industry. To control for the possible confounding influences associated with the size of the industry, this variable is operationalized as the natural log of the number of individuals employed in securities and commodities brokers (in thousands) for each annual period. This measure should have a positive effect on each of the three endogenous measures. The final strictly exogenous variable is a dummy variable, which represents the possible effects of the 1987 stock market event on the regulatory system, and which equals 0 in value for every year before 1988 and 1 for 1988 and for each year thereafter.[13]

Predicting the results of the forthcoming analysis seems difficult in this instance since, at first glance, the agency design (independent regulatory commission) lends itself to easier political manipulation by Congress vis-à-vis the president, while the technical complexity and the constant high level of industry support it receives appears to lend a substantial amount of bureaucratic discretion to the SEC. Based upon Khademian's (1992: 206–07) descriptive and anecdotal evidence, one cannot a priori predict (nor should one, given the vast amount of behavioral complexity that requires the use of exogeneity tests and dynamic simulations) these results since the author contends that political influence and bureaucratic discretion are roughly equal.[14] Some broad assertions, however, can be made. An independent regulatory commission such as the SEC should, ceteris paribus, be more responsive to signals and the institutional behavior of Congress vis-à-vis presidential administrations since these bureaucratic institutions are designed to mitigate executive influence.[15] Moreover, the amount of information asymmetry between the SEC and its political principals will shed light on the nature of causal and responsive behavior on the part of these institutions. In chapter 2 it was alleged that, as the information asymmetry (i.e., advantages on the part of the agency) between agency and political principals becomes greater, it will be easier for any given agency to affect the behavior of its political principals. As the size of the information asymmetry (in favor of the agency) increases, it will be more difficult for political principals to affect agency activity in a predictable or unpredictable manner.

Although the SEC is an agency that has a great advantage in policy expertise over political institutions, at the same time it is a relatively small entity and a highly centralized administrative organization. As a result, one cannot make any clear-cut predictions concerning the nature of agency-political relations within this policy setting. This is where the dynamic systems model allows for a range of theoretical relations that are often viewed as in conflict with one another (e.g., political control versus bureaucratic autonomy). Hopefully, the data analysis will lend insight into these theoretical matters and substantive issues.

Statistical Findings

This subsection involves empirically testing the dynamic systems model of agency-political relations in three different models of SEC regulatory enforcement behavior (total administrative proceedings, total investigations, and total injunctive actions). Because the model relaxes restrictive behavioral assumptions, the empirical results it produces will have more general theoretical implications for agency-political relations than those produced by past research. Considering the logged-differenced nature of the data employed here, the explanatory power of these models is quite robust.[16] The results of the diagnostic tests in appendix D also lend further evidence that the model specifications presented in this analysis are more than adequate.[17]

The first set of analyses focuses on the impact of variables that are treated as exogenous to the system. The second set of results provides information on the temporal (causal) sequence of presidential budgetary signals, congressional appropriation signals, and SEC enforcement behavior signals. Next, the contemporaneous correlation matrix of the signal innovations emanating from each of these institutions is examined. This matrix captures immediate behavioral responses to unanticipated changes in the behavior of these actors. The final two sets of results—innovation accounting and decomposition of the forecast error variance—involve a dynamic historical simulation analysis where each institution within the dynamic system responds to positive one-standard-deviation shocks emanating from one another for eight years following the original perturbation to the system.

The Effects of Exogenous Variables on the President-Congressional-SEC System

The findings of this model are presented in table 4.1. The coefficients and t-statistics associated with the endogenous variables are not presented here, for reasons outlined in appendix C. The impact of these deterministic (or strictly exogenous) variables on each of the endogenous left-hand side variables is listed in table 4.1. In both the president and the Congress equations, relative oversight policy liberalism of congressional committees exerts a negative significant impact on the political (budgetary) signals of each electoral institution in the Administrative Proceedings model formulation, while having a similar meaningful impact on only congressional appropriation signals in the Injunctive Actions model. These seemingly counterintuitive results suggest that more conservative oversight committees in the area of securities regulation, relative to the chamber's floor, will result in more positive budgetary signals on the part of the president and of the Congress as a whole body.[18]

There are three possible explanations for such findings. First, if committee policy ideological behaviors have an adverse effect on both the president and the entire Congress, this may suggest that the latter "lean against the wind"—that is, try to counterbalance the ideological effects of congressional committees. Also, it may reveal that conservatives actually favor greater resource allocations for the SEC to catch those in the market who do not play by the rules. This is not completely astonishing considering Khademian's (1992) assertion that Republicans responsible for overseeing the SEC demonstrate strong support for the agency and its policy mission.[19] Finally, the relationship of oversight committee ideology with congressional appropriations may indicate the possibility of a policy "turf" battle within Congress, between the oversight committee and the general appropriation decisions concerning the SEC.

The presidential partisanship variable indicates that, in all instances, there are no significant differences in presidential budget requests for the SEC, congressional appropriations to the SEC, and SEC enforcement activity along the lines of Democratic versus Republican administrations. The industry size variable is not statistically significant except in one equation (Congress equation in

TABLE 4.1 The Impact of Deterministic Variables on Presidential and Congressional Budgetary Preferences, and SEC Regulatory Performance (1949–1992)

Deterministic Variable	Administrative Proceedings Model			Investigations Model			Injunctive Actions Model		
	President (eq. 1)	Congress (eq. 2)	SEC (eq. 3)	President (eq. 4)	Congress (eq. 5)	SEC (eq. 6)	President (eq. 7)	Congress (eq. 8)	SEC (eq. 9)
Constant	-68.71 (-1.39)	-36.27 (-1.18)	296.94 (1.29)	54.04 (1.35)	86.46*** (3.68)	35.96 (.53)	-.78 (-.02)	47.18 (1.65)	205.13* (1.78)
Senate Subcomm.$_t$	-.18** (-2.48)	-.15** (-3.31)	-.10 (-.31)	-.07 (-1.00)	-.04 (-1.04)	.09 (.13)	-.14 (-1.54)	-.13* (-2.04)	.04 (.14)
House Subcomm.$_t$	-.30** (-2.41)	-.24*** (-3.08)	.21 (.37)	—	—	—	—	—	—
Economic Growth$_{t-1}$	—	—	—	—	—	—	-.07 (-.10)	.45 (.96)	-.81 (-.42)
Presidential Partisanship$_t$	9.95 (1.70)	4.73 (1.30)	-36.35 (-1.33)	3.25 (.74)	-.74 (-.29)	-2.84 (-.38)	1.17 (.27)	-5.07 (-1.60)	-13.30 (-1.04)
LN Industry Size$_t$	5.65 (1.42)	3.01 (1.21)	-22.10 (-1.19)	-4.05 (-1.26)	-6.49*** (-3.50)	-2.61 (-.48)	.16 (.05)	-3.80 (-1.61)	-15.30 (-1.61)
1987 Stock Market Crash$_t$	—	—	—	3.93 (.78)	7.25** (2.51)	5.52 (.64)	—	—	—

Goodness of Fit Statistics for Complete VAR Specifications:

R^2	.70	.84	.61	.71	.87	.68	.72	.79	.65
σ	6.36	3.98	29.66	6.30	3.62	10.74	6.24	4.53	18.26

NOTES: t-statistics are listed inside parentheses. The technical details and empirical results of these tests are discussed in appendix D.
* $p < .10$ ** $p < .05$ *** $p < .01$

the Investigations model). Finally, although congressional budgetary signals are responsive to the enforcement-oriented needs of the SEC in the post-1987 stock market crash, neither presidential budgetary signals nor SEC investigations activity has exhibited a corresponding increase resulting from this exogenous event.

F-Block Tests of Multivariate Granger Causality for President-Congress-SEC System

The multivariate F-block tests of Granger exogeneity (i.e., temporal causality) among the endogenous variables in the various Vector Autoregression

(VAR) model formulations are presented in table 4.2 (see appendix C for methodological design and VAR models). The findings generated from these multivariate causality tests shed a great deal of light on the complexity and heterogeneity of behavioral relations among the agency, president, and Congress. For instance, the F-block tests for the SEC equation are capable of demonstrating support for the notion of incrementalism reflected in administrative behavior (Crozier 1964; Downs 1967; Tullock 1965), and more generally in matters of public policy (Lindblom 1959; Wildavsky 1964). Incrementalism in this study means that an institution's current behavior is affected, at least in part, by its recent past (lagged) behavior. Thus, governmental agencies will update or modify their current actions based upon the institution's recent past actions. Empirical support for this thesis is garnered for presidential budgetary signals (Administrative Proceedings and Investigations models), congressional appropriation signals (Administrative Proceedings, Investigations, and Injunctive Actions models), and SEC enforcement activities (Administrative Proceedings and Investigations models).

Both the president and the Congress equations reveal that the past behavior of all three institutions plays an important role in explaining current presidential and congressional budgetary signals in both the Administrative Proceedings and the Investigations VAR models. The joint significance of these respective blocks of budgetary signal variables demonstrates that presidential and congressional budgetary signals are interdependent (i.e., "Granger cause" [see appendix C]) with respect to one another for the former model—and barely misses obtaining this condition in the latter model, given Congress→President ($p \approx .11$). This result supports the findings and contentions of past research on budgetary politics (Cox, Hager, and Lowery 1993; Davis, Dempster, and Wildavsky 1966; Kiewiet and McCubbins 1985, 1988, 1991: 197–206; Wildavsky 1964). Moreover, this finding is consistent with the view that suggests executive-legislative relations are often intertwined (Bond and Fleisher 1990; Light 1991; Peterson 1991). These results are consistent with the notion that the president plays a major role in setting federal regulatory priorities through his annual (OMB) budget request (Carpenter 1992, 1996; Kiewiet and McCubbins 1991; Padgett 1980, 1981); however, the results also suggest that congressional appropriations assist presidential administrations with the formulation of the president's budgetary requests. In the Injunctive Actions model, however, each political institution fails to respond to lagged changes in the budgetary signals emanating from the others. A more subtle relationship—such as sophisticated

TABLE 4.2 F-Block Tests of Direct Causal Relations Between the President, Congress, and the SEC (1949–1992)

Block of Coefficients	Administrative Proceedings Model—VAR (4)			Investigations Model—VAR (4)			Injunctive Actions Model—VAR (4)		
	President (eq. 1)	Congress (eq. 2)	SEC (eq. 3)	President (eq. 4)	Congress (eq. 5)	SEC (eq. 6)	President (eq. 7)	Congress (eq. 8)	SEC (eq. 9)
President	3.92[a]**	3.29**	.71	3.80**	8.81***	.57	1.35	1.53	1.64
	(.02)[b]	(.03)	(.59)	(.02)	(.00)	(.69)	(.28)	(.23)	(.20)
Congress	3.72**	4.85***	.82	2.18	7.97***	.77	.65	4.14**	2.12
	(.02)	(.01)	(.53)	(.11)	(.00)	(.56)	(.63)	(.01)	(.11)
SEC	2.72*	6.04***	3.83**	3.77**	8.23***	4.92***	3.61**	3.85**	1.08
	(.06)	(.00)	(.02)	(.02)	(.00)	(.00)	(.02)	(.02)	(.39)

NOTES: a. F-statistics for determining Granger Causality.
b. Significance levels are listed inside parentheses. They are rounded out to the nearest hundredth decimal place.
*** $p < .10$ ** $p < .05$ * $p < .01$

response—may possibly exist, but cannot be ascertained by focusing on the lagged adaptive aspects of administrative politics.

As a matter of fact, past variations in agency enforcement output signals are influenced by this institution's own past values in a manner consistent with incrementalism in both the Administrative Proceedings and the Investigations models. All three SEC equations reveal that current regulatory enforcement behavior is not temporally dependent upon the budgetary signals the agency receives from either the president and Congress. This is borne out by the fact that neither presidential nor congressional budgetary signal variables are jointly significant in the SEC equations for each of the three statistical models.

Based upon the theoretical framework proposed in chapter 2, these tests indicate that each agency-political dyadic relationship of SEC-president and SEC-Congress for all three VAR models follows the *bureaucratic influence hypothesis* —that is, past SEC regulatory enforcement behavior significantly influences current presidential and congressional budgetary signals separately, but the opposite does not hold true. Thus, the behaviors of democratic institutions are not independently determined as implied in the systematic research noted earlier. Instead, both executive and legislative democratic institutions are *conditioned* by the regulatory behavior of the agency responsible for policy administration—the SEC. Through its regulatory enforcement activity, administrative agencies can alter the manner in which elected officials signal support for the agency's policy mission. These results are in direct contrast to past empirical findings of principal-agent formulations of the political control over the bureaucracy thesis, which finds the nature of temporal causation flows from political principal(s) to the administrative agency (Carpenter 1992, 1996; Hedge and Scicchitano 1994; Moe 1982, 1985a; Ringquist 1995; Scholz, Twombly, and Headrick 1991; Wood 1988, 1990; Weingast and Moran 1983; Weingast 1984; Wood and Waterman 1991, 1993, 1994). As a result, these past works incorrectly presume that bureaucratic organizations are not capable of emitting stimuli of their own to affect political principals. The results presented in this section dispel this commonly accepted notion when examining the vigor of aggregate securities regulatory enforcement.

Contemporaneous Correlation of Innovations for
President-Congress-SEC System

The contemporaneous residual correlation matrix for the Administrative Proceedings model is presented in table 4.3. There is strong reciprocal behavior concerning contemporaneous innovations between presidential and congressional budgetary signals ($r = .51$, Administrative Proceedings model; $r = .60$, Investigations model; and ($r = .59$, Injunctive Actions model). This suggests that current (contemporaneous) period innovations on behalf of one institution will be matched with a response in the same direction. This finding could be interpreted as implying that political principals may not always be competing with one another for political control but, instead, will exhibit solidarity or cooperation in times of unanticipated changes in the budgetary-preference signaling behavior on the part of either institution. This is hardly surprising, given that agencies will attempt to play political principals off against one another in order to gain greater autonomy (Bryner 1987; Dahl and Lindblom 1953; Wilson 1989). Such a finding indicates that political principals are aware of this potential dilemma. Thus, political institutions' contemporaneous responses to a shock will result in a reciprocal shift toward each other. Political principals appear to exhibit solidarity or cooperation (at least in the short run) in times of unexpected changes in behavior.

In the Injunctive Actions model, where neither the president nor Congress "Granger cause" each other's budgetary signals, the significant positive contemporaneous correlation among these institutions' innovations is possibly indicative of evidence of rational expectations between these institutions, pertaining to SEC injunctive action outputs. The correlation of the contemporaneous policy innovations between SEC-president dyad ranges from $-.04 \leq r \leq .19$,

TABLE 4.3 Contemporaneous Policy Innovation (Residual) Correlation Matrices for VAR Models for Securities Regulatory Enforcement (1949–1992)

	Administrative Proceedings Model			Investigations Model			Injunctive Actions Model		
	President (eq. 1)	*Congress (eq. 2)*	*SEC (eq. 3)*	*President (eq. 4)*	*Congress (eq. 5)*	*SEC (eq. 6)*	*President (eq. 7)*	*Congress (eq. 8)*	*SEC (eq. 9)*
President	—	$.51^{***}$	-.04	—	$.60^{***}$	.16	—	.59***	.19
Congress	—	—	-.07	—	—	.06	—	—	.08
SEC	—	—	—	—	—	—	—	—	—

NOTES: These entries represent the contemporaneous correlation of policy innovations (errors) on behalf of the President, Congress, and the SEC.
*** $p < .01$

and between $-.07 \leq r \leq .08$ for the Congress-SEC dyad. These results indicate that these institutions respond in an anemic manner. The lack of a potent correlation may reflect a substantial lack of information, as well as a limited degree of acquiescence displayed by these institutions toward one another.

Simulated Response to a Shock in the President-Congress-SEC System

A dynamic simulation (Moving Average Representation [MAR] innovation accounting) exercise is conducted to see how behavior emanating from each of these institutions responds to an innovation (unexpected change) emanating from each institution. In the MAR exercise a contemporaneous causal ordering among perturbations is employed, based on the temporal sequence of the annual agency performance–political budgetary process (Williams and McGinnis 1992). The contemporaneous ordering of presidential (OMB request) behavior, congressional (appropriations) behavior, and SEC (enforcement) behavior was selected—since presidents initially set budgetary priorities for all administrative agencies through their annual budget request, Congress alters this request and appropriates it to the agency in question, and the agency uses these appropriated funds to administer policy.[20] The MAR response analysis is usually presented in graphical form; this study does not depart from conventional practice.[21]

The dynamic response graphs are displayed in figure 4.1. The columns of the graphs show the response of each institution to a one-standard-deviation shock (innovation) in a particular institution's behavior, while a row-wise interpretation pertains to the response of a particular institution to shocks coming from each of the three institutions contained in the model. The first row of graphs reveals that presidents respond in a reciprocal manner to shocks coming from Congress and the SEC before eventually approaching zero. Thus, presidents appear to play a conciliatory role in this relationship (Kiewiet and McCubbins 1985; but see Kiewiet and McCubbins 1991). This finding, in conjunction with the positive contemporaneous correlation of the innovations between president and congressional budgetary signals (r = .51), suggests that Congress and the president's budgetary signal innovations are congruent initially before fluctuating and moving toward equilibrium as they meet environmental and institutional demands.[22] However, the congressional response to a presidential budgetary shock does not have as clear a temporal pattern. Thus, the long-run dynamics are not consistent with the prevailing view displayed in the short run.[23]

Presidents respond in a reciprocal manner to SEC output innovations for a sustained period of time (through five years after the original shock). Thus, presidents do respond to agency behavior in a clear fashion and to unexpected deviations in the behavior of the latter. The same can be said of congressional response to SEC enforcement shocks, though not to the same extent. The initial response of Congress to an SEC policy shock is positive, then eventually becomes negative in later periods before tapering off toward zero. These results portray a different portrait of administrative politics, since they demonstrate the sophisticated interplay between agency and political institutions responsible for policy administration. Although bureaucratic agency-political institution relationships may be in equilibrium, there are also unexpected shifts in behavior that will result in a disequilibrium state. Eventually, however, this system will equilibrate over time as institutions gradually adapt to such disturbances. This is consistent with the perspective of both classic public bureaucracy treatises (Barnard 1938; Simon 1947) and modern-day principal-agent-based theories of agency-political relations (Mitnick 1980; Moe 1984; Perrow 1986) that acknowledge the necessity of these relationships' resting on some general level of agreement.

SEC enforcement activity signals (in the form of administrative proceedings) display an anemic response to presidential budgetary shocks. This could in fact reflect the agency's attempt to flex its discretionary muscles by not altering its enforcement output activity in response to unanticipated changes in presidential wishes.[24] SEC administrative proceedings activity responds in a positive manner to unanticipated changes in congressional budgetary (appropriation) signals for four years following such shocks. This result provides clear

FIGURE 4.1 Simulated Dynamic Response of the President-Congress-SEC System to an Orthogonal-ized, One Standard Deviation Shock in Each Institutional Variable (SEC Administrative Proceedings Model)

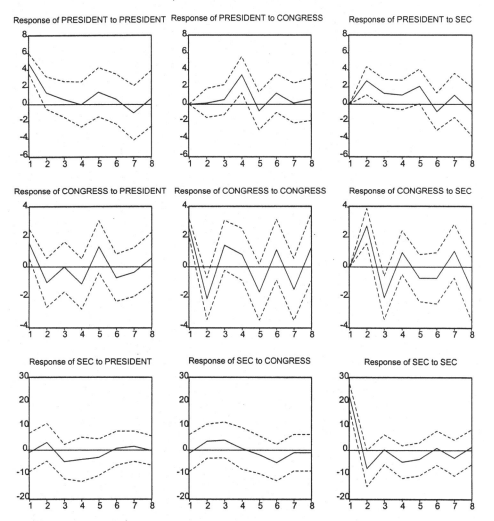

Response to One S.D. Innovations ± 2 S.E.

NOTES: Four annual lags of the variables were used in the VAR model so as to satisfy the white noise condition for each of the three equations in the system. The order of the variables is President, Congress, and SEC. The solid line is the point estimate of the dynamic response and the dashed lines represent the confidence bands generated using Monte Carlo integration procedures involving 1,000 resamples of the data.

empirical support for the institutional proximity thesis, which states that the SEC enforcement output is more responsive to congressional signals vis-à-vis presidential signals, given this agency's legislative and budgetary bypass authority with respect to the executive branch.

The dynamic simulation exercise is conducted to see how behavior emanating from each of these institutions would respond to a policy innovation (shock) on the part of each institution with respect to SEC Investigations. As in the preceding model, the contemporaneous ordering—of presidential (OMB request) behavior, congressional (appropriations) behavior, and SEC enforcement behavior (total investigations)—was selected, for reasons stated earlier.[25] The dynamic response graphs are displayed in figure 4.2.

In accordance with the Administrative Proceedings model, presidential budgetary signals exhibit a consistent, strong positive escalation in their (budgetary) behavior following a shock emanating from either Congress or the SEC in the Investigations model. This result, in conjunction with the positive contemporaneous correlation of these institutional innovations (r = .60), indicates that presidents play a conciliatory role in this relationship (Kiewiet and McCubbins 1985; but see Kiewiet and McCubbins 1991). One possible explanation for such behavior is that presidents do not wish to sharply disagree with Congress over the political (budgetary) signals toward the SEC, since they may want to save their political capital for larger battles on the legislative front, while also mitigating the opportunity of the SEC to play political principals off against one another.[26] Another plausible explanation for this pattern of behavior is that presidents follow the lead of Congress, because of the latter's closer institutional proximity to the SEC.[27]

The lack of a consistent positive congressional response to presidential shocks is in line with the analogous results obtained and also corroborates the parallel finding from the previous model. The SEC total investigations activity does not move in a manner congruent with presidential and congressional budgetary shocks. This view differs from those asserting that presidents exercise a great deal of influence over the SEC (Kohlmeier 1969; Moe 1982), and from the views of others who claim that Congress controls SEC regulatory behavior (Weingast 1984). Converse to this body of past research, the dynamic simulation analysis for this model clearly shows that presidential and congressional influence over agency behavior is modest in the area of securities regulation.

Finally, the dynamic simulation exercise is conducted to see how behavior

FIGURE 4.2 Simulated Dynamic Response of the President-Congress-SEC System to an Orthogonalized, One Standard Deviation Shock in Each Institutional Variable (SEC Investigations Model)

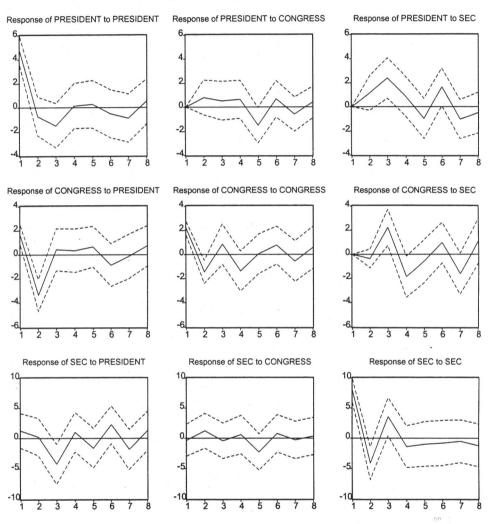

Response to One S.D. Innovations ± 2 S.E.

NOTES: Four annual lags of the variables were used in the VAR model so as to satisfy the white noise condition for each of the three equations in the system. The order of the variables is President, Congress, and SEC. The solid line is the point estimate of the dynamic response and the dashed lines represent the confidence bands generated using Monte Carlo integration procedures involving 1,000 resamples of the data.

FIGURE 4.3 Simulated Dynamic Response of the President-Congress-SEC System to an Orthogonalized, One Standard Deviation Shock in Each Institutional Variable (SEC Injunctive Actions Model)

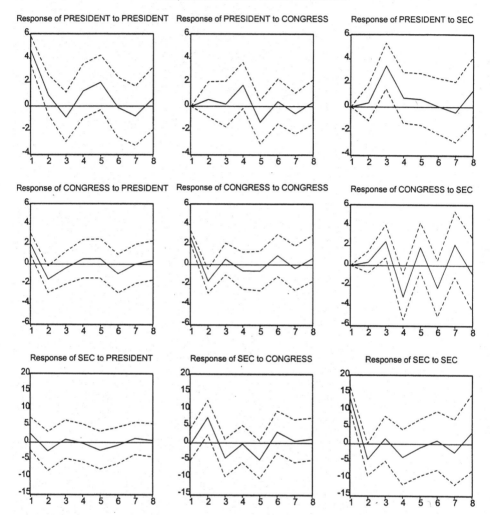

NOTES: Four annual lags of the variables were used in the VAR model so as to satisfy the white noise condition for each of the three equations in the system. The order of the variables is President, Congress, and SEC. The solid line is the point estimate of the dynamic response and the dashed lines represent the confidence bands generated using Monte Carlo integration procedures involving 1,000 resamples of the data.

emanating from each of these institutions would respond to a policy innovation (shock) on the part of each institution pertaining to SEC Injunctive Actions activity. Once again, the contemporaneous causal ordering of innovations was based on the temporal sequence of the annual agency performance–political budgetary process—that is, the contemporaneous ordering of presidential (OMB request) behavior, congressional (appropriations) behavior, and SEC enforcement behavior (total injunctive actions).[28] The MAR impulse responses are presented in graphical form in figure 4.3.

In accordance with the prior two models, presidential budgetary signals respond in a consistent, positive fashion to shocks emanating from both Congress and the SEC. After an initial reciprocal response in the period following the presidential budgetary signaling innovation, congressional budgetary signals oscillate in a random fashion around zero before tapering off and approaching equilibrium. Thus, one can conclude that congressional responses to presidential signals are short-lived. This initial reciprocity indicates unified political support in obtaining administrative objectives, since political principals are probably well aware that administrative agencies may try to play one against the other so as to gain discretion (Bryner 1987; Dahl and Lindblom 1953; Hammond and Knott 1993, 1996; Wilson 1989). This reciprocity, however, is short-lived as is the situation in the previous models.

SEC injunctive actions behavior exhibits an initial positive response to a presidential shock before oscillating around zero, then tapering off toward zero. This finding is consistent with the analogous result from the SEC investigations model. Substantively, this response pattern implies that SEC enforcement behavior (in the form of injunctive actions) is not very sensitive to unanticipated budgetary signal changes coming from the president. Therefore, the empirical models in the SEC case study suggest that, although presidential influence over administrative behavior may exist to some extent, it is of a rather limited nature. As in the Investigations model, the initial responses in SEC injunctive actions behavior are reciprocal to an innovation in congressional budgetary signals. In the subsequent periods, however, the agency's response does not follow a clear, consistent pattern.

Decomposition of the Forecast Error Variance for the President-Congress-SEC System

The decomposition of the forecast error variance lends additional insight into the causal nature of agency-political relations that cannot be gleaned from multivariate tests of Granger exogeneity since the former statistical tests are based on *unanticipated* changes in behavior, while the latter pertains to *anticipated* changes in behavior. These results can be found in table 4.4. The first equation (president) clearly reveals that presidential budgetary signals' forecast error variance are mostly explained by this institution's own innovations (approximately 47 percent in the Administrative Proceeding model, 60 percent in the Investigations model, and 59 percent in the Injunctive Actions model). This in turn supports the multivariate Granger exogeneity tests of lagged causal relations in both the Administrative Proceedings and Investigations models, which convincingly demonstrate that past presidential behavior does influence current presidential behavior. Moreover, the forecast error variance associated with presidential budgetary signals appears to be relatively more receptive to SEC enforcement innovations than congressional budgetary innovations. This, in turn, implies that presidents are sensitive to their own relatively distant position from the SEC, based on its lack of institutional proximity.

The decomposition of the forecast error variance in the Congress equations indicates that innovations in each of the three institutions play an important role in explaining congressional responses.[29] The investigations model shows presidents' budgetary signal innovations to play a strong role in explaining the forecast error variance in congressional appropriation signals. This is consistent with F-block causality tests since it suggests that, when it comes to investigation activity at the SEC, the president plays a large role in shaping aggregate congressional behavior through his annual budget request and the general setting of regulatory priorities.[30] Such a finding is consistent with much of the literature on presidential-congressional budgeting noted earlier. In the two other models (Administrative Proceedings and Injunctive Actions), both Congress and SEC innovations are critical for understanding the temporal dynamics of unanticipated shifts in congressional behavior for each type of regulatory enforcement activity (approximately 84 percent of the forecast variance in congressional appropriation signals in each VAR model are jointly explained by these two institutions' innovations). This receptivity on the part of Congress may be due to its relative institutional closeness to the SEC.[31] Furthermore, the important role of SEC enforcement shocks in explaining the forecast error variance in both political institutions' budgetary signals provides additional support for the bureaucratic influence thesis found earlier.[32]

The decomposition of the forecast error variance of each of these three types of SEC regulatory enforcement output corroborates the findings of the

TABLE 4.4 Decomposition of the Forecast Error Variance as a Result of Policy Innovations Emanating from the President, Congress, and the SEC

		Innovations in								
		Administrative Proceedings Model			Investigations Model			Injunctive Actions Model		
Forecast Error Variance in		President	Congress	SEC	President	Congress	SEC	President	Congress	SEC
President	t+1	100.00	.00	.00	100.00	.00	.00	100.00	.00	.00
	t+3	72.30	.88	26.82	75.62	2.82	21.57	65.61	1.04	33.35
	t+5	49.30	23.64	27.06	66.87	9.70	23.43	61.51	11.06	27.42
	t+8	47.13	24.39	28.48	60.29	10.50	29.21	59.00	11.53	29.47
Congress	t+1	26.32	73.68	.00	35.60	64.40	.00	35.26	64.74	.00
	t+3	12.18	46.51	41.31	52.78	28.13	19.09	28.56	45.60	25.84
	t+5	18.11	45.71	36.19	44.50	28.56	26.94	18.91	29.94	51.15
	t+8	16.38	47.07	36.55	39.74	26.48	33.78	16.26	25.08	58.66
SEC	t+1	.19	.29	99.54	2.39	.16	97.45	3.53	.12	96.35
	t+3	5.69	5.41	88.90	17.20	1.58	81.22	4.77	25.79	69.44
	t+5	8.64	5.50	85.85	18.40	5.91	75.70	5.69	29.45	64.85
	t+8	8.54	9.11	82.35	23.85	5.93	70.22	5.88	30.22	63.90

NOTES: Each cell entry is the percentage of forecast error variance t years ahead in the column variables produced by a policy innovation in the variable on the far left-hand side of the column. The order of the variables for the innovation accounting simulation are President, Congress, and SEC. Due to rounding error, the numbers in the rows do not always sum up to exactly 100.

lagged multivariate tests of Granger exogeneity. The innovations in SEC enforcement vigor explain from nearly 64 percent to slightly more than 82 percent of its own forecast error variance, eight years following the initial perturbation. At the same time, the budgetary innovations of the president and Congress roughly explain a combined 18 percent, 29 percent, and 36 percent of the forecast error variance in (respectively) SEC administrative proceedings, investigations, and injunctive actions enforcement activity. These findings provide rather modest support for political influence over SEC enforcement behavior.

Based on the decomposition of the forecast error variance results, the enforcement behavior of SEC appears to be causally prior to the budgetary signals it receives from its political principals. However, the decomposition of the SEC's forecast error variance supports the earlier results testing anticipated behavioral linkages by indicating that the behavior of political principals is not causally prior to SEC behavior. These findings run counter to past systematic empirical research, which argues that politicians control or influence bureaucratic behavior, and not vice versa. This is a very important result since it demonstrates that political principals—in terms of their political (budgetary) signals—cannot always be assumed to be causally prior to agency behavior as past research has posited. On a substantive level, these empirical findings provide robust support for the view that, through its regulatory enforcement vigor, the SEC influences the resource signals it receives from political institutions, which allows the SEC to pursue its policy mandate in a manner consistent with the *bureaucratic influence hypothesis*. Therefore, the aggregate vigor by which the SEC pursues its enforcement activities reflects a proactive bureaucratic institution that shapes its political environment.

Applying the Dynamic Systems Model of Administrative Politics to Antitrust Regulation

This section applies the dynamic systems model of administrative politics to the case of antitrust regulation in the United States. The focus is on *to what extent* and *in which ways* is each of these theories accurate? Previous studies give different answers to this question. The framework presented here lends a more realistic portrayal of president-congressional-agency relations by placing each institution on an equal footing at the onset of the study. By constructing a theoretical framework that attempts to encompass the most salient features contained within existing theories of administrative politics (e.g., institutional-choice, principal-agent, and bureaucratic politics [as discussed in chapter 3]), one can simultaneously make less confining assumptions and more sensible statements about the nature of behavioral relations between democratic institutions and the bureaucracy. Moreover, one may recall that at the foundations of this model is the relaxation of three key oversimplifying assumptions of past studies—one-way interaction from elected officials to the agency, no interaction between elected officials, and the preclusion of sophisticated behavior. The pertinence and substantive reality for each of these elements in the area of antitrust regulation is explained at greater length in the subsequent sections of this chapter.

The Dynamic Systems Model of Administrative Politics and Its Relevance to Antitrust Regulation

This model of administrative politics contains three main components, which make it unique among the existing research. The first novel component deals with considering the possibility of mutual adaptation between elected officials and the agency. This appears true in the case of antitrust regulation, even though much of the research, conducted by political scientists, ignores this dimension. The interviews uncovered anecdotal evidence suggesting that mutual adaptation and endogenous interaction represent the norm. A CBO analyst in the area of antitrust regulation notes that policy signals are exchanged between the Antitrust Division and its political principals (interview with author, June 1993). Furthermore, the disparate findings on the subject—most notably the writings of Eisner and associates (Eisner and Meier 1990; Eisner 1991) compared to those of Wood and Anderson (1993)—provide a stark contrast in terms of what forces actually drive antitrust regulation in the United States.[33] The cogent works from both intellectual camps, while being quite forceful, do not supply us with adequate insight for constructing a unified model of public bureaucracy.

As a result of the theoretical discordance surrounding this body of research, it is necessary to utilize a framework that treats each institution equitably with respect to policy administration.[34] This more objective approach will, it is hoped, move toward reconciling these conflicting explanations of behavior and, by doing so, should unearth unnoticed subtleties of administrative politics by clarifying the relationships between the president, Congress, and the Antitrust Division in the enforcement of antitrust regulation. Anecdotal support for the tenets of this framework were provided by my interview subjects, representing each of the institutions under investigation. This is consistent with the characterization found in the dynamic systems model of administrative politics. Furthermore, sophisticated behavior and reaction on the part of these institutions, reflecting unanticipated behavioral responses among institutions, can be empirically assessed within this framework. Evidence of any pair of institutions responding to shocks from the other, either instantaneously or in a dynamic fashion, can be empirically investigated by the statistical analysis of the data.

Operationalization of the Dynamic Systems Framework:
The Case of Antitrust Regulation

The application of the dynamic systems model to the case of antitrust regulation allows for dynamic interaction between the president, Congress, and the Antitrust Division. These relations allow for the possibility of bidirectional causality (feedback) running between the participants. In total, there are six possible bidirectional causal linkages between these institutions. They consist of the following pairs of potential dyadic relationships: president-Congress, president–Antitrust Division, Congress–Antitrust Division. As a result (as in the case of securities regulation studied previously in this chapter), one can test hypotheses relating to the causal and responsive mechanisms that underlie these relationships. These tests will involve assessing lagged adaptive behavior from the recent past, as well as sophisticated behavior in response to shocks to the president-Congress-AD system.

As in the SEC case study, the AD models employ analogous constant-dollar presidential budgetary (OMB) requests and congressional appropriations for the Antitrust Division. The AD measures of regulatory enforcement are (1) the total annual number of antitrust cases initiated by the agency for each year, and (2) the total annual number of antitrust investigations initiated by the agency for each year. The research I have conducted indicates that these measures were defined in the same manner throughout the sample period. Thus, variations in these measures do not represent changes in the definition of these policy outputs.[35]

The *"deterministic"* component for each model specification represents the environmental and intra-institutional forces that shape not only agency behavior but also the institutional behavior for both the president and Congress. The ideological composition of the relevant congressional oversight committees for both the House and Senate chambers are incorporated into each model.[36] These measures are operationalized as the relative median ADA score in a given year for each relevant committee or subcommittee located in each chamber.[37] These variables should have a positive effect on agency behavior, congressional appropriations, and presidential budgetary requests. More liberal committee policy ideology is postulated to result generally in higher rates of enforcement and to spur greater regulatory support on behalf of the president and Congress separately. These variables should also have a positive effect on agency behavior, congressional appropriation, and presidential budgetary request signals for the agency. In addition, a political event variable is employed that takes into account variations in antitrust behavior on the part of the Antitrust Division (political principals) during the Reagan presidency (Eisner and Meier 1990). Although *"vertical"* related enforcement activities rose (e.g., mergers and monopolies), and the regulation of *"horizontal"* antitrust practices (e.g., price-fixing) declined during this period, it is generally thought that aggregate enforcement dropped during the Reagan administration.[38] Thus, the event (i.e., dummy) variable should exert a negative effect on the regulatory behavior of the Antitrust Division (political principals).

Internal bureaucratic factors associated with regulatory efforts at the Antitrust Division are also associated with the Economic Policy Office (EPO).[39] Following Eisner and Meier's (1990: 279) lead, the EPO may have both a single onetime impact as well as a long-term gradual effect on aggregate enforcement activity. The former variable is operationalized as the ratio of economists to attorneys in the Antitrust Division following the creation of the EPO in 1972. The latter variable is measured as a linear trend that takes on a value of one for the first year following the creation of the EPO (1973) and increases by units of one for each subsequent year. The purpose of these variables is to account for variations in the regulatory behavior of the agency and political principals that may be attributable to bureaucratic policy change.[40]

Although one may expect antitrust enforcement to be negatively related to the increased prominence associated with economic modes of analysis within the Antitrust Division, the hypothesized relationships between these variables and the endogenous measures of institutional behavior are potentially unclear since the frequency of certain types of cases (e.g., monopoly and merger cases) declined during this period, whereas the frequency of others (most notably price-fixing cases) rose. It is much clearer that bureaucratic policy change (i.e., Meier and Eisner's institutional hypothesis) could very well threaten political principals, because one of their main administrative functions is to oversee and direct the regulatory (policy) mission of bureaucratic agencies. Under such conditions, these internal administrative factors should be negatively related to the budgetary signals of political principals. Put in simple terms, the more prominent these internal factors are within the agency, *holding all else constant,* the less support elected officials will supply to the regulatory mission of the agency.

General macroeconomic conditions may play a role not only in affecting the behavior of the agency, but also in shaping the behavior of political principals (see Posner 1970 for an opposing viewpoint).[41] According to the private interest theory of economic regulation (Amacher et al. 1985; Eisner and Meier 1990; Shugart 1990; Stigler 1971; Wood and Anderson 1993), both inflation and unemployment may exert an effect on each government institution's view of antitrust regulation and enforcement. Inflation should be positively related to the vigor of antitrust enforcement since charges of price-fixing and other anticompetitive actions are more likely to rise with the onset of higher rates of inflation. The directional effect of the unemployment variable is less obvious (Wood and Anderson 1993). On one hand, stringent antitrust regulation will exacerbate unemployment by reducing inefficiencies in economic markets. In response to this situation, public-minded regulators may slacken enforcement endeavors as the unemployment rate rises. On the other hand, merger and acquisitions activity could result in layoffs and claims of anticompetitive behavior. This, in turn, could thrust antitrust regulators toward more vigorous enforcement behavior. Finally, a dummy variable, which represents the possible effects of the Hart-Scott-Rodino Antitrust Improvements Act of 1976 on the regulatory system that equals zero for every year before 1977 and equals one in 1977 and for each year henceforth, is considered in each model specification.[42] One expects that this act has resulted in a rise in the number of AD enforcement outputs and budgetary signals emanating from both political institutions.

Speculation regarding the results of the forthcoming analysis seems rather difficult in this instance. According to the institutional proximity thesis, the agency design of the Antitrust Division (executive bureau) should lend itself to easier political manipulation by the president vis-à-vis Congress, while its technical complexity and internal administrative factors would seem to grant this institution a sizable amount of discretion (Eisner and Meier 1990; Eisner 1991; Katzmann 1980; Weaver 1977). In addition, since the AD is an executive branch bureau, one should observe the unanticipated behavior of both president and congressional budgetary signals to be less correlated than in the SEC case. The reason for this is that the SEC enjoys greater independence compared to the AD due to its institutional design as an independent regulatory commission. Therefore, presidents and Congress will have a greater incentive to act in concert to reign in the SEC relative to an executive bureau such as the Antitrust Division.

Furthermore, an executive bureau such as the Antitrust Division should be more inclined to respond in a reciprocal fashion to budgetary signals emanating from the president vis-à-vis Congress, holding all else constant, since these bureaucratic institutions are designed to mitigate legislative influence.[43] After all, presidents define the broad contours of antitrust policy through the regulatory tone they set (Shepherd 1985: 138). On a more specific plane, presidents expose their antitrust enforcement activities through the budgetary process (Katzmann 1980; Weaver 1977). This assertion would also appear to be consistent with Eisner's (1991: 45–46) charge that the Antitrust Division is relatively immune from congressional pressures since it is shielded by presidential administrations.

The degree of information asymmetry between the Antitrust Division and its political principals will also shed light on the nature of causal and responsive behavior on the part of these institutions. In chapter 2, it was hypothesized that the larger the information asymmetry (i.e., advantages on the part of the agency) between agency and political principals, the easier it should be for any given agency to affect the behavior of its political principals. As the size of the information asymmetry (in favor of the agency) increases, it will be more difficult for political principals to affect agency activity in an anticipated and/or unanticipated manner. Although the Antitrust Division is an administrative institution that has a great advantage in policy expertise over its political masters, it is at the same time a relatively small entity and a highly centralized organization.

Statistical Findings

The dynamic systems model of administrative politics is tested for two aggregate types of antitrust regulatory activity: total antitrust cases and total antitrust investigations. As in the previous analysis of securities regulation, the results generated by this empirical analysis should be more valid than those of past studies examining the same phenomena, because it is a more realistic conceptualization, which considers the dynamics and complexity inherent in the institutional politics of policy administration. Once again, the explanatory usefulness of these models is well above that of just simply examining the mean of these respective dependent series in isolation. This is especially remarkable considering the transformed nature of the data for the endogenous portion of the model. The diagnostic checks in appendix D also furnish additional evidence that these model specifications are more than adequate.

The Effects of Exogenous Variables on the
President-Congressional-AD System

The effect of the deterministic variables that appear exogenous to the system of institutions is presented in table 4.5. The coefficients and t-statistics for the endogenous system variables are not reported here. In the AD cases model, presidential budgetary signals are higher during the Reagan administration period than otherwise. Conversely, the congressional appropriation signals are lower during this same period than otherwise. Why is this the case? It may reflect that the AD's regulatory effort was receiving greater support from the Reagan administration during this period since the rise of economic analysis within the agency resulted in different types of cases being pursued by the agency (see Eisner and Meier 1990). It is less clear on the surface, however, why congressional budgetary signals declined during this period. There are two possible explanations for this result. First, Congress had a genuine interest in scaling back economic regulatory efforts throughout the 1980's—for many reasons including, but not limited to, adhering to presidential wishes, the opin-ion of the mass public, economic and technological changes, and a broad philosophical change in the way elites viewed economic regulation (Derthick and Quirk 1985a, 1985b; Gerston, Fraleigh, and Schwab 1988; Hammond and Knott 1988; Meier 1985; Quirk 1988). Second, Congress was not trusting of the Reagan White House administration, thus they chose to emit negative signals to counteract the positive ones emanating from the administration. However, the rate of change in antitrust cases was not significantly altered during this era. In tandem, these empirical findings imply that the AD's antitrust cases enforcement activity was not responsive to the changes in either presidential and congressional budgetary signals during the Reagan administration era.[44]

The positive and significant sign associated with the unemployment variable in the Congress equation implies that legislators seek to raise agency funding in order to induce heightened regulatory vigor during periods of high unemployment. The reason for this response is based on the view that merger and acquisitions activity could lead to joint increases in layoffs and charges of anti-competitive behavior. Given that unemployment has no significant impact on agency performance in this particular model, one can presume that Congress's responsiveness to fluctuations in the unemployment rate does not translate into enhanced bureaucratic responsiveness in this specific instance. Since the inception of the Hart-Scott-Rodino Antitrust Improvements Act of 1976, only presidential budgetary signals have been substantially altered (declined) in support of the AD's cases enforcement activity. However, this decline in budgetary signals has not translated into a decrease in the vigor of regulatory outputs for the AD. Once again, this demonstrates the gulf between what makes political institutions responsive to regulation vis-à-vis the agency administering the policy.[45]

In the Antitrust Investigations model, increases in the balance of economists to attorneys within the agency result in a rise in congressional appropriation signals, yet cause a decline in investigations activity that barely misses ob-

TABLE 4.5 The Impact of Deterministic Variables on Presidential, Congressional, and Agency Behavior Antitrust Cases VAR Model (1949–1992)

Deterministic Variable	Antitrust Cases Model			Antitrust Investigations Model		
	President (eq. 10)	Congress (eq. 11)	AD (eq. 12)	President (eq. 13)	Congress (eq. 14)	AD (eq. 15)
Constant	-13.04 (-1.69)	-17.45* (-1.74)	-8.57 (-.28)	.15 (.06)	1.51 (.73)	2.51 (.45)
Economists/Attorneys$_t$	—	—	—	95.89 (1.29)	112.39* (1.87)	-271.73 (-1.68)
EPO$_t$	—	—	—	-1.41* (-1.80)	-1.21* (-1.91)	2.48 (1.46)
Reagan Administration$_t$	19.58*** (3.06)	-15.47* (-1.86)	-5.78 (-.23)	—	—	—
Unemployment$_{t-1}$	1.99 (1.25)	4.50** (2.17)	3.43 (.55)	—	—	—
Hart-Scott-Rodino Act$_t$	-13.59*** (-3.47)	-4.38 (-.86)	-6.96 (-.46)	—	—	—
Goodness of Fit Statistics for Complete Specifications						
R2	.88	.56	.36	.79	.70	.61
α	6.54	8.51	25.59	8.47	6.85	18.46

NOTES: t-statistics are listed inside parentheses. The technical details and empirical results of these tests are discussed in appendix D.
* p < .10   ** p < .05   *** p < .01

taining statistical significance at conventional levels. Conversely, since the advent of the Economic Policy Office within the AD, political budgetary signals toward the agency have steadily declined across time, holding all other factors constant. Thus, this particular institutional change within the agency appears to have hampered the political (budgetary) support it receives. The creation of this office, however, has also led to a nonsubstantial rise in AD Investigations activity.[46]

F-Block Tests of Multivariate Granger Causality for President-Congress-AD System

The multivariate F-block tests of Granger Causality among the endogenous variables in the VAR antitrust cases and investigations models are presented in table 4.6. In both models, past congressional budgetary signals influence the

TABLE 4.6 F-Block Tests of Direct Causal Relations Between the President, Congress, and the Antitrust
Division (1949–1992)

Block of Coefficients	Antitrust Cases Model-VAR (5)			Antitrust Investigations Model-VAR (5)		
	President (eq. 10)	Congress (eq. 11)	AD (eq. 12)	President (eq. 13)	Congress (eq. 14)	AD (eq. 15)
President	6.29***	.25	.87	3.98**	2.36	1.02
	(.00)	(.94)	(.52)	(.01)	(.08)	(.43)
Congress	18.36***	.61	.86	6.14***	3.95**	2.25
	(.00)	(.69)	(.52)	(.00)	(.01)	(.09)
Antitrust Division	4.38***	.40	.79	.70	4.08**	2.16*
	(.01)	(.84)	(.57)	(.63)	(.01)	(.10)

NOTES: a. F-statistics for determining Granger Causality.
b. Significance levels are listed inside parentheses. They are rounded out to the nearest hundredth decimal place.
* $p < .10$ ** $p < .05$ *** $p < .01$

current budgetary signals emitted by the president, yet the opposite holds true
only for the AD Investigations model. Nonetheless, these empirical results are
consistent with the SEC results in that they clearly demonstrate that political
institutions' budgetary preferences concerning administrative behavior are
not formed exogenously from one another as all empirical studies and many
theoretical works on the subject implicitly assume. In three out of four instances, political institutions' budgetary signals exhibit incremental behavior
manner—as predicted by many theories of public policy and its administration (Cohen and Axelrod 1984; Feldman 1989; Lindblom 1959; March and
Olsen 1976, 1984, 1989; March and Simon 1958).[47]

In only a single instance is there any evidence that indicates that political
budgetary signals may affect the vigor of AD regulatory enforcement. In this
case, congressional appropriation signals significantly shape AD investigation
activity. However, this result is not a robust one so this inference cannot be
definitively gleaned from the data. In two instances, however, both consistent
and strong empirical evidence exists demonstrating that variations in AD cases
(investigations) initiated are causally prior to movements in presidential (congressional) budgetary signals. Therefore the tests of lagged causal relations reveal support for the *bureaucratic influence* hypothesis with respect to presidential (congressional) budgetary signals in the Antitrust Cases (Investigations)
model. The relationship between the president and agency with respect to the
AD Investigations model reflects *bureaucratic autonomy,* whereas the relation-

ship between congressional and administrative agency with respect to AD investigations activity is indicative of *mutual adaptation*.[48]

AD enforcement behavior evolves in a comparatively less incremental manner vis-à-vis the overall SEC findings. This may indicate that the former agency's regulatory activities generally move in a self-determined manner, which may involve unanticipated forms of behavior (e.g., strategic reaction and sophisticated adaptation). This contrasts with the findings of the SEC model, where two of the three models revealed an incremental form of institutional behavior. Although the agency's status as an independent commission leads one to believe it is less susceptible to gradual adjustment or adaptation, both the SEC's relatively well-defined target group (the securities and commodities industry) and its sole jurisdictional domain over administering its policy area could in fact make such behavior more feasible. Additional investigation into this pattern of dynamic relationships requires an inspection of policy innovations emanating from each institution, and its impact on AD behavior.

Contemporaneous Correlation of Innovations for President-Congress-AD System

The contemporaneous residual correlation matrix for the antitrust cases and antitrust investigations models is presented in table 4.7. The correlation between the presidential and congressional budgetary signals variables in both instances is positive. This correlation coefficient just misses obtaining statistical significance at the ten percent level in the AD Cases model ($r = .23$), while attaining statistical significance at the five percent level in the AD Investigations model ($r = .35$). Although the positive correlations indicate that both institutions' innovations (i.e., shocks) move together in a contemporaneous fashion, it is not as strong as the SEC models discussed earlier in this chapter. This supports the hypothesis that the SEC—being an independent regulatory commission with budgetary and legislative bypass authority from the executive branch administrative apparatus—forces political principals to reciprocate immediate unanticipated responses (at least in a contemporaneous fashion) in order to provide a unified front to the agency.[49]

The contemporaneous innovations in each AD model between the president and the agency are positive, but not significantly correlated to one another ($r = .14$ in the AD Cases model; $r = .01$ in the AD Investigations model).[50] For all practical purposes, this means that presidents and the AD act in a weakly

TABLE 4.7 Contemporaneous Policy Innovation (Residual) Correlation Matrices for VAR Models of Antitrust Regulatory Enforcement System (1949–1992)

	Antitrust Cases Model-VAR (5)			Antitrust Investigations Model-VAR (5)		
	President (eq. 10)	Congress (eq. 11)	AD (eq. 12)	President (eq. 13)	Congress (eq. 14)	AD (eq. 15)
President	—	.23	.14	—	.35**	.01
Congress	—	—	-.19*	—	—	-.47***
Antitrust Division	—	—	—	—	—	—

NOTES: These entries represent the contemporaneous correlation of policy innovations (errors) on behalf of the President, Congress, and the Antitrust Division.
*** p < .10   ** p < .05   *** p < .01

reciprocal manner in response to a shock, which implies that these institutions do not feel the need to respond to innovations emanating from the other institution, or are not capable of responding to these shocks in a contemporaneous manner. This anemic response may be due to the exceptionally close institutional proximity between the AD and the White House, and does not necessitate a significant response since they are closely aligned. Specifically, this result may be attributable to the greater number of checkpoints within the executive branch (Department of Justice and the White House) that must approve AD regulatory performance proposals, which in turn could reduce the amount of uncertainty and subsequently mitigate unanticipated changes between these two institutions.

However, the current period shocks between congressional appropriation signals and AD enforcement behavior are negatively correlated in both instances, yet only significant in the Investigations model (r = −.47 [p < .01]).[51] This finding is not startling when one considers the institutional distance of the Antitrust Division from Congress. In many administrative and policy matters, this agency often deals with Congress indirectly through the shield of the DOJ, the White House, or the OMB.

In sum, these results exhibit some indirect support for the institutional proximity thesis since the policy surprises of an executive bureau (Antitrust Division) are positively correlated—i.e., policy congruence—with those of the chief executive, and are also negatively correlated—i.e., policy divergence—

with those belonging to the legislature. In addition, these empirical results in conjunction with the F-block tests of Granger Causality reveal that the possibility of rational expectations within this context is most unlikely.

Simulated Response to a Shock in the President-Congress-AD System

The dynamic simulation (MAR innovation accounting) exercise is conducted to see how behavior emanating from each of these institutions responds to an innovation (shock) on the part of each institution. The contemporaneous causal ordering among these innovations is based on the temporal sequence of the annual agency performance–political budgetary process—that is, the contemporaneous ordering of presidential budgetary (OMB request) signals, congressional appropriation signals, and AD enforcement behavior (total antitrust cases and total investigations). The MAR impulse responses are presented in pictorial form (figures 4.4–4.5).

In the first row of figure 4.4, the response of presidential budgetary signals to various system shocks in the AD Cases model is graphically portrayed. The most clear, consistent response is that of the president to a congressional appropriation innovation. In this case, presidents initially respond in a positive manner to such shocks in years t+1 and t+2 before both oscillating around and tapering off towards zero. In the second row, only congressional shocks appear to have any impact on congressional behavior. This implies some evidence of incremental behavior displayed on behalf of Congress, in terms of unanticipated behavioral responses, that are not captured in those tests examining anticipated behavior presented earlier in this section. The impulse responses of the agency (AD) to congressional appropriation shocks is slightly negative for the first two periods following the shock. This is consistent with the negative contemporaneous correlation coefficient between these two institutions shown in Table 4.7. These results indicate that AD cases activity are not responsive to presidential or congressional budgetary signal shocks.[52] This same general finding is also uncovered in the SEC empirical models.

The AD Investigation impulse response graphs are displayed in Figure 4.5. In the first row, there is evidence that presidents generally respond in a positive (reciprocal) manner for the periods subsequent to a shock in congressional appropriation signals. Furthermore, the president's budgetary signaling response to a shock in AD investigations activity is slow, yet is briefly positive in years t+3 and t+4 before both oscillating and tapering off towards zero. The second row shows that not only is congressional budgetary behavior respon-

FIGURE 4.4 Simulated Dynamic Response of the President-Congress-AD System to an Orthogonalized, One Standard Deviation Shock in Each Institutional Variable (Cases Model)

Response to One S.D. Innovations ± 2 S.E.

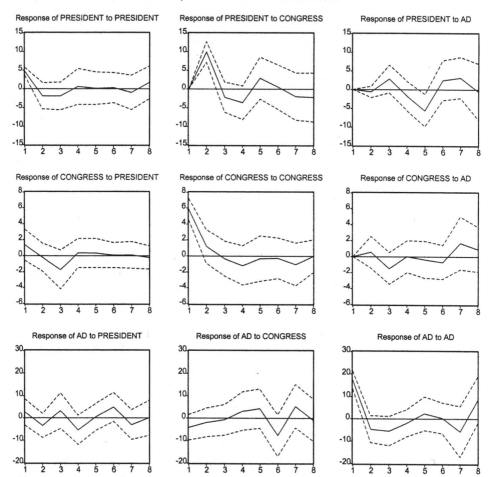

NOTES: Five annual lags of the variables were used in the VAR model so as to satisfy the white noise condition for each of the three equations in the system. The order of the variables are President, Congress, and Antitrust Division. The solid line is the point estimate of the dynamic response and the dashed lines represent the confidence bands generated using Monte Carlo integration procedures involving 1,000 resamples of the data.

FIGURE 4.5 Simulated Dynamic Response of the President-Congress-AD System to an Orthogonalized, One Standard Deviation Shock in Each Institutional Variable (Investigations Model)

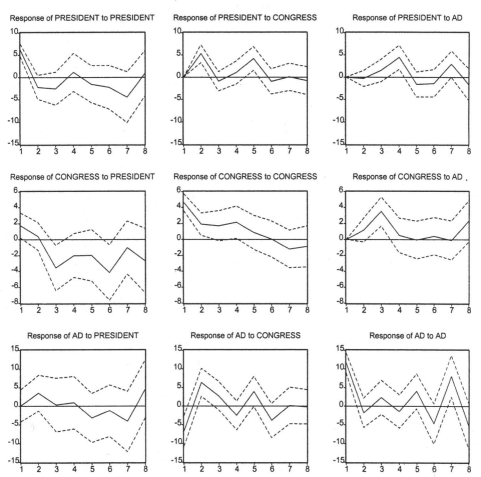

Response to One S.D. Innovations ± 2 S.E.

NOTES: Five annual lags of the variables were used in the VAR model so as to satisfy the white noise condition for each of the three equations in the system. The order of the variables are President, Congress, and Antitrust Division. The solid line is the point estimate of the dynamic response and the dashed lines represent the confidence bands generated using Monte Carlo integration procedures involving 1,000 resamples of the data.

sive to its own shocks, it also moves in a positive manner in response to a shock in AD investigations activity. This evidence is consistent with the F-block tests presented earlier in that this agency's regulatory performance can play a vital role in shaping the budgetary preferences of this political principal. AD investigations initially respond in a positive manner to a shock in presidential budgetary signal preferences in years t+1 and t+2, while this response is initially strongly negative in year t+1 with respect to a congressional appropriation shock.[53] This evidence supports the view that the AD's relations with Congress are more confrontational relative to the president. This is not surprising given that the executive branch system serves as a shield for the AD, and also that it is much more institutionally proximate vis-à-vis Congress.

Decomposition of the Forecast Error Variance for the President-Congress AD System

The variance decomposition of the forecast error variance for each of the dependent series/equations for both Antitrust Division models is listed in table 4.8. In the AD Cases model, nearly 60% of the forecast error variance in presidential budgetary signal innovations after eight years is explained by innovations in congressional appropriation signals while only about 10% of the forecast error variance in congressional appropriation signals after eight years is explained by the president's budgetary signal innovations. Moreover, nearly 77% of the forecast error variance in the Congress series can be accounted for by its own innovations. These findings support the lagged F-block tests of causal relations discussed earlier which indicate that anticipated congressional behavior is insensitive to anticipated presidential behavior in this instance. The fact that the AD innovations explain 67% of its own forecast error variance after eight years is further proof that these particular agency outputs are consistent with the *bureaucratic autonomy* hypothesis.[54]

The variance decomposition of the forecast error variance for each series in the AD Investigations model also yields interesting results. Presidential budgetary signal innovations account for slightly less than half (47%) of its own forecast error variance after eight years. These same signal innovations account for almost the identical amount of forecast error variance in the congressional appropriation signals' series. Unlike the AD cases model, these results indicate that presidential innovations are more dominant in explaining political budgetary signals relative to congressional innovations. This pattern is consistent with the analogous findings for the SEC Investigations model dis-

TABLE 4.8 Decomposition of the Forecast Error Variance as a Result of Policy Innovations Emanating from the President, Congress, and the Antitrust Division

		Innovations in					
		Antitrust Cases Model			Investigations Model		
Forecast Error Variance in		President	Congress	AD	President	Congress	AD
President	t+1	100.00	.00	.00	100.00	.00	.00
	t+3	20.48	73.46	6.07	61.07	35.91	3.03
	t+5	14.77	63.46	21.77	41.93	38.04	20.03
	t+8	14.58	59.24	26.19	47.10	29.74	23.16
Congress	t+1	5.14	94.86	.00	12.20	87.80	.00
	t+3	11.34	82.94	5.72	27.42	48.85	23.74
	t+5	11.41	82.80	5.80	33.39	47.03	19.58
	t+8	10.32	76.24	13.44	47.13	34.17	18.70
Antitrust	t+1	2.08	5.18	92.77	.01	25.12	74.87
Division	t+3	7.18	5.23	87.59	4.94	37.37	57.69
	t+5	12.32	10.61	77.07	7.79	38.28	53.93
	t+8	13.05	19.95	67.00	13.36	27.67	58.97

NOTES: Each cell entry is the percentage of forecast error variance t years ahead in the column variables produced by a policy innovation in the variable on the far left-hand side of the column. The order of the variables for the innovation accounting simulation is President, Congress, and Antitrust Division. Due to rounding error, the numbers in the rows do not always sum up to exactly 100.

cussed earlier. Therefore, it is possible that presidential budgetary signals, which precede congressional appropriation signals in terms of the stages of the agency budgetary process, provide a cue to administrative agencies to begin examining market activities since investigations typically precede other kinds of formal action taken on behalf of administrative agencies. Once again, AD investigations activity does not appear to be temporally dependent upon the budgetary signals of either political institution, given that its own innovations explain almost 60% of this series' forecast error variance after eight years.[55]

Summary of Empirical Findings

This chapter has focused on the empirical application of the dynamic systems model of administrative politics by focusing on both *anticipated* and *unanticipated* behavioral responses from the president, Congress, and an administrative agency. Moreover, the dynamics of agency-political relationships analyzed here are in the tradition of classic public administration theorists (Barnard 1938; Simon 1947) as well as from a principal-agent perspective (Mitnick 1980; Moe 1984), since both a "zone of acceptable behavior" and a "two-way street" among these institutions implies such behavior.

In sum, the results of the empirical analysis pertaining to president-Congress-SEC relations contain some novel and theoretically provocative findings. First, both the multivariate tests of Granger Causality and the decomposition of the forecast error variance question the assumptions of past research by demonstrating in several instances that presidential and congressional budgetary signals in relation to bureaucratic agencies are interdependent. The contemporaneous correlation of the innovations in the SEC models indicates that presidential budgetary signals elicit an immediate, positive (reciprocal) response by Congress.[56] Second, the SEC appears (initially) more responsive to unanticipated congressional appropriation signals relative to unanticipated presidential bud-getary signals. Finally, agency regulatory performance signals are critical for understanding the budgetary signals of its political institutions, especially in the case of securities regulation.

These empirical results reveal that bureaucratic agencies are not only "proactive" organizations that, through their enforcement activity, help shape the political stimuli they receive. In terms of democratic accountability, the institutional proximity of these organizations bears a close correlation with predictions of their dynamic behavior. For instance, the SEC will generally (though not always) be more sensitive to Congress than to presidential administrations because of its institutional design. These findings provide empirical support for the "new institutionalism" of scholars studying the bureaucracy, who maintain that politicians battle over the design and structure of administrative agencies and that the war is often won before the agency even begins to administer policy (Knott and Miller 1987; Moe 1988, 1989, 1990).

Contrary to the vast majority of previous research, the SEC case study presented here demonstrates that a single institution will not always dominate policy administration. The findings establish conclusively that the political tools versus bureaucratic factors dichotomy is an oversimplified way to understand administrative behavior. Instead, the behavior of each institution is a function of a dynamic interrelations process involving all the governmental institutions regularly involved in the administration of securities regulation. The findings of this chapter are less consistent with Weingast (1984) and Moe

(1982) who make quantitative declarations that SEC behavior is separately controlled by Congress and the president respectively.[57]

Khademian's (1992) anecdotal claims, however, that the SEC exhibits a great deal of policy expertise and discretion over securities regulation, while at the same time being responsive to both Congress and the president, are well grounded given the statistical evidence presented here. Former SEC chairman Manuel Cary (1961–1967) supports this latter point, contending that independent agencies are entities not truly independent from political pressures (Cary 1967: 139). Khademian's contention that Congress is generally more supportive of SEC regulatory behavior than the president is strongly supported by the empirical evidence of this study. Although she does not state why this is the case, it appears that the relative policy congruence and receptivity between these institutions is due to the fact that these organizations are more proximate to one another than the president-agency dyadic relationship.

Such a finding is not surprising when one considers issues centered on the structure and design of administrative agencies and how their behavior is often shaped by politicians before they start operations (Knott and Miller 1987; Moe 1988, 1989, 1990; Seidman and Gilmour 1986). One interesting (and important) subtlety not captured by Khademian's anecdotal evidence is the complex relationship between the SEC and the president. In general, the results of the causality tests and the decomposition of the forecast error variance of these models indicate that presidents respond to enforcement innovations coming from the SEC. However, the opposite does not usually hold true, as the SEC does not move in a reciprocal manner following "surprises" emanating from the White House. In this regard, the findings may suggest that the direct power of presidential administrations over this independent regulatory commission's behavior is quite limited. Much of the presidential influence will be more subtle and indirect through affecting the budgetary signals of Congress in these particular instances.

The results of the Antitrust Division Cases and Investigations models also produce several noteworthy findings regarding agency-political relationships. First and foremost, agency behavior (in terms of aggregate enforcement activity) is modestly responsive to the budgetary signaling behavior of political principals in both a lagged adaptive manner as well as in a more sophisticated fashion. However, the AD is relatively more responsive to these signals on the whole compared to the SEC. The SEC exerts a relatively greater impact on the budgetary signals that it receives from its political principals (president and

Congress) vis-à-vis the AD, given that the former agency is more consistently causally prior to current changes in political budgetary signals, and its innovations also explain a larger percentage share of the forecast error variance in these signals. Although neither administrative agency is a pawn of its political superiors (via budget signals), the empirical findings reveal that the SEC is relatively autonomous compared to the AD. This is hardly surprising given that the SEC is an independent regulatory commission that is designed to be more (politically) autonomous than an executive bureau. These empirical results support the contention that the Antitrust Division experiences a great deal of independence from its political superiors in a manner that is indicative of the *bureaucratic autonomy* and *bureaucratic influence* hypotheses, respectively (Eisner and Meier 1990; Eisner 1991; Katzmann 1980; Weaver 1977),[58] while rather limited evidence is garnered for the *mutual adaptation* hypothesis.[59] Consistent with the securities regulation empirical results, while there may exist a strong, formal hierarchical relationship between a political principal and an administrative agency, it will not invariably translate into political control of the volume of bureaucratic outputs that reflect regulatory vigor displayed by the Antitrust Division, as empirical research on the topic maintains (Lewis-Beck 1979; Wood and Anderson 1993). Also, although the results from the model examining Antitrust Division caseload activity demonstrate support for the claim that congressional budgetary behavior is not influenced by Antitrust Division aggregate caseload activity (Yandle 1988: 270–271), the findings generated by the Investigations model display empirical evidence to the contrary. This suggests that members of Congress (MCs) may view investigatory efforts as being a critical precursory enforcement activity of the Antitrust Division, which necessitates congressional action in the form of budgetary resource signals; however, subsequent actual cases that are brought up by the agency do not require the same degree of political support in this manner.

The statistical evidence, however, does not support the anecdotal claim made by individuals within both the OMB and CBO who assert that antitrust regulation evolves in an incremental manner. Rather, this outcome is congruous with a top level Antitrust Division official who maintained that antitrust enforcement efforts do not vary in an incremental manner (interview with author, June 1993). Based on the F-block tests of lagged causal relations and the dynamic impulse response graphs, this agency perspective contains greater empirical merit.

The contemporaneous budgetary innovations between Congress and the

Antitrust Division variables are negative in both AD models. This finding reveals that each institution's behavior contemporaneously diverges from the other in response to a policy surprise. Consistent with the institutional proximity thesis, these statistical results demonstrate that institutions that are further apart from one another will in fact have a greater tendency to exhibit policy divergence in a contemporaneous manner. This result, however, differs from the analogous relationship between the president and SEC. The latter relationship reflects modest levels of policy congruence in two of three instances. Such a finding is plausible given that the SEC does not have a formal shield from political principals, whereas the Antitrust Division does have one, in the form of DOJ and the White House respectively, when dealing with Congress. Furthermore, the contemporaneous responses to these innovations between the president and Congress are not as strongly and positively correlated in the AD models as in the SEC models. Although policy conflict does occur between Congress and the president, the empirical results indicate that the contemporaneous response to budgetary signaling innovations between each political institution will generally reflect reciprocity. This is not unusual when one considers that politicians realize that independent regulatory commissions enjoy a certain degree of additional discretion by design compared to executive branch bureaus and departments. Therefore, if political institutions hope to have influence over policy administration in this area, they need to appear as allies to one another in the presence of unanticipated movements in behavior (at least contemporaneously) in order to display a unified front to the bureaucratic agency in question.

The dynamic analysis involving the decomposition of the forecast error variance for each institutional participant once again provides interesting evidence when it comes to unanticipated behavior. Regarding congressional-Antitrust Division relations, Eisner (1991: 43) asserts that the former's part of the budgetary process appears to have little, if any, relationship with the enforcement behavior of the latter. Except for the significant, negative contemporaneous correlations among the residuals found in both models (especially in the AD Investigations model), Eisner's assertion does contain considerable empirical merit. In addition, the strong negative correlation between the contemporaneous budgetary signal innovations of Congress and the enforcement innovations of the Antitrust Division in each model indicate that agency behavior does not acquiesce to unanticipated changes in political signals, but instead moves away from them in a contemporaneous manner.

Chapter 5

Democratic Governance in the Modern Administrative State

The Politics of the Administrative State Reconsidered

Existing research implicitly assumes that bureaucratic institutions are not capable of shaping the behavior of political overseers. Moreover, bureaucratic agencies are not viewed as proactive organizations, capable of influencing the budgetary signals emitted by political institutions. The dynamic systems model of administrative politics set forth in this study, on the other hand, maintains that bureaucratic organizations not only are capable of responding to political stimuli (Carpenter 1996; Hedge and Scicchitano 1994; Moe 1982, 1985a; Ringquist 1995; Scholz, Twombly, and Headrick, 1991; Wood and Anderson 1993; Wood and Waterman 1991, 1993, 1994) but also are able to emit stimuli of their own toward political institutions.

The central purpose of this study has been to reconceptualize politics in the modern administrative state as a means to obtain accurate insights into the nature of agency-political relationships. The study suggests that political scientists need to create general models of administrative politics that are more comprehensive in nature. The forceful competing claims set forth by an array of students of American politics and public bureaucracy, using qualitative, quantitative, and formal modes of research, need to be reconciled in some orderly and objective fashion. A general framework that encompasses a variety of theoretical claims made in existing research on the topic has been set forth. Instead of using purely deductive modes of analysis to square these seemingly disparate findings, a theoretically driven inductive approach toward assessing behavioral relationships among the presidency, Congress, and administrative organizations has been adopted in this study. This strategy is appropriate, given the stark theoretical disagreements found in this area of administrative politics. The dynamic systems model does not predict a specific outcome that will always occur—e.g., bureaucratic agencies generally behave in an independent fashion from their political principals. Very few topics of interest in political science can boast a theory of behavior that predicts with great certainty that a specific outcome will always hold. Due to the excessive number of possible laboratories to investigate these behavioral relationships, it is even more difficult to achieve any level of unanimity. What can be achieved, however, is an examination of various phenomena using a general theoretical lens such as the dynamic systems model of administrative politics. This framework can not only be applied to other policies involving economic regulation, or social regulation for that matter, but can extend to other policy types such as distributive and redistributive policy environments as well.

Both the descriptive and quantitative evidence displays the dynamic complexity of administrative politics—on two distinct levels. The first level deals with the heterogeneity of behavioral relations between institutions in the enforcement of economic regulation. The empirical results of this study show that, in some instances, anticipated behavior may in fact differ for any given dyadic relationship. In this regard, the empirical evidence exhibits support for the *bureaucratic influence* hypothesis in all three models involving securities regulation. The case of antitrust regulation displays support for the *bureaucratic autonomy* hypothesis, *bureaucratic influence* hypothesis, and the *mutual adaptation* hypothesis. Although unabridged political influence (or control) consistent with the *political influence* hypothesis is a real possibility within this theoretical framework, no evidence of this type of relationship is garnered from the quantitative data from the SEC and Antitrust Division of the DOJ analyzed in this study. By no means do these findings indicate that political influence does not exist at all. Rather, it just means that the political control theory does not hold when it comes to the anticipated (i.e, predictable) aspects of institutional behavior for the two case studies analyzed. One can conclude from the statistical results obtained in this study that both the Antitrust Division and the SEC are robust administrative organizations that generally are not subject to political domination, as implied by those espousing a principal-agent view of political control or an "overhead theory of democracy" perspective.

These findings also suggest that dyadic relations between political principals (i.e., the president and Congress) are, in fact, heterogeneous. In some instances the anticipated component of budgetary-preference signals show that presidents may influence Congress, the latter may exert influence over the former, or they may jointly influence each other. These results also indicate that the political principal who is most proximate (in an institutional sense) to the administrative organization will generally be responsive to the past behavior of the more distant political principal. One possible explanation may be that this institutionally "closer" political principal may serve as a shield for the administrative body in question.[1] If this is the case, then a political principal may function as a buffer (or shock absorber) for the agency, to protect it from its more "distant" political counterpart by being responsive to the latter institution's budgetary signals. An alternative rational choice–based interpretation of this same pattern of behavioral relations might infer that this transpires for strategic reasons. The political principal that is institutionally closer may generally wish to view the behavior of the relatively more distant political principal so that it can react for its own policy purposes. This is quite plausible since the (institutionally) more proximate of the political principals may perceive its relatively solid position will enable it to respond to unanticipated changes in administrative behavior, though this may not necessarily be the case in all instances—as the results for the Antitrust Division seem to indicate. After all, this latter line of reasoning would be consistent with the proponents of the politics of institutional choice who insist that politicians intentionally design administrative organizations so as to create an environment in which the former can best control the latter (Knott and Miller 1987; Moe 1988, 1989, 1990).

The second level involves the distinction between anticipated behaviors versus unanticipated behaviors. The former entails preference and behavior variations that each governmental institution in the system can readily observe on its own. In other words, presidents, Congress, and administrative agencies can effortlessly examine budgetary behavior and bureaucratic policy outputs from previous years by examining agency annual reports, disclosures at congressional hearings, or the *Budget of the United States Government*, for example. The latter form of behavioral relations pertains to unanticipated movements in the behavior for each governmental institution in the system. This type of behavior means that these participants cannot formulate their expectations by simply extrapolating from the past history and records of the agency—as dynamic (lagged) adaptation or adaptive expectations would imply from the tradition of bounded rationality and adaptive learning espoused by public administration scholars from over a generation ago (March and Simon 1958; Simon 1947, 1955). An institution can respond to these unanticipated fluctuations (also termed "policy innovations" or "policy shocks") emanating from other institutions within the same system. In these instances, institutions will respond in a sophisticated manner by altering their own current and future paths of behavior. The results of the contemporaneous correlation between policy innovations and the subsequent dynamic response analysis indicates that the pattern of relationships may vary quite a bit between these two distinct types of dynamic behavior.

Although analyses of specific aspects of agency-political relations (e.g., principal-agent political control–based model of a politician and an agency) are insightful, the general explanatory power of these frameworks is limited to an important—yet narrow—set of problems. Reconsidering administrative politics in a democratic system of government means that there are three broad issues incorporated and discussed at length in this study that merit serious attention from those of us examining the functioning of public bureaucracy within the confines of our governmental system. There follow three key considerations that have been all but ignored in previous empirical research investigating the nature of agency-political relationships: (1) *a primary emphasis allowing for endogenous agency-political behavior across time,* (2) *sophisticated or "unanticipated" forms of behavioral response,* and (3) *a comprehensive framework of analysis that views policy implementation as a product of a dynamic system of government institutions.* It is essential that future research on this topic treat each of these facets with the utmost consideration, or else it will risk making tenuous (even erroneous) assertions concerning bureaucratic politics. Failure to recognize the fundamental importance of these three aspects to the study of administrative politics will hinder our understanding of administrative agency-political institution relationships.

Institutional Dynamics and the Administration of Public Policy

Previous studies downplay, or in some cases even ignore, the role of governmental institutions in the policy administration milieu, at the expense of highlighting incident specific events and/or conditions. Because they are the fundamental basis for governmental organisms and political life (March and Olsen 1984, 1989), institutions cannot be ignored or relegated to an ancillary capacity. Furthermore, institutional analysis is preferable to the individual-level or discrete-event analysis for two critical reasons.

First, institutions by their very design and purpose are much steadier than individual-level policy actors. As a result, institutions outlast the individual personalities and predilections of policy actors within the policy environment. Also, discrete policy changes may not necessarily reflect an institution's general behavior, but they can serve to disguise what is actually transpiring if such discrete occurrences are relatively rare or anomalous. To illustrate this point, a majority of the descriptive and empirical studies claiming presidential control over the bureaucracy view the manner in which policy outputs fluctuated in response to Ronald Reagan's assuming office in 1981. Students of public bureaucracy try to infer such findings to mean that presidents generally exert control over the bureaucracy through the latter's output. Such a claim is unfounded since it is possible that the Reagan administration may well have been the exception to the rule. This is supported in classic works on bureaucratic politics from the preceding decade during the Nixon-Ford administrations (Aberbach and Rockman 1976; Heclo 1977), which suggests that presidents are often not successful in manipulating the bureaucracy for their policy intentions.[2] A broader shortcoming of administrative politics research to date has been its tendency to base conclusions on whether the bureaucracy is autonomous or subject to political influence (or domination) for any given short, recent period of time in American politics and policy.[3] Since many of the studies inspect only two or three adjacent presidential administrations, they are not historical analyses in the purest sense. Instead, a preferable term to describe this genre of research would be "longitudinal" because they are studies of behavior across a time span, but the interval is relatively short and the emphasis is on discrete events or shifts in the policy environment via key political appointments and the like.

Second, most political research questions are concerned with broader issues of constitutional design and the practice of democratic government. This is most true for research on the public bureaucracy by political scientists. For example, determining whether presidents generally influence (or control) an administrative agency can provide us with a deeper understanding of bureaucratic politics compared to investigating whether a key political appointment has brought about change in policy administration. In other words, most political scientists who study governmental organizations are trying to tap into (at

· least on some level) the general behavior of these institutions. This does not preclude individuals who reside within these entities at some point in time, but neither does it make them of central importance in explaining regulatory performance. The failure of past research to fervently seek answers to these broader concerns implicitly leads to a preoccupation with discovering tools of political control, and how comparatively effectively each one performs. This is not to say that these research questions are not fruitful endeavors, they clearly are. It is just that the obsession has made those scholars who are empirically investigating administrative agency-political institution relationships lose sight of the larger, surrounding questions that have broader theoretical and substantive value.

In recent years, institutional-choice theories of public bureaucracy have given institutions well-deserved and much overdue attention by recognizing the intrinsic significance attached to how politicians and interest groups bargain to arrive at an administrative design that is both favorable to their interests and agreeable at some minimum acceptable threshold level. Those coming from this tradition assert that bureaucratic institutions are not designed to be efficient, well-oiled machines of policy administration. Instead, bureaucratic organizations are designed to reflect the power of political interests through the use of rules (Kettl 1993: 418). The scholars from this approach acknowledge that the design and rules constructed for administrative bodies will necessarily constrain their behavior to a significant extent in a proscribed way that exhibits the balance of political interests. The main thread underlying its theoretical foundations is the greater relative importance of institutions over individuals. This point is not made just because of the transience of individuals. Rather, the individuals participating in the execution of public policy via the bureaucracy are heavily constrained by the rules that are largely designed by politicians. Institutional-choice theories note the central role institutions perform in the theater of American government. These theories often focus on the effects of agency creation (Moe 1988, 1989, 1990) and the static micro-analytic underpinnings of relations among administrative agencies and political institutions under various scenarios (Hammond and Knott 1993, 1996). One thing that is consistent with these works is that they are generally static in nature and do not focus on administrative outcomes. An exception to this former observation is Bendor and Moe (1985). In their study, however, they examine only the dynamics of conventional adaptive behavior (March and Simon 1958; Simon 1947) via computer simulation models.[4]

Institutional dynamics are an important, required area of inquiry because most, if not all, scholars studying public bureaucracy realize both the value of institutions and that politics in the administrative state often require us to employ a broad historical lens so that a general pattern of behavior can be discerned and accurately portrayed. Considering how institutional behavior evolves dynamically across time is an inherently closer representation of social reality on the political as well as the administrative level. This is not to say that static theoretical models of individual actors fail to make significant contributions to our base of knowledge.[5] These studies perform an essential function by exploring basic (i.e., fundamental) individual and institutional motivations on a micro level. Beyond the purview of such inquiry, however, these studies are not designed to reveal the dynamic complexity and heterogeneity of governmental institutions from a macro-level perspective.

The Role of Sophisticated Behavior in Agency-Political Relationships

Political actors and the institutions to which they belong are able to respond in a sophisticated manner to changes in their political and policy environment. Nonformal research on the politics of the administrative state has virtually ignored the importance of sophisticated (unanticipated) forms of behavior as well as expectations. Formal theories of public bureaucracy are correct in placing an emphasis on how sophisticated behavior can be used for both strategic purposes as well as how it can reflect information uncertainty on behalf of governmental institutions. In the area of administrative politics, both bureaucratic organizations and institutions of democratic governance do not anticipate each other's behavior with complete certainty. This does not mean that institutions/actors operate in an information-sparse environment where they can adapt only to tangible or observable behavior. The quantitative analysis and anecdotal evidence obtained from the interviews conducted with relevant governmental actors unanimously agree that the lines of communication between these institutions are open, which suggests that institutions often operate in an information-rich policy environment where they are in the position to respond to unanticipated movements in another institution's behavior (Krause 1997).

Although evidence suggestive of rational expectations is uncovered in only a single instance throughout this study (between president and Congress budgetary-preference signals in the SEC Injunctive Actions model), there were some other situations where this possibility may have been almost achieved. It seems quite possible, however, that future research using the dynamic systems model to analyze agency-political relationships may uncover this type of behavior. In doing so, it would lend even greater credence to the theoretical arguments made in positive political theory research on the topic than can be uncovered by the approach undertaken in this particular study.

Some public bureaucracy scholars construct theoretical and empirical models with lagged adaptation (alternatively conceptualized as being dynamic adaptation or adaptive expectations) as their centerpiece (Bendor and Moe 1985; Carpenter 1992, 1996; Wood and Waterman 1993, 1994). These approaches posit that current agency performance (measured by its policy output) responds to past political and environmental signals because the agency experiences inertia, operates under uncertainty, lacks complete information, and possesses limited cognitive (processing) capabilities to assimilate policy signals. The intellectual foundations of these models are heavily influenced by classic works on organization theory (March and Simon 1958; Simon 1947). These approaches are very informative, and also constitute a significant improvement over preceding research efforts on the topic, because of their introduction of expectational behavior and explicit consideration of information processing into the study of administrative behavior. At the same time, research must progress to account for the genuine complexity and subtlety found in the operations of government, which cannot be solely attributable to conventional lagged adaptation. This study extends this theme to include sophisticated behavior and adaptation, which entail that governmental organizations both initiate and respond to policy perturbations emanating from one another.

The Necessity for Comprehensive Theory Building in the Study of Administrative Politics

Theoretical development in administrative politics has been quite slow relative to other areas in political science. The main source of this problem can be attributed to oversimplified models, which contribute to our knowledge base but also obscure the more important, broader issues needing our attention—such as bidirectional interaction among political and administrative institutions, and the distinction between "anticipated" and "unanticipated" forms of behavior. Another minor source of this problem is the lack of dialogue between those employing formal theory, quantitative-empirical analysis, and qualitative approaches (e.g., see Kettl 1993 for an excellent discussion of this issue). Each of these methods of inquiry has something of value to offer. In this study alone, the existing formal research on the topic has contributed greatly to the notion of strategic behavior with respect to institutional relations. Qualitative, quantitative, and formal modes of analysis have each made a significant contribution to our base of knowledge.

One important consequence of comprehensive theory building in the study of bureaucratic politics is that it can take into account joint influence between political institutions and administrative agencies. As the empirical evidence suggests, allowing for this possible type of behavior is vital, because it reflects the symbiotic relationship often exhibited in policy administration in other environments (i.e., distributive and redistributive policy).[6] Existing theories of administrative politics cannot capture this type of influence since they restrict behavioral relationships in a unidirectional or a "one-way street" manner based upon hierarchical considerations. These existing models of agency-political institution relationships, in terms of approach, are noncomprehensive theories by nature (for an exception see Hammond and Knott 1993, 1996). As a result, such theories may lead to misleading and sometimes even erroneous conclusions since they are not consistent with the actualities of policy administration in a democratic system of governance.

For theoretical development to progress at a more rapid pace, greater attention to the finer aspects of substantive realities is required. In the case of the politics of the administrative state, the many existing theories of administrative politics serve as partial explanations as outlined earlier in chapter 2 of this book. For example, principal-agent models that espouse political control over bureaucratic organizations are valid but serve only as one special case of relations between administrative agencies and political institutions. The same is true for models espousing bureaucratic autonomy. We need to strive toward encompassing various theories of administrative politics into a singular framework of analysis, which it is hoped will in turn lead us toward a unified theory of administrative politics. If we do not construct comprehensive analytic frameworks, the quest toward developing theoretical unity and substantive consensus on these macro-level relationships will be made more difficult. This study attempts to serve as the first step in this direction.

Summary of Case Study Findings

This study examines administrative politics involving two salient areas of economic regulation that have been explored by political scientists: securities and antitrust regulation. Past research on these substantive areas arrives at various different conclusions as to which institution drives administrative behavior. In the area of securities regulation, it has been argued that presidents (Moe 1982), Congress (Weingast 1984), and the SEC (Khademian 1992) are *the* driving force behind SEC regulatory behavior. This same discordance occurs in the area of antitrust regulation, where some maintain that elected officials control regulatory enforcement activity over the Antitrust Division of the Department of Justice (Lewis-Beck 1979; Wood and Anderson 1993), and others claim this agency exhibits a relatively high degree of autonomy and influence in its policy domain (Eisner and Meier 1990; Eisner 1991; Katzmann 1980; Weaver 1977).

The dynamic systems model of administrative politics has been employed to assess the validity of the various competing theories of bureaucratic behavior. This model encompasses the assumptions (implicit or explicit) found in the theoretical models used to explain bureaucratic behavior. Analysis of annual time-series data on regulatory performance (policy outputs) and the budgetary-preference signals of the president and Congress for the 1949–1992 sample period yields an investigation into the general nature of presidential-congressional-agency relations pertaining to the overall vigor of enforcement efforts in each policy area. The results of these case studies can be summarized in the following manner:

1. Both environmental and intra-institutional factors are capable of playing a vital role in shaping the behavior of institutions in the regulatory system. For instance, both the Reagan administration and the unemployment rate exert a significant effect on the congressional budgetary signals pertaining to the Antitrust Division in the Antitrust Cases model, where the balance of economists to attorneys and the Economic Policy Office of the AD help shape these congressional budgetary signals in the system where the focus of enforcement effort is on Antitrust Investigations. The empirical evidence contained in this study suggests that these types of influences are more important in understanding the formation of political institutions' budgetary signals vis-à-vis agency enforcement activity. In sum, the various empirical models presented in this study reveal that these budgetary signals toward administrative agencies are shaped by a myriad of factors including oversight committee ideology, presidential administrations, industry size, administrative innovation through the creation of a specialized economic policy office, macroeconomic conditions, regulatory legislation, and major industry events.

2. Both bureaucratic agencies investigated in this study display support for

the notion that these institutions do not merely respond to democratic institutions in a Pavlovian fashion but instead actively shape their respective policy environments through their enforcement activities. In no single case is there empirical support for the conventional notion of political control over the bureaucracy that is found in principal-agent models espousing this perspective. The SEC empirical models exhibit strong unified support for the *bureaucratic influence hypothesis.* The Antitrust Division empirical models yield support for the *bureaucratic influence* hypothesis with respect to president-agency relations (Antitrust Cases model), *bureaucratic autonomy* hypothesis with respect to president-agency (Antitrust Investigations model) and Congress-agency (Antitrust Cases model) relations. Furthermore, there is some evidence that the relationship between congressional appropriations signals and Antitrust Division investigations, based on lagged adaptive behavior, reflects the *mutual adaptation* hypothesis.

3. The notion of presidential-congressional interdependence has not been explicitly considered in systematic studies of administrative politics. Both sets of case studies indicate that the budgetary-preference signals of presidents and Congress are strongly interrelated. The lagged tests of multivariate Granger exogeneity clearly demonstrate in several instances that presidential-congressional budgetary-preference signals are not formed independent of one another—as has been presumed in much of the formal literature and in all of the quantitative-empirical literature on the subject. Thus, future research focusing on the general nature of agency-political relations must consider this facet when formulating theoretical and empirical models. The one interesting distinction between these case studies is that the contemporaneous policy innovations of these institutions in the SEC models exhibit consistent strong positive correlations, while this relationship is much more attenuated in the AD models. These results may suggest that political institutions feel a greater need to initially cooperate in response to unanticipated movements in budgetary-preference signals emanating from one another in the SEC models vis-à-vis the AD models because these democratic institutions will feel a greater need to demonstrate a unified front to an independent regulatory commission, which is designed to have relatively more independence from political influence than an executive bureau or department.

4. For the most part, administrative agencies and political institutions are, at best, weakly related to one another in terms of contemporaneous movements in their innovations. In the one instance where there is a strong contem-

poraneous correlation in the unanticipated behaviors of an agency and political institution, it is a negative relationship. Overall, these statistical results imply that there are limits to controlling bureaucratic behavior via sophisticated behavior on the part of political institutions. This, in turn, suggests that some degree of information asymmetry exists between administrative agencies and political institutions. The dynamic simulation results also provide us with some novel insights into unanticipated forms of behavior displayed by these governmental institutions. For example, presidential budgetary-preference signals often move in a reciprocal manner for the periods immediately following an unanticipated movement (shock) in the congressional budgetary-preference signals. Thus, in terms of aggregate bureaucratic outputs, presidents play a *reactive role* in both the administration of securities and antitrust regulation. Also, the SEC appears relatively more responsive in a reciprocal manner to congressional shocks vis-à-vis presidential shocks for only the initial periods following such events.

In essence, these findings provide a similar general portrait of agency-political relations. Administrative agencies, through their regulatory performance, can help shape their political environment. This is borne out by the empirical fact that the SEC and Antitrust Division each play a notable role in affecting the budgetary-preference signals received by each agency from its political principals. Also, both case studies demonstrate that presidential and congressional budgetary-preference signals are not distinct from each other. Instead, the behavior of these political institutions is intertwined. Finally, agency-political relations uncover sophisticated forms of behavior (in the form of policy innovations and subsequent responses) that may differ from inferences drawn from conventional empirical models of bureaucratic behavior premised on lagged adaptation. One clear example is the SEC's generally modest, yet positive dynamic response for the initial periods following a congressional shock. This pattern of political responsiveness was not uncovered by either the F-block Granger Causality coefficient tests or the contemporaneous correlations of each institution's innovations.

Although the general findings for these case studies are quite common, there are some distinctions between these sets of models. First, each agency's institutional design differs from the other. The SEC is an independent regulatory commission that has legislative and budgetary bypass authority from the executive branch of government whereas the Antitrust Division must get its policy plans cleared with the DOJ and the OMB. As a result, it is not surprising that the SEC—compared to the Antitrust Division—exhibits stronger, more positive ties with Congress vis-à-vis presidents. Second, the agencies also differ in the nature of the clientele they serve. The SEC serves a narrowly defined, well-specified industry (securities and commodities markets) whereas the Antitrust Division enforces its regulations across a plethora of industries. The net effect is that presidential-congressional relations in securities regulation will exhibit greater cooperation in the face of unanticipated fluctuations in SEC enforcement outputs, compared to those from the Antitrust Division, because the SEC enjoys more formal independence due to its institutional design and can more easily galvanize support from the securities and commodity industry to shield it from political pressures.

The causal connection between political principals, however, may differ in terms of institutional proximity to the agency responsible for administering policy. Under such circumstances, the results from the F-block tests of Granger Causality for both sets of models customarily demonstrate that a political principal institutionally farther from the bureaucratic agency will play a significant role in shaping the anticipated behavior of the political institution that is more proximate to the agency. The implication of this phenomenon is that "closer" institutions will generally allow more "distant" institutions to take the policy lead and respond to it in some manner appropriate to this institution for strategic purposes discussed earlier in this chapter. The analysis of unanticipated behavior, however, reveals that presidential budgetary innovations will elicit a moderately consistent, positive contemporaneous response from Congress. This reciprocity is also generally returned in the form of positive responses by presidents to innovations involving congressional budgetary signals for the subsequent periods following the shock to the latter political institution.

Conventional wisdom on bureaucratic behavior maintains that there exists a significant incremental component to the manner in which agency outputs respond to change in their political environment (Carpenter 1992, 1996; Moe 1985a; Wood and Waterman 1991, 1993, 1994). Relatedly, the two case studies analyzed here display some striking differences between the SEC and AD models concerning incremental components of agency enforcement behavior. Evidence of such behavior is significant in two out of the three SEC models tested, while it is not found in either of the AD models.

Why should there be such differences with respect to incremental behavior exhibited by these agencies? The SEC's well-defined (i.e., concentrated) target group and exclusive administrative authority over the securities and commodities markets will afford it the opportunity to adjust its own institutional behavior in a more gradual manner. On the other hand, the Antitrust Division's shared jurisdictional responsibilities with the FTC and the well-dispersed target group that it regulates will require that this administrative agency place a premium on organizational flexibility so that it can alter its behavior in response to changing conditions within the policy environment.[7]

The empirical evidence from these two case studies indicates that a hierarchical relationship between political principals and the SEC and the Antitrust Division respectively may hold in a constitutional design sense (Moe 1984; Redford 1969). Empirically, this type of formal hierarchical structure, however, does not appear to have a strong substantive bearing on the level of enforcement vigor with which either securities or antitrust regulation is administered. These statistical findings raise serious questions concerning the theoretical underpinnings of principal-agent models of political control over bureaucracy that are used to explain administrative behavior in these areas of regulatory policy. This is not to say there is no validity to these models with respect to substantive prediction.[8] Additional analyses applying this type of theoretical framework and empirical methodology to numerous policy areas may reveal support for this popular and intuitively appealing theory. In all likelihood, the principal-agent theory of political control over bureaucracy is an oversimplification of social and political realities, which represent a particular class of administrative agency-political institution relationships from a broader spectrum.

"Runaway" Bureaucracy or Democratic Control?
Responsiveness in the Modern Administrative State

The nature of influence among administrative organizations and their political principals has been the central focus in this study. Do elected officials control bureaucratic performance (outputs) in the form of the regulatory vigor with which the latter pursues its policy mission? Or do administrative agencies operate with a free rein where accountability to democratic institutions is, in general, severely limited? The nature of political control (or lack thereof) has long been a debate among scholars. While the findings are mixed, these past research efforts have found varied evidence for both political control and bureaucratic autonomy perspectives. The cases analyzed in this study lead one to conclude that a more temperate, symbiotic relationship transpires among agencies and their political overseers. Although bureaucratic influence over the (budgetary) behavior of democratic institutions is pervasive, this does not mean the administrative apparatus in the United States could best be characterized as a "runaway" bureaucracy. Simply, it would be in the best interest of administrative agencies not to behave in a manner that elicits a hostile response by political institutions since such action may serve to harm bureaucratic organizations.

The empirical findings of this study have clear and general theoretical implications—bureaucratic behavior may often play a significant role in shaping the budgetary-preference signals that the agency receives from political institutions, especially when it comes to anticipated forms of behavior. Therefore, the budgetary means by which political institutions attempt to control administrative agencies is shaped by the latter. However, this does not translate into a runaway bureaucracy because the behavior of administrative agencies is still constrained by their own internal organizational limitations, as well as by how they wish to be perceived by elected officials according to their actions (Krause 1998: 10).[9] To put it simply, political influence over the bureaucracy exists; however, it is less direct and more subtle than previous studies have claimed.

At the same time administrative agencies are not passive receptors of political stimuli as past research has posited, but rather can play an active role in shaping their policy environment. From a normative perspective, a systems view of bureaucratic agency-political institution relations is desirable since it provides a balanced view of agencies' pursuit of flexibility and discretion that is simultaneous with politicians' desire to make the bureaucratic institutions democratically accountable and responsive to their needs. Even though this relationship is not always a cooperative one, especially in many areas of regulatory policy, it does provide balance to our system of policy administration by suggesting that these institutions are inextricably linked to one another. This broader portrait of agency-political relations to the policy administration system suggests that we live in a democratic system of governance in which the administrative apparatus of the state and its democratic institutions cannot singularly dominate or control how public policy is administered.

Administrative Politics and Democratic Governance

Policy administration is a vital function for governance. This is especially true for democratic systems where it can significantly affect the meaning and intent of public policy being made by electoral institutions and the judiciary. During our nation's history, expansion of the administrative state have generally paralleled both macroeconomic and population growth. This should come as no surprise since the needs of the American polity has risen dramatically since the late nineteenth century (Skocpol 1992; Skowronek 1982). The spiraling growth of the administrative state in the United States during the past hundred years has required the bureaucracy to play a more co-equal role with democratic institutions of governance than during the nation's first hundred years. This growth in power is embodied by administrative institutions' ability to implement laws constructed and passed by the three branches of government, and is further enhanced by a general trend of increased delegation of authority and responsibility to administrative agencies over the content of public policy (Dodd and Schott 1979; Lowi 1969). Research on the topic reveals that much of this increased power stems from policy expertise exhibited by administrative agencies and pertaining to their relevant domains (Eisner 1991; Khademian 1992; Meier 1987, 1993; Mosher 1968; Rourke 1984).

The theoretical framework proposed in this book has two implications for the study of agency-political relationships in the modern administrative state. First, these relationships are continuous in nature, with institutions constantly adjusting to one another across time. Second, although hierarchy does formally matter in bureaucratic agency-political institution relations, it does not necessarily consign public bureaucracies to a subordinate role where they are subject to political manipulation. The constitutional foundations of public bureaucracy in the United States suggest that these institutions do contain a certain degree of legitimate power separate from the three branches of government. The degree to which the bureaucracy is independent from political forces is an empirical question that can be answered only by examining a a variety of both agency and policy types. The framework of analysis set forth in this study allows students of American political institutions and public bureaucracy a general way to address this issue from a common theoretical ground.

On the Continuity of Public Policy

Public policy is an evolving process. Kenneth Meier describes a more complex relationship involving the politics of "sin" policies by suggesting that a linkage between political institutions and bureaucratic agencies exists, whereby the institutions all influence one another and each structures its own responses to the others (Meier 1994: 7). This outlook is more consistent with both the dual notions of a "two-way street" and an "acceptable zone of behavior"—coming from Simon (1947) and Barnard's (1938) view of administrative politics, as well as from this study—than with much of the recent scholarly research on the topic. In a similar vein, Ringquist, Worsham, and Eisner (1994) aptly note that administrative politics are not characterized by a one-shot game. Instead, agency-political relationships are inherently dynamic, which means that the rules of the game and the behavior of the institutional participants will vary across time.

This continuity was borne out by the empirical analysis conducted in this study—in two distinct ways. First, the traditional concept of lagged adaptive behavior and adaptive expectations (also referred to as dynamic adaptation by students of public bureaucracy)[10] was inspected more thoroughly than in existing studies, by means of dynamic empirical tests involving the temporal-causal nature of these relationships. Second, the analysis of policy innovations (and subsequent responses) from these institutions reveals that an even more sophisticated process of dynamic adaptation occurs where each institution not only instantaneously reacts to a policy shock emanating from another institution but also responds in a differential manner across time.

Even though a dynamic model of bureaucratic politics is proposed in this study, static theories do advance our knowledge because they can play an important role in basic theory building by (1) exposing the micro-based motivations of relevant institutions and/or individuals, and (2) eliminating superfluous explanations of behavior. These micro-based models of individual and institutional behavior are limited, however, in that they are not adequately equipped by themselves to interpret the macro dynamics of bureaucratic agency-political institution relationships. The theoretical model presented in this book is epistomologically analogous to modern macroeconomic theories in that, while it is an inherently macro-level model, its foundations are also informed from the micro-level insights concerning agency-political relationships (e.g., sophisticated behavior and interaction). By creating a framework that consists of the elements of micro foundations of agency-political relationships embedded within the aggregate portrait of administrative politics, behavioral complexity is not obtained through forsaking the continuous nature of public policy and its administration.

Most, if not all students of public policy acknowledge the continuous nature of public policy. However, most of the existing research to date ignores this practical reality, and this oversight leads students of American institutions to make near-sighted claims regarding the nature of administrative politics. Some of these analyses are limited in historical scope since they do not emphasize public policy as a continuous process, but rather assert that a series of discrete events are largely responsible for explaining these behavioral relationships. Therefore, these studies cannot safely make claims that presidents control the bureaucracy based upon changes from one presidential administration to the next (such as Carter to Reagan). In order to be consistent with the concept of continuity in agency-political relationships, the strength and the position of presidents, Congress, and administrative agencies can best be ascertained by examining the dynamic historical evolution of these institutions across a sufficiently long period of time.

Hierarchy and the Politics of Policy Administration

Dating all the way back to Woodrow Wilson's classic work on the dichotomy between politics and policy administration, students of American public bureaucracy have been concerned with the structure between democratic and administrative institutions. One such area of concern has been the concept of hierarchy between political institutions and bureaucratic agencies. Generally, research on this topic before the 1980s did not deny the constitutionally designed hierarchy that exists between these institutions, but at the same time emphasized that administrative institutions were distinct entities whose performance was subject to internal organizational factors, and that they played a proactive role in policy administration (Barnard 1938; Crozier 1964; Downs 1967; Kaufman 1956; Lowi 1969; March and Simon 1958; Mosher 1968; Simon 1947).

Research since the early 1980s has emphasized the role of hierarchy between these entities as the theoretical basis of its models. This body of research has viewed electoral institutions as constitutionally superior to the bureaucracy. Therefore it is assumed that the former can manipulate the latter through various devices and mechanisms at their disposal (e.g., Hedge and Scicchitano 1994; Mitnick 1980; Moe 1982, 1984, 1985; Redford 1969; Scholz, Twombly, and Headrick 1991; Weingast and Moran 1982, 1983; Wood and Anderson 1993; Wood and Waterman 1991, 1993, 1994). The foundations of these principal-agent models of political control over the bureaucracy either posit or imply that a strict hierarchical relationship exists between politicians and bureaucrats (Mitnick 1980; Moe 1984). Although it may seem to be an appropriate theoretical assumption to make in a constitutional design sense, it does not accurately represent the modern-day realities of politics in the administrative state, since there are limits to politicians' ability to control the bureaucracy (Bendor, Taylor, and Van Gaalen 1985, 1987; Eisner and Meier 1990; Eisner 1991; Hammond and Knott 1993, 1996; Khademian 1992; Knott and Miller 1987; Miller 1992).

The model presented in this study allows one to test whether these hierarchical relations between electoral and administrative institutions hold true as the political control theorists (especially from the principal-agent paradigm) would maintain. Because it views administrative agencies as capable of proactive institutional behavior in implementing public policy, the dynamic systems model does not make restrictive behavioral assumptions about causal relationships based upon hierarchy. Although the empirical results from both case studies analyzed here may not be generalizable across every case, they nonetheless reveals that a strict principal-agent relationship between political institutions and administrative agencies does not hold to form. These findings are of great importance since they challenge the theoretical foundations of existing principal-agent based models of political control that are commonly used to analyze agency-political relationships.

From a practical perspective, scholarly research on this topic must realize that hierarchy is not necessarily unabridged. There are myriad factors such as information asymmetries, policy expertise, delegated authority and responsibility that may undermine to varying degrees the hierarchical structure between politicians and bureaucrats. These factors, however, cannot satisfactorily address the issue of political control versus bureaucratic autonomy since they are indirect means of assessing agency behavior. The complexity of administrative politics makes it increasingly difficult to discern whether hierarchy exists, and if so in what manner. The body of research on administrative politics is full of controversy regarding the basic issue of political control versus bureaucratic independence. As a result of this theoretical conflict and the seemingly convincing arguments made for both perspectives, it is necessary to treat these claims in an encompassing manner that recognizes the possibility of hierarchical relationships without falsely assuming they exist. Only through the use of a comprehensive framework can more accurate answers be obtained to this behaviorally complex causal relationship. This framework, in turn, not only serves as a battlefield for future research examining issues relating to hierarchy in administrative politics, but also makes possible a unified approach to the study of public bureaucracy.

Fusion of Methodological Approaches and Varying Insights into the Study of Agency-Political Relations

This project attempts to remain somewhat eclectic to the various approaches and tools of studying administrative politics. This research is informed by qualitative, quantitative, and formal research. Each research style makes unique contributions to our understanding of the politics of the administrative state. A major problem found in research on public bureaucracy is that it is isolated according to the methodological approach taken. For example, many political scientists who utilize formal modes of analysis to examine agency-political relations fail to draw upon the rich reservoir of work done by both traditional public administration and quantitative-empirical scholars. This point is not intended to singularly castigate the use of formal analysis in administrative politics. Conversely, the individuals conducting both qualitative and quantitative-empirical research are also guilty of ignoring the insights obtained not just from mathematical models of agency-political relationships but also by one another.

This study attempts to synthesize all three approaches for investigating policy administration. For instance, many substantive insights have been acquired from previous qualitative works on administrative politics as well as from the policy areas of interest (i.e., securities and antitrust regulation). This approach is extended through the use of elite interviews, which provided invaluable guidance, not only theoretically but also on issues of measurement and statistical analysis. Although a formal theoretical model is not presented here,[11] this brand of research informed the dynamic systems model of administrative politics proposed here with respect to the nature and importance of sophisticated behavior on the part of governmental institutions. The quantitative-empirical approach to the study of administrative politics yields the greatest source of influence, for one obvious reason: it is the prominent method of analysis employed in this study. The body of research generated from this tradition has been useful in examining the plurality of interests, individuals, events, and institutions actively shaping the administration of public policy.

Methodological pluralism in the social sciences is desirable. It should not be diminished in the name of scientific advancement, from epistemological bias, or from philosophical arrogance. This is especially true for research in the area of administrative politics. This field must be more open to harvest the benefits acquired by other forms of research. Through fruitful discourse, which leads to the exchanging of ideas and approaches in inspecting administrative politics, not only will our understanding of public bureaucracy become more unified, it will also be more inclined to progress at a more rapid pace than exists today. Future research can only benefit from the use of comprehensive theoretical frameworks that attempt to relax cumbersome assumptions. In doing so, models can be constructed that are applicable to different policy settings (e.g., distributive and redistributive policy environments, or parliamentary versus presidential systems of government), which in turn will facilitate many types of comparative analysis regarding policy administration. As a result, our understanding of the differences in bureaucratic agency-political institution relationships across different policy environments, institutional arrangements, and democratic systems will be enhanced in a profound manner.

Subsequent research also requires us to construct theoretical models (whether they are formal or nonformal) that are a closer fit to social and political reality. In this study an attempt to take one step in this direction has been made by focusing on the general nature of institutional relations between the president, Congress, and administrative agencies. Research on administrative politics also needs to place a greater premium on theory building. This is essential, given the comparably slower pace of theoretical development in administrative politics.[12] For instance, where many other fields have been successful in defining the battlefield in which theory is made, research on the relationship between public bureaucracy and political institutions has not been able to arrive at an agreement on fundamental issues. To get a better idea of the fundamental issues and concepts about which there can be some general consensus (i.e., define this battlefield), scholars studying administrative politics need to step back and test the assumptions and claims associated with such existing theories. Therefore, prospective inquiries into the nature of bureaucratic agency-political institution relationships should entail comprehensive modes of analysis, or we risk losing focus of the substantive realities associated with the product and processes involved in the creation of public policy. Otherwise, dialogue within this field of study will continue to be discordant. Such continued practices will result in further stagnation of scholarly inquiry into the nature of behavioral relations among the governmental institutions that are responsible for creating and administering public policy.

Where Do We Go From Here? Implications for the Current State of Theory in Administrative Politics

The current state of research on administrative politics requires a broader view of relationships among bureaucratic agencies and political institutions. In essence, there is a need to strive toward theoretical unity in explaining these relations. The models used to explain phenomena in this area of political science vary a great deal—by both substance and implicit or explicit assumptions being made concerning behavioral relations. Besides the three cornerstones of the dynamic systems theory proposed in this study, existing research tries to gauge bureaucratic autonomy by assessing the significance of indirect factors (e.g., creation of a specialized policy office). This mode of analysis shows a similar type of short-sightedness as conventional political control theses, which emphasize discrete shifts in behavior at the expense of longer and more subtle strands of influence. Based upon the arguments advocated in this body of research, an absence of bureaucratic autonomy is revealed if the agency under examination operates in an environment without significant bureaucratic policy change in one form or another (e.g., SEC). In this study, one can potentially observe whether administrative organizations display autonomy, power, incrementalism, joint influence with political principals, or some combination thereof under various circumstances not addressed by existing research.

The findings presented here also exhibit tenuous support for traditional theories of administrative politics. Political control studies coming under the rubric of the principal-agent paradigm (including Redford's "overhead theory of democracy") appear deficient in their simple premise that politicians have control over the bureaucracy because of their hierarchical position. One can plausibly argue that, in theory, elected officials behave as principals who delegate authority to administrative agencies, which in turn faithfully execute the preferences of politicians (Moe 1984; Weingast and Moran 1982, 1983). In practice, however, agencies have their own culture and professional norms, which lead them to implement public policy in a manner that is not always consistent with the principal-agent paradigm of political control. This is not to say that political control of any variety (including the traditional conceptualization of principal-agent based theories) cannot take place. What the theoretical framework and subsequent quantitative analysis from this study does indicate is that this form of rigid unidirectional (political) control will not always hold in the style described in principal-agent based models of political control. Instead, if political influence does occur, it may do so in a joint manner with bureaucratic influence (i.e., mutual adaptation or joint influence). It may also transpire in a more subtle fashion through sophisticated (i.e., unanticipated) behavior as the findings of this study have shown.

The dynamic systems model goes beyond claims of bureaucratic autonomy made in prior research. Bureaucratic autonomy theories posit that administrative agencies are unresponsive to political influence, but the opposite is not true (Aberbach and Rockman 1976; Eisner and Meier 1990; Eisner 1991; Heclo 1977; Ogul 1976). This study's empirical results forcefully demonstrate that in some instances bureaucratic behavior (reflected through policy outputs) will help shape the budgetary signaling behavior of political principals. These findings have two meaningful ramifications. On a theoretical level, the conceptualization of relationships found in bureaucratic politics (ranging from political control to bureaucratic autonomy) must be extended to include bureaucratic influence or power. On an empirical level, previous models of administrative politics may well suffer from problems relating to model misspecification.

The lack of comprehensive analyses displayed in the existing body of research on the topic unintentionally skews the empirical results that are generated. Although discrete events such as changes in presidential administrations, political appointments, bureaucratic policy change, and so on are important explanatory considerations, they suffer from the problem of being incident specific. These incident-specific factors cannot demonstrate a general pattern of institutional behavior across time. The conceptual model set forth in this study is devised to capture this integral dimension of governmental behavior. For one to make meaningful general declarations concerning political control or bureaucratic autonomy, one must explore these relationships across a fairly long historical period of time from an institutional perspective so that generalizable statements about these concepts can be made with an adequate amount of validity.

Scholars examining the foundations of the administrative state in the United States arrive at the same general conclusion: that bureaucratic organizations can be viewed as being political—and not purely managerial—entities (Nelson 1982; Skocpol 1992; Skowronek 1982). Such a portrait of American bureaucracy demonstrates why the analysis of administrative organizations in political environments is requisite to understanding policy administration.[13] Although most of the existing research correctly notes that administrative behavior must be examined in some type of pluralist-based model (e.g., multiple political principals, competing interest groups, etc.), none of the quantitative-empirical body of research to date has truly given the bureaucracy a legitimate role in matters of policy administration, as has been done in many descriptive studies. Future quantitative-empirical research must conceptualize the bureaucracy as a proactive institutional entity in its own right for research to progress in the study of administrative politics.

In closing, the implications for future study of administrative politics are quite simple—greater thought and reflection must go into future theories of politics in the administrative state. This means that scholars conducting research on this topic need to take a few steps back to see the broader picture. By doing so, the subtleties of macro agency-political relationships that are not visible in existing research can be assessed. Theory in administrative politics currently suffers from a tunnel-vision-like fixation with the tools of control/determinants of administrative behavior. Such a narrow focus is akin to the small child visiting an art gallery who cannot see the works in full because her face is pressed ever so tightly to the paintings. The further construction of dynamic theories that emphasize institutional behavior from a systems perspective do relax implausible behavioral assumptions, which will yield more realistic insights regarding agency-political relationships than currently exist. The hope is that students of public bureaucracy who are interested in understanding the broader aspects of administrative politics will be able to then place accurate theoretical and behavioral restrictions on the action of governmental institutions once the theoretical battlefield is more fully developed beyond its present state.

Appendix A: Interviews

The purpose of these interviews was both to guide this research theoretically and to suggest possible alternative explanations where applicable. Interviews were conducted during June 1993 in Washington, D.C. with individuals who shape policy administration within the environments under study. Interview subjects in each case study consisted of individuals holding positions as staff members in relevant House congressional committees; various administrative agency personnel serving in public affairs, regulatory enforcement, and budgetary matters; and policy analysts from the OMB and the CBO. The interviews were useful in both the refinement of the concepts related to this theoretical framework and as a subsequent means to operationalize the concepts utilized in this project.

Interviews were conducted in sessions of forty-five to ninety minutes, in person (with one exception—a telephone conversation that lasted twenty minutes with a House Judiciary Committee staff member). The identities of the respondents are not revealed since most desired anonymity. The interview format was semi-structured, in that substantively similar questions were posed to all interview subjects. However, the questions were raised in such a manner that elicited an open-ended response, which placed a premium on informativeness. The main focus of the questions concerned the three cornerstones of the dynamic systems theory of administrative politics proposed in this study. Inquires were also made regarding whether the respondents felt that budgetary variables and regulatory enforcement variables were accurate indicators of aggregate political and agency behavior. For the most part, the questions involved general matters relevant to all interviewees, irrespective of their institutional position. This, in turn, yielded a "systems" perspective of how their institutions interdependently functioned in the administration of public policy.

Because of its emphasis on open-ended responses, this information was not used in a survey data analytic format; rather, it was used as a qualitative guide for theoretical and substantive elaboration.

Notable statements were made with some degree of consensus by the interview subjects. For instance, all interview subjects acknowledge that lines of formal as well as informal communication are quite strong. These statements, in turn, were quite consistent with one of the major propositions of the dynamic systems theory of administrative politics, concerning sophisticated behavior on the part of institutional participants involved in policy administration.

In sum, the interview subjects were designed to reflect the diversity of individuals and institutional positions in administrative politics. Interviews in the SEC case study involved members within the enforcement division, budget shop, and public affairs offices within the agency. In addition, individuals in the OMB and CBO who worked in the areas of securities regulation were interviewed, as well as staff members of the House Energy and Commerce and Appropriation committees, which oversee the SEC and its policy mission. The study of antitrust regulation at the Antitrust Division of the DOJ entailed interviews with employees who worked in the budget shop and enforcement offices. As in the SEC case study, personnel in the area of antitrust regulation in the OMB and CBO were interviewed, as well as staff members of the House Judiciary and Appropriation Committees, which oversee the Antitrust Division and its policy mission.

Appendix B: Measurement

The general types of variables employed within this framework are utilized for all the models covered in this analysis. These variables are treated as being either *endogenous* or *deterministic* (i.e., strictly *exogenous*). The endogenous variables are the budgetary-preference signals of each political principal and various forms of aggregate regulatory enforcement activity undertaken by the relevant administrative agencies. The deterministic variables are those environmental and intra-institutional considerations that influence each of the endogenous variables in a deterministic manner. What follows is the descriptive evidence for selecting the endogenous variables employed in the ensuing models.

Background and Justification for Endogenous Variables

The individuals interviewed for this study acknowledge that the budgetary behaviors of political principals are instrumental in molding agency behavior. A CBO policy analyst in the area of securities regulation contends that "budgetary decisions affect the scope of the [agency's] mission." A staff member who deals with antitrust matters on the House Appropriations committee contends that congressional appropriations reflect congressional behavior. He adds that Congress cuts agency budgets to send a message that they are not satisfied with an agency's behavior. This same individual contends that "appropriations decisions reflect agency enforcement behavior."[1] This implies that congressional appropriations may be thought of as generally representing the budgetary preference behavior of Congress as an aggregate institution.

Real OMB budgetary requests for each agency are one important indication of the behavior displayed by presidents (Carpenter 1992, 1996; Padgett 1981). An OMB policy analyst specializing in securities regulation supports this out-

look by stating that "money [budgets] sets policy—this is [the] most important [consideration]." Aggregate measures of regulatory enforcement are used
to capture agency behavior.[2] This is quite reasonable, given that most empirical studies on the subject of agency-political relationships have used these policy output measures to represent bureaucratic behavior (Carpenter 1992; Hedge
and Scicchitano 1994; Meier 1994; Moe 1982; Scholz and Wei 1986; Scholz,
Twombly, and Headrick 1991; Wood 1988, 1990; Wood and Waterman 1991,
1993, 1994; Wood and Anderson 1993).[3]

Moreover, the anecdotal evidence obtained from the interviews also supports this viewpoint. For example, an SEC official involved in regulatory enforcement notes that agency performance and regulatory success are often
measured by broad aggregate enforcement measures. This individual also
claims that presidents and Congress exhibit a "sensitivity to the number of enforcement cases since it measures [agency] productivity in their eyes." An individual involved in regulatory enforcement at the Antitrust Division furnishes a
similar sentiment by inferring that aggregate enforcement data serve as an accurate reflection of the division's regulatory activity. A committee staff member on the House Judiciary Committee contends that aggregate enforcement
statistics (e.g., number of civil cases, number of criminal cases, and number of
investigations) serve as a "good barometer which are used by the oversight subcommittee."

Not all people interviewed for this study viewed aggregate enforcement
data as being flawless. One such person was a staff member on the House Energy and Commerce Committee (dealing with securities regulation and legislation). This individual admits that aggregate enforcement statistics are not perfect measures of regulatory enforcement.[4] The same person, however, acknowledges that these measures are often the only evaluative data available to assist
politicians in forming regulatory preferences. An OMB budget/policy analyst
insists it is nearly impossible to measure—let alone successfully disseminate—
more detailed regulatory performance measures; therefore, the use of aggregate agency policy outputs are widespread. An experienced employee of the
SEC echoes this sentiment by terming aggregate enforcement statistics as
measures that give a digestible numerical summary, even though these data do
not reflect the finer details such as employee hours per case.[5] A senior staff
member involved in regulatory enforcement activities at the SEC repeats this
opinion by asserting that not all enforcement cases are equal, but that aggregate enforcement statistics are the most reliable source and appraisal of agency
activity that are available.

Each of these individuals, however, acknowledged that while being imperfect, these aggregate measures do reflect agency behavior to a considerable extent. Also, they recognize that these factors help shape the behavior of political principals and agencies since they are easily digestible and are readily available for dissemination. Descriptions of the variables considered in the various SEC and AD models appear in tables B.1 and B.2, respectively.

TABLE B.1 Variable Definitions for the SEC Regulatory Enforcement Models

Endogenous System Variables

(1a)   Total Administrative Proceedings$_t$: the total annual number of administrative proceedings initiated in year t.
(1b)   Total Investigations$_t$: the total annual number of investigations conducted in year t.
(1c)   Total Injunctive Actions$_t$: the total annual number of injunctive actions issued in year t.
(2a-c) Presidential Preferences$_t$: the annual OMB/presidential real budgetary request for the SEC for year t.
(3a-c) Congressional Preferences$_t$: the annual congressional real appropriation to the SEC for year t.

Deterministic Variables

(a-c)   House Oversight Committee Relative Policy Liberalism$_t$: the difference in median ADA scores between the House Interstate and Commerce (later Energy and Commerce) Committee's Subcommittee on Securities Regulation and the entire House in year t.
(a-c)   Senate Oversight Committee Relative Policy Liberalism$_t$: the difference in median ADA scores between the Senate Banking Committee's Subcommittee on Securities Regulation and the entire Senate in year t.
(a-c)   Real Economic Growth$_{t-1}$: the annual real growth rate of Gross National Product (GNP) in year t-1.
(a-c)   Presidential Partisanship$_t$: a dummy variable coded 1 for Democratic administrations, 0 for Republican administrations.
(a-c)   Log of Industry Employment$_t$: the natural log of the annual number of individuals employed as securities and commodities brokers (in thousands) in year t.
(a-c)   Stock Market Crash of 1987$_t$: a dummy variable coded 0 for 1949–1987, and 1 for 1988–1992.

TABLE B.2 Variable Definitions for the AD Regulatory Enforcement Models

Endogenous System Variables

(1a)   Antitrust Cases$_t$: the total annual number of antitrust cases initiated by the Antitrust Division (DOJ) in year t.
(1b)   Total Investigations$_t$: the total annual number of investigations conducted by the Antitrust Division (DOJ) in year t.
(2a-b) Presidential Preferences$_t$: the annual OMB/presidential real budget request for the Antitrust Division (DOJ) for year t.
(3a-b) Congressional Preferences$_t$: the annual congressional real appropriation to the Antitrust Division (DOJ) for year t.

(table continues)

TABLE B.2 *(continued)*

Deterministic Variables

(a-b) House Oversight Committee Relative Policy Liberalism$_t$: median difference in ADA scores between the House Judiciary Committee's Subcommittee on Monopolies and Commercial Law and the entire House in year t.

(a-b) Senate Oversight Committee Relative Policy Liberalism$_t$: median difference in ADA scores between the Senate Judiciary Committee's Subcommittee on Antitrust and Monopolies and the entire Senate in year t.

(a-b) Economic Policy Office (EPO) Trend$_t$: a linear trend variable coded as 0 before 1973; as 1 in 1973; as 2 in 1974, etc.

(a-b) Economists/Attorney Ratio after EPO creation$_t$: coded as 0 before 1973; as the ratio of economists to attorneys for each subsequent year.

(a-b) Unemployment Rate$_{t-1}$: median annual national civilian unemployment rate in year t-1.

(a-b) Inflation Rate$_{t-1}$: annual percentage change in consumer price index between years t and t-1.

(a-b) Reagan Administration Dummy Variable$_t$: a dummy coded as 1 in 1981–1988 for the Reagan presidency; 0 otherwise.

(a-b) Hart-Scott-Rodino Antitrust Improvements Act of 1976$_t$: a dummy variable coded as 0 for 1949–1976; as 1 for 1977–1992.

Appendix C: Statistical Methodology

In this appendix, both the methodological design and the logic underlying the quantitative diagnostics are discussed. In selecting the appropriate methodological design, substantive weight was given to meshing the real-world complexities of policy administration in a democracy together in a tractable model that would be suitable for statistical inference. The obvious design involves selecting a quantitative tool that is appropriate for examining time series observations in a dynamic systems framework. The quantitative diagnostics associated with this statistical technique (as well as for time series analysis in general) are also addressed in this appendix. The description of the quantitative diagnostic checks is important, since the validity with which statistical inferences are made relies upon properly estimated models that must meet certain conditions. Both VAR methodology and the quantitative diagnostic tests employed in this study are discussed at greater length and in greater technical detail in the subsequent sections of this appendix.

Methodological Design

A dynamic multiple equation statistical technique termed Vector Autoregression (VAR) (Sims 1980) is utilized for testing the complex nature of agency-political relations. The nonstructural VAR methodology has three distinct advantages over structural equation approaches. First, this approach serves as a theoretically driven inductive statistical technique that does not place a priori assumptions regarding the autoregressive nature of behavior on the part of political principals and the agency. Second, VAR models do not assume a well-developed unified theory of behavioral relations; therefore, they serve as an especially useful quantitative time series technique when there are competing theories for any given phenomena. This is truly helpful, given the present state of the debate between political control and bureaucratic autonomy perspectives of administrative politics. For example, it is difficult to accurately assume a causal order of relations between the president and Congress in the area of bureaucratic agency-political institution relations. This point is especially true given the conflicting body of research in this subfield.[1]

The quantitative analysis of these relationships within a VAR context is consistent with the widely held notion that public policy is the result of endogenous interaction between bureaucratic and political institutions subject to environmental forces (Anderson 1990; Dye 1966; Jones 1984).[2] In sum, the main advantage of the VAR approach is that it reproduces the dynamic properties of the data while allowing for weak assumptions concerning functional form and model specification.[3]

Since the central hypothesis of this paper is concerned with finding out whether agencies, presidents, and Congress influence each other in a systematic manner, variables representing these institutional players are treated as being endogenous within the VAR system. In order to determine causal linkages between these policy actors, the VAR analysis focuses on multivariate generalizations of Granger causality[4] (see Granger 1969; Freeman 1983; and Wood 1992 for bivariate applications) via an F-block test of the coefficients associated with the endogenous variables in the VAR system.[5] The multivariate Granger causality tests are much superior to the conventional bivariate Granger causality tests, which can produce misleading results due to omission of other relevant variables if great care is not taken in modeling such relationships (Lutkepohl 1982). Mathematically, relations among the president, Congress, and bureaucratic agency can be represented in matrix algebra notation by the following dynamic reduced form:

$$Y_t = ALY_t + \beta X_t + v_t \qquad\qquad\qquad (C\text{-}1)$$

where LY_t is a matrix of lagged stochastic or endogenous system variables representing both agency regulatory enforcement activity and the budgetary behavior of the president and Congress, separately; X_t is a vector of nonstochastic or strictly exogenous variables representing a deterministic nature;[6] and v_t is a six-dimensional vector in which each of the error terms is identically and independently distributed with a mean of zero. In more substantive terms, the dynamic systems model of administrative politics proposed here can be represented in a general manner by the following set of equations:

$$President_t = a_{10} + \Sigma\, a_{11i}President_{t-i} + \Sigma\, a_{12i}Congress_{t-i} +$$
$$\Sigma\, a_{13i}Agency_{t-i} + X\beta_{1t} + e_1 \tag{C-2}$$
$$Congress_t = a_{20} + \Sigma\, a_{21i}President_{t-i} + \Sigma\, a_{22i}Congress_{t-i} +$$
$$\Sigma\, a_{23i}Agency_{t-i} + X\beta_{2t} + e_2 \tag{C-3}$$
$$Agency_t = a_{30} + \Sigma\, a_{31i}President_{t-i} + \Sigma\, a_{32i}Congress_{t-i} +$$
$$\Sigma\, a_{33i}Agency_{t-i} + X\beta_{3t} + e_3 \tag{C-4}$$

where each institution's current behavior can be explained by its own recent past behavior (as determined by the appropriate lag length) and by the behavior of its fellow institutions, a vector of deterministic variables, and a residual term that accounts for "unanticipated" behavior (i.e., policy innovations or shocks) by system participants.

Before performing any estimation on this system of dynamic reduced-form equations one must address three important issues concerning proper model specification for the endogenous portion of the VAR model. First, these variables must be a stationary time series, that is, have a constant and finite mean and variance, as well as covariances that are time independent and solely the function of lag length. The use of logged-differenced data will help ensure stationarity for the endogenous portion of the VAR model.[7] Second, lag lengths must be determined for each endogenous variable appearing in the right-hand side of an equation. This is done by performing a modified likelihood ratio test proposed by Sims (1980) and by performing a serial correlation test to ensure that the residuals are white noise. Finally, the coefficients of the model must not exhibit *permanent* instability within the sample period.[8]

After the proper stochastic process has been established, a vector of nonstochastic (deterministic) variables can be added and the system subsequently reestimated, thus representing the final model. The test statistics should possess the usual asymptotic properties if the system has been properly estimated (Judge et al. 1988; Sims, Stock, and Watson 1990). Because of the small number of degrees of freedom in each equation, a quasi-model reduction strategy is employed that arrives at the most parsimonious specification (Hendry, Qin, and Favero 1989; Judge et al. 1985). This strategy will ensure that the generated results do provide valid statistical inferences. The use of Wald F-tests for omitted variables as well as the Schwarz criterion (SC) will be used to determine model specification.

This analysis tests for behavioral relations in five ways. First, F-tests for lagged causal relations pertaining to anticipated behavior from the recent past serve to test notions of block (multivariate) exogeneity. These statistical tests may mask the presence of causality between these two endogenous variables since they only take into account past behavior.[9] Second, conventional t-tests on the regression coefficients are analyzed for those variables that appear in a strict deterministic fashion to the VAR system.[10]

Third, the contemporaneous innovation (i.e., residual) correlation matrix is presented in order to partially shed light (in conjunction with the multivariate Granger exogeneity tests) on whether these institutions possibly exhibit rational expectations.[11] This matrix gives information about the nature of shared contemporaneous policy innovations among institutions.[12] The sign of this correlation among the residuals demonstrates whether these institutions respond in a manner that is reciprocal (positive correlation) or antagonistic (negative correlation) to a contemporaneous innovation emanating from some other institutional participant in the current period.[13]

Fourth, a dynamic simulation exercise called *innovation accounting* is employed, which traces the expected path of future behavior of institutions in response to policy innovations. This method entails a recursive moving average representation (MAR) of the sum of orthogonalized shocks in the variables in the system, and their subsequent impact on each of the left-hand-side variables in the VAR system.[14] The MAR traces the dynamic impulse response of the fitted model to an unanticipated movement or shock in one of the variables that correspond to a one standard deviation orthogonalized shock emanating from the respective residuals in the VAR system.[15] Moreover, the MAR takes into account the responses of all variables in the VAR system to an orthogonalized positive one standard deviation shock in a single variable.[16] Some have questioned the accuracy of impulse responses generated from an unrestricted VAR model (Runkle 1987a, 1987b; Lutkepohl 1990). A Monte Carlo integration approach—which relies upon Bayesian statistical theory to derive valid confidence bands surrounding the point estimates of the impulse responses—is employed in this portion of the empirical analysis (Hammersley and Handscomb 1964; Geweke 1989; Kloek and Van Dijk 1978; Van Dijk, Kloek, and Boender 1985; Zellner 1971). To derive these series of Bayesian estimates using Monte Carlo simulation, one thousand draws from a Normal-inverse Wishart distribution are used to compute each standard error estimate.

Finally, the decomposition of forecast error variance serves as a complement to innovation accounting by providing an estimate of the amount of influence each variable has on another variable in the system. The impacts variables have on one another through time can be traced by inspecting the proportion of one variable's forecast error variance, which can be accounted for by any given variable's innovations or shocks. This, in turn, can provide additional information on the issue of causal relations among endogenous variables. The next section presents the technical details associated with the quantitative diagnostic tests employed for each model tested in this study.

The Methodology of Quantitative Diagnostic Tests

Constructing such a complex model requires one to conduct preliminary analysis and diagnostic checks to ensure that the results generated from these models are valid. This portion of the statistical analysis is concerned with various issues that will be dealt with sequentially. First, all the endogenous VAR variables (i.e., budgetary and regulatory performance measures) were examined to find out whether they were stationary variables—whose values were not a function of time (i.e., variables whose mean, variance, and actual values were not a function of time). This examination is conducted by performing Augmented Dickey-Fuller unit root tests (Cromwell, Labys, Terreza 1994: Dickey and Fuller 1979) of the following form:

$$\Delta_t = \rho Y_{t-1} + \gamma \Delta Y_{t-1} + \epsilon_t\text{—random walk;} \tag{C-5}$$

$$\Delta Y_t = \alpha + \rho Y_{t-1} + \gamma \Delta Y_{t-1} + \epsilon_t\text{—random walk, plus drift;} \tag{C-6}$$

and

$$\Delta Y_t = \alpha + \rho Y_{t-1} + \gamma \Delta Y_{t-1} + \phi t + \epsilon_t\text{—random walk, plus drift and}$$
a deterministic trend. $\tag{C-7}$

where $\alpha, \rho, \gamma,$ and ϕ are parameters and ϵ_t is assumed to be independently and identically distributed with a zero mean and constant variance. The corresponding hypotheses for this test are:

$H_0: \rho = 1$
$H_A: \rho < 1$

where the null hypothesis purports that a unit root does exist for any given variable (i.e., nonstationarity is present) and the alternative hypothesis indicates that the variable in question does not contain a unit root (i.e., stationarity is achieved). More specifically, an AR(1) process is stationary if $-1 < \rho < 1$. Thus, if the null hypothesis that $\rho = 1$ cannot be rejected, then it is inferred that the time series contains a unit root and the model in (C-5) can be thought of as a random walk, the model in (C-6) represents a random walk with drift, and (C-7) reflects a random walk with a deterministic trend. If the absolute value of ρ exceeds one, then the series is explosive—i.e., the variance of Y is solely a function of time.

Second, in instances where variables display nonstationarity, there may be some linear combination of these variables that is stationary. Mathematically, this can be represented by the following linear expression:

$$u_t = Y_t - \alpha - \beta X_t \qquad\qquad (C-8)$$

where the disturbance term u_t is a linear combination of Y_t and X_t. Engle and Granger (1987) term this phenomenon "cointegration"; if u_t is stationary, Y_t and X_t are said to be cointegrated. Simply put, this means that both variables will tend to move together across time as they approach infinity. Engle and Granger have developed a procedure that tests whether a linear combination of these variables is stationary by applying a Dickey-Fuller (DF) or an augmented Dickey-Fuller (ADF) unit root test to the residuals from a cointegrating regression.[17]

On the other hand, Johansen and associates (Johansen 1988, 1991; Johansen and Juselius 1990) propose a cointegration test designed for endogenous variables by determining the rank of the long-run matrix (p) in a multi-equation framework. This alternative approach, unlike the residual-based cointegration tests, is robust to variable orderings in the cointegrating regression (Hamilton 1994: 601). Therefore, the Johansen method of testing for the presence of cointegration is preferable when the model being constructed represents a system of endogenous variables. This approach is estimated via the method of maximum likelihood to determine the rank of p. This is determined by the maximum eigenvalue statistic with small-sample correction (Reimers 1992).[18]

If these aforementioned test statistics are significant, then cointegration will exist between the series in question, and some would advocate an error correction approach to facilitate proper statistical estimation (Beck 1987; Davidson et al. 1978; Durr 1992a, 1992b; Engle and Granger 1987; Granato and Smith 1994; Granger and Newbold 1986; Ostrom and Smith 1993; but for a different opinion in a VAR context please see Freeman 1993: 9; Sims 1988; Williams 1993). One thing clear is that, if these test statistics fall short of statistical significance, the variables in question can be thought of as not being cointegrated. In this case, one needs to difference the data in the appropriate fashion in order to obtain variables that exhibit a stationary time series (Hamilton 1994: 652).

After addressing the issues of unit roots and cointegration for the endogenous portion of the model, the next step is to properly specify this component of the VAR model. For a VAR to yield reliable estimates, it must follow a strictly "white noise" process (i.e., no significant residual correlation), with parameters (coefficients) that do not exhibit temporal instability of a permanent nature (Freeman, Williams, and Lin 1989; Goldstein and Freeman 1990, 1991). This means that one has to select a parsimonious lag length for each of the endogenous variables in the VAR system of equations, while at the same time satisfying both statistical criteria. Traditionally, time series modelers have used information (model) selection criteria such as Akaike (Akaike 1974; Amemiya 1985; Judge et al. 1988) and Schwarz (Judge et al. 1988; Schwarz 1978), or the modified likelihood ratio test statistic (Sims 1980) to determine the appropriate yet most parsimonious lag length (p) for VAR models.

Monte Carlo econometric evidence suggests, however, that these methods consistently underparameterize time series models (Nickelburg 1985). Inder's (1993) Monte Carlo investigation of small sample properties of time-series-related estimators infer that the problems associated with underparameterization far exceed those associated with overparameterization. In other words, strict adherence to the sole use of information criteria or likelihood ratio statistics as a method of selecting lag lengths in time series models—without examining whether the conditions of a strictly "white noise" residual vector (i.e., no significant residual correlation) hold true—is a precarious methodological practice.

For each VAR model, the lag length for the endogenous portion was determined by finding a lag length for each of the three equations that was the most parsimonious yet contained white noise residuals. From a practical standpoint, this was determined by a rigorous process that involved (1) inspecting the Ljung-Box Q-statistic with six degrees of freedom[19] to determine if significant residual correlation did exist; (2) executing tests of parameter (model) instability using both recursive residuals and the CUSUM plot tests; and (3) using the Sims Modified Likelihood Ratio statistic to find the most parsimonious lag length for each system that satisfies the white noise residual assumptions (Freeman, Williams, and Lin 1989; Sims 1980).[20]

Once these conditions are met for the endogenous portion of the VAR model, each exogenous variable is subsequently added to each equation to determine whether these factors have a significant effect on reducing the residual sums of squares in the relevant equation. This procedure involves use of an omitted variable Wald F-test. Both this statistic and the model specification exhibiting the lowest possible Schwarz criterion value were used to assess the proper dimension of the model.[21] After it was determined which deterministic variables were to be incorporated, the VAR system of equations was reestimated with the appropriate exogenous variables.

In addition, an even more exhaustive set of diagnostic checks was employed to test the validity and reliability of this final estimated system. In order to test for residual serial correlation, the Ljung-Box Q-statistic described earlier was utilized as a χ^2 statistic with six degrees of freedom. Tests to determine whether the errors were timewise homoskedastic included the autoregressive conditional heteroskedasticity (ARCH) test proposed by Engle (1982). The ARCH test examines those instances where the magnitude of the residuals appears to be related to the recent size of the residuals. This test statistic is distributed as a χ^2 with the number degrees of freedom equal to the number of lagged squared residual terms specified. The White (1980) test is performed to detect heteroskedasticity of some unknown form. The Ramsey (1969) RESET test presumes that the model specification in question contains a disturbance vector that is distributed as multivariate normal, that is, $N(0, \sigma^2 I)$. This assumption implies that the residuals will be homoskedastic, serially uncorrelated, and normally distributed. This test also detects other specification errors such as omitted right-hand-side variables, incorrect functional form (e.g., nonlinearity), and correlation between the X_t (regressors) and u_t (disturbance) vectors. This statistic is distributed as an F-test. The stability of the model's parameters is determined by inspecting the recursive residual and CUSUM plots discussed in the preceding paragraph. Testing the statistical assumptions for each of the final VAR models is important since they are estimated via OLS. The results of these quantitative diagnostics and preliminary analyses for each complete model in the SEC and AD case studies respectively are described in appendix D.

Appendix D: Preliminary Analysis and Diagnostic Results

The preliminary analysis of these variables and subsequent empirical models is important in determining the efficacy of inferences that are generated. These various tests allow us to have confidence in the statistical results presented in chapters 3 and 4. In this appendix all of the diagnostic results for the SEC models and AD models are presented. These results provide empirical support for the model specification choices made for each set of models presented in chapters 4 and 5.

Preliminary Analysis and Quantitative Diagnostics for the SEC models

In formulating the empirical analysis, one must begin by analyzing the properties of the dependent variables being examined. Thus the order of integration and possible existence of cointegration among endogenous variables in the VAR model is investigated. The results of the unit root (integration) and cointegration tests for the levels of these variables are listed in table D.1.

The outcomes for the various Augmented Dickey-Fuller (ADF)[1] reveal that none of the regulatory enforcement measures, nor either of the political (budgetary) variables, is a stationary time series when expressed in levels. In other words, these series contain a unit root (i.e., an integrated time series). Although one could use differenced versions of these variables to achieve stationarity, it has been demonstrated that cointegrating relationships between series can render it inappropriate to use statistical analysis employing only differenced data—since the long-run dynamics of the endogenous variables under examination are ignored (Durr 1992a, 1992b; Engle and Granger 1987; Granato

TABLE D.1 Augmented Dickey-Fuller Unit Root Tests and Cointegration Tests for the Endogenous Variables in the SEC VAR Models

Variable(s)	ADF (1) Tests—Levels			ADF (1) Tests—Percentage Changes			E-G & Johansen Cointegration Tests		
	Constant	Constant & Trend	No Constant or Trend	Constant	Constant & Trend	No Constant or Trend	Constant	Constant & Trend	Maximum Eigenvalue
Administrative Proceedings	-.33 (-2.55)	-.34 (-2.57)	-.01 (-.23)	-1.35** (-6.20)	-1.34** (-6.07)	-1.35** (-6.26)	—	—	—
Investigations	-.27 (-2.08)	-.44 (-2.66)	-.02 (-.88)	-1.04** (-4.23)	-1.04** (-4.22)	-1.02** (-4.18)	—	—	—
Injunctive Actions	-.10 (-1.40)	-.34 (-2.31)	.02 (.53)	-.96** (-3.87)	-1.00* (-4.02)	-.86** (-3.65)	—	—	—
Presidential Request	.07 (2.69)	-.05 (-.44)	.05 (3.45)	-.79** (-3.76)	-.81* (-3.79)	-.54** (-2.90)	—	—	—
Congressional Appropriation	.07 (2.69)	.04 (.35)	.05 (3.70)	-.41 (-2.34)	-.42 (-2.39)	-.23 (-1.60)	—	—	—
Congressional Appropriation (1st Difference)	—	—	—	-1.75** (-6.64)	-1.75** (-6.57)	-1.73** (-6.60)	—	—	—
Administrative Proceedings Model	—	—	—	—	—	—	-.35 (-2.68)	-.34 (-2.49)	14.23
Investigations Model	—	—	—	—	—	—	-.42 (-2.66)	-.45 (-2.77)	15.41
Injunctive Actions Model	—	—	—	—	—	—	-.35 (-2.15)	-.39 (-2.42)	16.57

NOTES: t-statistics are listed inside parentheses. The Augmented Dickey-Fuller (ADF) cointegration tests are those presented by Engle and Granger (1987) with critical values generated by MacKinnon (1990). The critical values for the Johansen (1988) and Johansen and Juselius (1990) cointegration tests (maximum eigenvalue statistic) are based upon Reimers (1992) small-sample correction method. None of these tests indicates that cointegration exists.
** p < .01   * p < .05

and Smith 1994; Granger and Newbold 1986; Phillips 1988; Ostrom and Smith 1993). The Engle-Granger and Johansen cointegration tests among the three series for each VAR specification are reported in table D.2.[2]

The ADF test that includes both the constant and the trend are listed, since the test statistic generated is independent of the value of the intercept term of the cointegrating regression.[3] Both the insignificant ADF and maximum eigenvalue test statistics indicate that these endogenous variables in each VAR

TABLE D.2 Model Diagnostic Test Results for SEC VAR Models

Diagnostic Test	Administrative Proceedings Model			Investigations Model			Injunctive Actions Model		
	President (eq. 1)	Congress (eq. 2)	SEC (eq. 3)	President (eq. 4)	Congress (eq. 5)	SEC (eq. 6)	President (eq. 7)	Congress (eq. 8)	SEC (eq. 9)
Preliminary VAR Specification									
Ljung-Box Q	5.34	4.97	9.22	3.28	1.71	6.67	5.06	2.36	1.22
χ^2 (6)	(.50)a	(.55)	(.16)	(.77)	(.94)	(.35)	(.54)	(.88)	(.98)
MLR Test (Full Model)		13.67			9.99			10.57	
χ^2 (21)		(.88)			(.98)			(.97)	
Complete VAR Specification									
Ljung-Box Q	3.34	2.32	6.02	2.83	5.21	7.56	5.84	3.89	1.59
χ^2 (6)	(.77)	(.89)	(.42)	(.83)	(.52)	(.27)	(.44)	(.69)	(.95)
ARCH	.00	.14	.44	.90	.61	2.42	.42	.15	1.79
χ^2 (1)	(.99)	(.71)	(.51)	(.34)	(.44)	(.12)	(.52)	(.70)	(.18)
ARCH	.06	1.12	.73	1.01	1.32	2.41	.56	.44	4.69
χ^2 (2)	(.97)	(.57)	(.69)	(.60)	(.52)	(.30)	(.76)	(.80)	(.10)
White	34.12	32.00	31.00	28.34	30.35	26.51	30.54	28.51	31.70
χ^2 (32, 31, 32)	(.32)	(.42)	(.47)	(.55)	(.60)	(.65)	(.49)	(.60)	(.43)
Ramsey RESET	.57	.72	.26	.04	1.89	2.71	.08	3.00	.25
F (1,21)	(.46)	(.41)	(.62)	(.84)	(.18)	(.12)	(.79)	(.10)	(.63)
Ramsey RESET	.96	.55	.28	.12	1.19	2.53	.43	1.47	.50
F (2, 20)	(.40)	(.59)	(.76)	(.89)	(.33)	(.11)	(.66)	(.26)	(.62)
Wald F Stat	.58	.31	.65	.11	1.98	1.38	.44	1.25	.07
	(.57)	(.74)	(.53)	(.90)	(.17)	(.28)	(.65)	(.31)	(.93)

NOTES: Probability levels are listed inside parentheses and rounded to nearest hundredth decimal place. The modified likelihood ratio (MLR) test proposed by Sims (1980) was performed to compare the efficacy of VAR(4) and VAR (5) processes. The null findings indicate that each model is best analyzed as a VAR(4) process.

specification are not cointegrated (i.e., there does not exist a linear combination of these variables that is stationary).

From these results one can conclude that the endogenous variables analyzed here follow an I(1) (integrated of order one) process. Instead of taking the simple first difference of these variables to induce stationarity, all the measures were converted into annual percentage changes.[4] This makes theoretical and intuitive sense, since many students of bureaucratic agency-political institution relationships note that elected officials send *"signals"* to administrative agencies (Bendor and Moe 1985; Carpenter 1992, 1996; Khademian 1992; Padgett 1980, 1981; Weingast and Moran 1983).[5] This annual percentage change was given by the following formula:

$$(LN(X_t) - LN(X_{t-1})) * 100 \qquad (D\text{-}1)$$

where $LN(X_t)$ is the natural log of the endogenous variable in question at time t, and $LN(X_{t-1})$ is the natural log value of this same variable from the previous period.[6]

After recalculating these endogenous variables with the given formula in (D-1), ADF unit root tests are implemented to see whether these variables achieved the stationarity conditions that are necessary to validate tests of statistical inference (e.g., multivariate Granger exogeneity tests, t-tests on exogenous variables, dynamic simulation exercise). The significant results of these tests for all of the endogenous variables (with the lone exception of real congressional appropriations) do indicate that each of these series is integrated of order one and becomes stationary time series after differencing.[7] The transformed logarithmic variable for real congressional appropriations was first-differenced. The significant ADF test statistic reveals that this variable achieved stationarity after its second differencing procedure—that is, I(2).

Once the order of integration was determined and stationarity was achieved, the next step in properly estimating the VAR models was to determine the proper lag length, so that the disturbances satisfy the condition of a strict "white noise" residual vector. Recent Monte Carlo evidence indicates that conventional means of determining lag lengths in time series models (e.g., information criteria and likelihood ratio tests) can result in an underspecified model if not used in tandem with residual diagnostics (Inder 1993; Nickelburg 1985). Therefore, the "white noise" assumption associated with the proper specification of the VAR model is explicitly dealt with by conducting (1) a Ljung-Box Q test for serial correlation (with six degrees of freedom); (2) time series plots of recursive residuals and CUSUM tests to assess model stability[8] (i.e., parameter constancy)[9] for each of the three equations in each VAR specification; and (3) the Sims modified likelihood ratio test statistic to find the most parsimonious lag length for each system that satisfied the white noise residual assumptions (Sims 1980). The appropriate lag length for the entire VAR system is the one in which each equation satisfies these conditions, that is, exhibits a strictly "white noise" residual vector and no permanent instability.

The results of the first two tests used to assess appropriate lag length are listed in table D.2 for each VAR model. The insignificant Ljung-Box Q-statistics indicate that the disturbances are not serial correlated. In sum, the results of these preliminary VAR specifications revealed that the appropriate lag length for each SEC model was four years—that is, VAR(4).

The deterministic (or strictly exogenous) variables in the VAR were subsequently added for each model and reestimated. The SEC Administrative Proceedings model indicates that the best specification—that is, one in which any variables in at least one equation significantly reduced the residual sum of squares, based on a significant Wald F-statistic—was included in each of the equations for a given VAR model, for each of the equations consists of both Senate and House subcommittee policy liberalism, the natural log of the number of brokers both in the securities and commodities industry and in the presidential partisanship dummy variable (both the GNP growth measure and stock market crash dummy variable are excluded from the final specification).[10] In order to ensure that the results generated from this reestimated system for the Administrative Proceedings model are valid, another (and more extensive) battery of diagnostic checks were implemented for each equation within each model. The results of these diagnostic tests for the administrative proceedings model clearly demonstrate that all of these equations within the dynamic VAR model are properly specified. In other words, the residuals are well behaved (i.e., with no significant residual correlation; they are homoskedastic, and are normally distributed); the model does not suffer from an omitted variables problem; the regressors and disturbance terms are not correlated; and the linear functional form is deemed appropriate. In sum, these diagnostic checks reveal an extremely well-specified final estimated system of equations for the Administrative Proceedings model.

The SEC (total) Investigations model indicates that the best specification (based on the same Wald test criterion noted above) for each of the equations consists of both Senate subcommittee policy liberalism, presidential partisanship, and the natural log of the number of brokers in the securities and commodity industry, and the 1987 stock market crash dummy (the real GNP growth and House subcommittee policy liberalism variables are excluded from these final specifications).[11] In order to ensure that the results generated from this re-estimated system for the total investigations model are valid, once again a second (and more extensive) round of battery of diagnostic checks were conducted for each equation within each three-equation VAR model. These tests suggest that each of these equations within the dynamic VAR model is accurately specified. In other words, the residuals are well behaved (i.e, with no significant residual correlation and homoskedastic, normally distributed errors), the model does not suffer from an omitted variables problem, the regressors and disturbance terms are not correlated, and the linear functional form is deemed appropriate.

The SEC (total) Injunctive Actions model indicates that the best specification for each of the equations consists of Senate subcommittee policy liberalism, real GNP growth from the preceding year, presidential partisanship dummy, and the natural log of the number of brokers in the securities and commodities industry (both the House subcommittee policy liberalism variable and 1987 stock market crash dummy are excluded from these final specifications).[12] In order to ensure that the results generated from this reestimated system for the total investigations model are valid, a second (and more extensive) round or battery of diagnostic checks was conducted for each equation within each model (three equations). The results of these diagnostic tests for the total investigations model suggest that each of these equations within the dynamic VAR model is properly specified. In other words, the residuals are well behaved (i.e, strictly Gaussian "white noise" vector), the model does not suffer from an omitted variables problem, the regressors and disturbance terms are not correlated, and the linear functional form is deemed appropriate. In sum, these diagnostic checks reveal an adequately specified final estimated system of equations for the total injunctive actions model.

Preliminary Analysis and Quantitative Diagnostics for the Antitrust Division Models

The results of the unit root (integration) and cointegration tests for the levels of the endogenous variables are listed in table D.3. The results of the various augmented Dickey-Fuller tests reveal that no single time series reflects a stationary process when expressed in levels.[13] In other words, each of these series contains a unit root (i.e., integrated). The Engle-Granger and Johansen cointegration tests between the three series for each VAR specification are also reported in this table. The ADF statistic that includes both the constant and the trend are listed, since the test statistic generated is independent of the value of the intercept term for the cointegrating regression.[14] The insignificant ADF and maximum eigenvalue statistics for each endogenous VAR specification in-

TABLE D.3 Augmented Dickey-Fuller Unit Root Tests and Cointegration Tests for the Endogenous Variables in the AD VAR Models

Variable(s)	ADF (1) Tests—Levels			ADF (1) Tests—Percentage Changes			E-G & Johansen Cointegration Tests		
	Constant	Constant & Trend	No Constant or Trend	Constant	Constant & Trend	No Constant or Trend	Constant	Constant & Trend	Maximum Eigenvalue
Antitrust Division Cases	-.27 (-2.19)	-.72** (-4.39)	-.01 (-.37)	-1.28*** (-5.50)	-1.28*** (-5.43)	-1.27*** (-5.54)	—	—	—
Antitrust Division Investigations	-.07 (-.97)	-.06 (-.75)	-.01 (-.45)	-1.08** (-4.23)	-1.16*** (-4.46)	-1.08** (-4.29)	—	—	—
Presidential Request	-.07 (-1.26)	-.15 (-1.43)	-.01E-01 (-.02)	-1.17*** (-4.77)	-1.21*** (-4.79)	-1.12*** (-4.67)	—	—	—
Congressional Appropriation	-.06 (-1.48)	-.18 (-2.78)	-.02E-01 (-.12)	-.54** (-3.45)	-.55* (-3.45)	-.49*** (-3.22)	—	—	—
Antitrust Division Cases Model	—	—	—	—	—	—	-.55 (-2.51)	-.55 (-2.49)	10.90
Antitrust Division Investigations Model	—	—	—	—	—	—	-.48 (-2.40)	-.46 (-2.22)	10.41

NOTES: t-statistics are listed inside parentheses. The Augmented Dickey-Fuller (ADF) cointegration tests are those presented by Engle and Granger (1987) with critical values generated by MacKinnon (1990). The critical values for the Johansen (1988) and Johansen and Juselius (1990) cointegration tests (maximum eigenvalue statistic) are based upon Reimers (1992) small-sample correction method. None of these tests indicates that cointegration exists.
* p < .10   ** p < .05   *** p < .01

dicate that these variables do not share a common stochastic trend (i.e., are not cointegrated time series).

Based on these results, one can conclude that the endogenous variables analyzed here are I(1) (i.e., integrated of order one). Instead of taking the simple first difference of these variables to induce stationarity, all the measures were converted into logged annual percentage changes. After recalculating these endogenous variables with the given formula in (D-1), ADF unit root tests were conducted to see whether these variables achieved the stationarity conditions that are necessary to validate tests of statistical inference (e.g., multivariate Granger exogeneity tests, t-tests on exogenous variables, dynamic simulation exercise). These results are also reported in table D.3. The significant results of these tests for all of the endogenous variables do indicate that each of these series is integrated of order one and becomes stationary time series after first differencing.

Once the order of integration was determined and stationarity was achieved, the next step in properly estimating the VAR models was determining the proper lag length so that the disturbances satisfy the conditions of a strict "white noise" residual vector. The appropriate lag length is determined in the same manner as it is in the VAR models analyzing the President-Congress-SEC system discussed in the preceding section. The results of the first two tests used to assess appropriate lag length are listed in table D.4 for each VAR model. The insignificant Q-statistics indicate that the disturbances are not serially correlated. In sum, the results of these preliminary VAR specifications reveal that the appropriate lag length was five years—, that is, VAR(5)—in both AD models.[15]

Next, the deterministic (or strictly exogenous) variables in the VAR are subsequently added for each model and re-estimated. Preliminary analysis of the AD Cases VAR model revealed that all of the deterministic variables (save the Senate and House relative median oversight policy liberalism measures, inflation rate variable, and the economist to attorney ratio and EPO time trend)[16] contribute to the goodness of fit to the data for the system.[17] Therefore, the Reagan administration dummy, the inflation and unemployment rates, and the Hart-Scott-Rodino Antitrust Improvements Act dummy are strictly deterministic (exogenous) variables that are included in the final VAR model specification. In order to ensure that the results generated from this reestimated system for the Antitrust Cases model are valid, another (and more extensive) battery of diagnostic checks were implemented for each equation.

The results of these diagnostic tests for the AD Cases model are also listed in this table. These tests clearly demonstrate that both the Congress and AD equations pass all the statistical diagnostic tests. The President equation also passes all diagnostic tests concerning the model's residuals, save the marginal significance associated with the second-order Ramsey RESET test (p = .07). On the whole, this VAR system appears to be well-specified and suitable for statistical inference.[18]

As in the previous model investigating the behavior of antitrust regulatory institutions with respect to cases, preliminary analysis of the AD Investigations VAR model reveals that the specification that provides the best statistical fit to the data is one that contains the economists/attorney ratio variable, EPO trend variable, inflation and unemployment rates, Reagan administration dummy, and Hart-Scott-Rodino Antitrust Improvements Act dummy as deterministic variables. Estimation of the Antitrust Investigations model was made more challenging by difficulty in estimating a statistical model that contained

TABLE D.4 Model Diagnostic Test Results for AD VAR Models

Diagnostic Test	Antitrust Cases Model—VAR (5)			Antitrust Investigations Model—VAR (5)		
	President (eq. 10)	Congress (eq. 11)	AD (eq. 12)	President (eq. 13)	Congress (eq. 14)	AD (eq. 15)
Preliminary VAR Specification						
Ljung-Box Q	5.48	.73	7.56	3.11	3.36	2.69
χ^2 (6)	(.48)	(.99)	(.27)	(.80)	(.76)	(.85)
MLR Test (Full Model)		11.72			13.32	
χ^2 (17)		(.82)			(.72)	
Complete VAR Specification						
Ljung-Box Q	5.83	3.47	9.69	4.42	8.03	5.92
χ^2 (6)	(.44)	(.75)	(.14)	(.62)	(.24)	(.43)
ARCH	.03	.13	.15	1.00	.00	.00
χ^2 (1)	(.87)	(.72)	(.70)	(.32)	(.99)	(.99)
ARCH	.08	1.26	.52	.81	.47	.05
χ^2 (2)	(.96)	(.53)	(.60)	(.67)	(.79)	(.98)
Ramsey RESET	2.27	.81	.47	.42	4.73**	.37
F (1,16)	(.15)	(.38)	(.50)	(.52)	(.04)	(.55)
Ramsey RESET	3.13*	.40	2.62	.77	5.95**	1.46
F (2,15)	(.07)	(.68)	(.10)	(.48)	(.01)	(.26)
Wald F-statistic	.67	.92	.85	2.50*	2.40*	.83
	(.65)	(.50)	(.54)	(.07)	(.08)	(.57)

NOTES: Probability levels are listed inside parentheses. The modified likelihood ratio (MLR) test proposed by Sims (1980) was performed to compare the efficacy of a VAR(5) and VAR (6) processes. The null findings indicate that each of these models is best analyzed as a VAR(5) process. The White test could not be performed for the Antitrust Division equations since there were an insufficient number of observations.
* $p < .10$ ** $p < .05$

no drawbacks in terms of passing the variety of diagnostics tests employed here. After estimating and analyzing several models, each with its own limitations, it was decided to use a parsimonious specification that contained only the economist to attorney ratio and EPO trend variables as deterministic variables in this VAR system. The VAR analysis for the Antitrust Investigations model is based on this specification. While this approach entails possible exclusion of other relevant deterministic variables,[19] each equation's residuals follow a white noise process and are also timewise homoskedastic. Plus, only the Congress equation failed to pass the Ramsey RESET tests at conventional levels of statistical significance. The other variants of this model suffered from deeper problems of serial correlation, ARCH residuals, and/or multiple occurrences of a significant Ramsey RESET. On the positive side, there is consistent evidence across each of the five variants of this model that were estimated in preliminary analysis concerning the causal nature of this model.[20] For instance, the F-block tests of Granger Causality reveal that current presidential budgetary signals are influenced by both its own past behavior as well as that of Congress in each case. Also, both the lagged behavior of the President and the AD also influence the current budgetary appropriation signals of Congress. Although the results reported in chapter 4 reveal that Congress's budgetary signals affect AD investigations activity, three of the five variant model specifications did not uncover support for this finding. The contemporaneous correlation of the innovations of this system reveal that findings are substantively similar across various Antitrust Investigation model specifications, except that the residual correlation between the President and Congress remains positive, but is not significant in two out of five alternative models. The innovation accounting portion of the analysis displayed consistent evidence across various alternative models that were estimated.[21]

Notes

1. Introduction

1. The term *control* is employed here since it is widely used elsewhere. Political control studies demonstrate influence to varying degrees, not necessarily complete domination over bureaucratic agencies.

2. Both these principal-agent approaches to the study of administrative politics will be discussed in more detail in the next section.

3. Congressional dominance scholars (Calvert, Moran, and Weingast 1987; Calvert, Mc-Cubbins, and Weingast 1989; McCubbins and Page 1987; McCubbins and Schwartz 1984; Shepsle and Weingast 1984; Weingast 1984; Weingast and Moran 1983) argue that such devices would indeed practically eliminate information asymmetries, whereas Niskanen (1971, 1975) suggests these devices are essentially impotent. A temperate response is echoed by Woolley (1993) who claims that these devices are only successful at limiting agency discretion if (1) committee and floor median preferences converge, and (2) House and Senate median committee policy preferences converge.

4. This study breaks down the literature according to the dominant viewpoints contained within each piece of research. For instance, many scholars—such as Meier (1987), Rourke (1984), Seidman and Gilmour (1986), and Wilson (1989)—acknowledge the potency of both bureaucratic strength and political controls. However, these works largely entail descriptive accounts of the various tools and/or means at the disposal of each institutional actor. Further, none of these works describe the degree of political control (or conversely bureaucratic autonomy) that agency-political relations occupy in actuality. Nor have these works been systematic studies analyzing the relative (or absolute) influence possessed by each institutional actor. At the same time, it is important to note that a great portion of the systematic analyses has not been nearly as temperate as the aforementioned research. The literature written by those supplying theories of bureaucratic autonomy, congressional dominance, and presidential control to explain administrative behavior has generally had an unbalanced perspective. Since my aim is to argue against previous heavily skewed views of political-bureaucratic relations (see Hammond and Knott 1993, 1996 for an exception to this observation), I define these works accordingly.

5. The general purpose underlying this framework is not to test every possible case for generalizability, but to present a general theoretical framework to serve as a more realistic portrayal of political-bureaucratic relations that can be applied to different agency types (such as regulatory, redistributive, and distributive).

6. Because of the restrictive assumptions embedded within these frameworks, existing models of political-bureaucratic relations (most notably principal-agent models) have come under well-justified criticism for their lack of generalizability to other types of agencies involved in distributive and redistributive policy (Meier 1993a, 1993b; Meier, Polinard, and Wrinkle 1995). The framework presented in chapter 2 circumvents these assumptions, thus making this framework applicable to nonregulatory agencies.

7. For example, Gildea (1990) provides strong empirical evidence to suggest that the monetary policy preferences of Board of Governor members of the Federal Open Market Committee (FOMC) are shaped by the academic institution from which they received their professional training.

8. Two clear illustrations reflecting internal professionalization change and its effects on regulatory performance were the Antitrust Division of the Department of Justice and the Federal Trade Commission (FTC), respectively. In the case of the Antitrust Division, Eisner and Meier (1990) and Eisner (1991, 1992) contend that the balance of economists to attorneys and the creation of the Economic Policy Office (EPO) within this same division explain substantive aspects of antitrust enforcement. The case of the FTC was quite similar to the Antitrust Division because of the emphasis placed on economic analysis in the wake of agency reorganizations during the 1970s. This was reflected by sharp increases in the number of economists hired during the post-reorganization period of the 1970s and 1980s as a means to facilitate case selection and decision making (Katzmann 1980; Eisner 1991, 1992; Wilson 1989). In addition, a policy-planning office and evaluation committee were created in both the Antitrust Division and the FTC to set long-term goals as it related to enforcement programs (Clarkson and Muris 1981; Eisner 1992).

9. The degree of severity associated with this asymmetry is a matter of much debate. This project seeks to shed some quantitative and anecdotal light on this debate. This topic will also be further discussed as a problem associated with principal-agent models of political control over the bureaucracy.

10. One example is William Niskanen's seminal research (1971, 1975). Central to Niskanen's argument is his claim that the combination of an informational monopoly and control of the agenda on the part of the agency permits these organizations to constrain legislators' choices to such a great extent that they are inclined to get whatever they desire from legislators in terms of budgets and slack resources. Niskanen's model rests upon the assumption that the agency is the superior of Congress through informational advantages.

11. Meier (1987: 43–45) notes that the agency can shape its political environment; however, it does so through less direct means such as expertise, cohesion, and leadership. He does not suggest that this influence may occur in a more direct tangible fashion through agency performance (as in policy outputs).

12. This study does not assume hierarchical relations from the outset (as is the case with

principal-agent models), nor is such a behavioral structure precluded. Instead, in this investigation I wish to explain the general nature of hierarchy through a theoretically guided inductive process. See Wood (1988) for possible limitations of hierarchy theory in administrative politics.

13. Similarly, Woolley (1993) does not acknowledge the possibility of hierarchy and its effect on congressional-bureaucratic relations. It is Woolley's assessment that agencies can and will take the "policy lead" as long as committee and floor median policy preferences and House and Senate median committee policy preferences are not too similar. Although this observation may be true in some cases, it ignores the often noted risk-averse nature of agencies (Bendor, Taylor, and Van Gaalen 1985). Agencies do want discretion over matters of policy and administration, but at the same time they want to maintain or enhance their reputation with elected officials (Kaufman 1981; Wilson 1989).

14. The theory of overhead democracy (Redford 1969) is a precursor to principal-agent based political control/influence theories of administrative politics.

15. Moe (1984) states that politicians may not be able to use "slack" resources as a means to control agencies since information asymmetries exist in favor of the latter. Moe adds, however, that politicians will rely on less demanding mechanisms such as those often studied in existing empirical studies (e.g., staffing and funding levels, selective monitoring, aggregate performance/agency output). Moreover, politicians can alleviate (if not overcome) much of these information asymmetries based upon agency reputation across time, and the feedback politicians receive from constituency groups is affected by agency behavior (McCubbins and Schwartz 1984; Twombly 1992; Weingast 1984; Weingast and Moran 1983).

16. Kaufman (1981) notes that, although the bureaucracy has its own distinct culture and is constrained by past commitments, it is also quite sensitive to the wishes of members of Congress.

17. Some scholars claim that the congressional dominance perspective has limited explanatory power for understanding bureaucratic behavior (Moe 1987a; Wilson 1989). Hammond and Knott (1993, 1996) aptly note that many of the quantitative studies conducted by the congressional dominance school (Calvert, Moran, and Weingast 1987; Weingast 1984; Weingast and Moran 1983) in their models ignore potential influence emanating from the presidents, thus possibly rendering faulty statistical inferences.

18. Although the early work of Weingast (1981) makes the case for little presidential involvement over regulatory policy administration, this strong viewpoint was tempered in a subsequent work by McCubbins, Noll, and Weingast (1989), in which they contend that Congress was more apt to use administrative procedural controls as a means to combat presidential dominance regarding political appointments.

19. There is no clear consensus whether *ex ante* or *ex post* controls over administrative agencies are more effective in the presence of multiple political principals (McCubbins, Noll, and Weingast 1987, 1989 favor *ex ante* controls, whereas Arnold 1987, Hammond and Knott 1993, Hill and Brazier 1991, Horn and Shepsle 1989, and Robinson 1989 make strong cases for the effectiveness of *ex post* controls).

20. Hammond and Knott (1993) note that Weingast's claim concerning MCs' power over

presidential appointments is rescinded to some extent by his later collaborative efforts (Mc-Cubbins, Noll, and Weingast 1987, 1989). These later works posit that congressional actors are more likely to employ administrative procedural controls as a means to combat presidential dominance in the area of political appointments.

21. Many regulatory agencies established in the pre–World War II period were designed to deal with economic regulation independent from presidential pressures. Social regulatory agencies created in recent years, however, tend to be more closely aligned to the executive branch (such as the Environmental Protection Agency, or the Office of Surface Mining Regulation, Occupational Safety, and Health Administration).

22. For a fine exception to this question, please see Hammond and Knott's (1993, 1996) elegant model of multi-institutional policy making. For a detailed critique of the strengths and weaknesses of Hammond and Knott's work and its implications for research on the dynamics of macro agency-political relations, please see Krause (1994).

23. Moe's theoretical contributions constitute an exception to this observation (1984, 1987a, 1987b, 1988, 1989, 1990). In addition, recent research has posed critiques and suggestions for future elaborations of principal-agent theories used to explain political control over administrative agencies (Waterman and Meier 1998; Waterman, Rouse, and Wright 1998; Worsham, Eisner, and Ringquist 1997).

24. In the tradition of Mosher (1968) and March and Olsen (1984, 1989), research by Eisner and Meier (1990) and Eisner (1991, 1992) lends insight into the effect of professionalization on the substance of agency performance in the area of antitrust regulation.

25. It has also been asserted that these factors are determined by "top-down" political forces (Wood and Anderson 1993).

26. This concept is borrowed from Simon's work on internal bureaucratic relations between employers and subordinates within the agency where the individuals at the top level of the hierarchy are "employers" while individuals in lower agency positions are "subordinates." According to both Barnard and Simon, this contractual authority will be bidirectional (a "two-way street"). This concept will be further explored in chapter 2.

27. This study does not attempt to suggest the complete abolition of bureaucratic autonomy or political control models of the bureaucracy as a heuristic device in analyzing agency-political relationships. Rather, it is argued here that the present conceptualizations of this approach are too narrow, thus serving as a special case for only one type of behavior. As a result, these existing theories must be encompassed within a larger theoretical framework, applicable to other types of policy (such as redistributive and distributive), and also to different forms of behavior.

28. In certain instances, this pattern of behavioral relations may be indicative of rational expectations (see Goldstein and Freeman 1991; Krause 1997: 531–32; Williams and McGinnis 1988). This is discussed in greater detail in chapter 2.

29. Both groups generally view budget and enforcement measures as being the most important (and commonly employed) phenomena in obtaining a broad understanding of relationships between administrative agencies and political institutions. For more detailed information on this assertion, see Appendix B.

30. Throughout this study, these notions are supported from a variety of academic and government sources.

31. It is true that administrative organizations are not monolithic entities. This study does not intend to suggest that bureaucratic institutions do not contain internal divisions, thus ignoring a possible source of administrative heterogeneity within a given agency. However, the aggregate behavior of various units will constitute aggregate regulatory performance (i.e., agency behavior). The dynamic systems model of administrative politics set forth in this study is explicitly designed to examine the macro-behavior of institutions administering public policy, while being informed by micro-level insights involving institutional interaction, and sophisticated reaction to unanticipated deviations in behavior quite possibly because of strategic considerations.

2. A Dynamic Systems Model of Administrative Politics

1. This point of contention has been supported by McCubbins, Noll, and Weingast (1987) and by Kiewiet and McCubbins (1991).

2. Hammond and Knott (1993, 1996) acknowledge the validity of these competing theories in their multi-institutional model of policy making and argue that these claims may hold true in certain instances but not in others. Their theory, however, focuses on policy proposals as a method to analyze the preferences of political principals and the agency. The framework presented here employs a more tangible mode of evaluation to study these institutional preferences through the analysis of budgetary preferences and agency output.

3. For the purposes of this analysis, institutional strength will constitute the bread-and-butter items of political-bureaucratic relations: resources (i.e., budgetary levels) and measures of agency policy outputs reflecting regulatory vigor. Other factors relating to political-bureaucratic relations (such as oversight-committee policy liberalism, economic conditions, and so on) will be introduced in a deterministic manner.

4. Much of the research on the "new institutionalism" school is in the form of institutional choice theory, which states that issues relating to administrative politics can best be addressed by examining the three-way interactions between agencies, politicians, and pressure groups. Past research within the institutional choice theoretical paradigm has largely focused on the design, structure, and processes for these agencies, not on their performance in terms of outputs and outcomes. This study focuses on budgetary and enforcement output signals by examining how institutions interact with one another to affect agency and political behavior.

5. In theory, the framework presented here could be more generally applied to non-budgetary preferences and non–agency output measures. For purposes of tractability, data limitations, and integration to most of the empirical research, these more tangible means of political and administrative behavior are examined in this study.

6. Contrary to the views of Niskanen (1971, 1975), bureaucrats are not always budget-maximizers (Johnson 1992). The willingness of an agency to vigorously pursue its mandate will, however, be reflected by the amount of budgetary resources it requests and the vigor of

their agency enforcement activities. This is supported not only by past research but also by governmental actors interviewed for this project.

7. Existing models of administrative politics make restrictions on behavioral relations. These models also presume that policy conflict between administrative agencies and their political principals is the norm that motivates administrative behavior.

8. A similar point is made by Hammond and Knott (1993: 53).

9. These institutions consist of the agency, president, and Congress as a whole. Although both Senate and House oversight-committee preferences are captured in a deterministic fashion, the floor preferences for each chamber are not considered separately as in both Hammond and Knott (1993, 1996) and Woolley (1993). Analysis of each chamber will allow us to examine not only whether legislative oversight-subcommittee ideology affects agency behavior, but also if it influences the behavior of political principals (Congress and president). The examination of budgetary signals within each chamber does not lend itself to such analysis because these figures infinitesimally differ between the Senate and the House floor chambers. Final appropriations (budgetary) decisions are often viewed as reflecting the aggregate institutional behavior for the entire Congress, and are distinct from presidential budgetary requests (Carpenter 1992, 1996). The difference between these two budgetary figures will be even greater when analyzed as signals (percentage rates of change) compared to absolute levels.

10. For instance, Wood and Waterman's (1994) study of water enforcement litigation referrals for EPA shows that the impact of Congress and president are substantially greater than that of the courts. For the two case studies examined in this book, courts are not viewed as typically affecting the *overall level or vigor of regulatory enforcement*, but instead the *type of cases that may be emphasized in certain select (isolated) cases*. This is a point consistent with past empirical research of antitrust regulation (Eisner 1991; Wood and Anderson 1993). In the case of antitrust regulation, for instance, judicial impacts are experienced according to the particular type of cases based on a variable (see Wood and Anderson's [1993] use of *United States v. General Dynamics Corporation* [1974: 415 U.S. 486]), not on various *aggregate* measures of enforcement activity (see Wood and Anderson's [1993] analysis of aggregate investigation and litigation activities that do not consider judicial factors, especially table 2: 24). Furthermore, the other empirical work on the subject (by Eisner and Meier [1990]) cited in this study does not include a courts variable in their disaggregate enforcement models—which some may view as an oversight on their behalf. Wood and Anderson (1993) in their study explicitly note that the Supreme Court's decision on the General Dynamics case would affect (i.e., result in a decline of) merger litigations—which are a specific disaggregate type of enforcement activity (see table 3: 28)—but not on other types of disaggregate activities (civil restraint of trade litigations, criminal restraint of trade litigations [see table 4, p. 32]; percentage of civil investigative demand investigations, percentage criminal litigations [see table 3: 28]). Therefore, the decision to exclude the courts is a sound one from a theoretical and substantive level, given this study's focus on aggregate enforcement caseload activities across time.

On a practical level, there are also three methodological issues that make the inclusion of the courts an extremely difficult (if not impossible) task for my empirical analysis. First, inclusion of a courts variable into this system of agency-political relations would require one to obtain a continuous measure. Accurate data on judicial impact of a continuous nature is an extremely difficult task. For instance, the percentage of cases won by the agency does not take into account the size of penalties awarded to these entities, thus it is a problematic measure for this type of analysis. Second, sample size constraints would mean not considering environmental and intra-institutional considerations. Third, given the extensive statistical analysis that was performed (including the exhaustive set of statistical diagnostics appearing in Appendix D to ensure the validity of the empirical results), there is strong reason to believe that each of the model specifications contained in this study is more than adequate representations of bureaucratic politics.

11. The oversight subcommittee can influence the budgetary decisions of relevant congressional appropriations committees, and this aspect can be captured within the dynamic systems model. This relationship in turn would address the influence of oversight subcommittees on the general (aggregate) behavior of Congress.

12. Administrative policy outputs can describe a significant portion, if not all facets, of administrative behavior (Ringquist 1995; Wood and Anderson 1993). The conclusions of most prior empirical research, however, are based on such data. For the purposes of this study, personal interviews—undertaken by the author—with agency personnel at the SEC and relevant staff at the OMB, the Congressional Budget Office (CBO), and on congressional committees generally concur that these outputs are an imperfect yet accurate reflection of agency performance.

13. Although enforcement actions involve differential amounts of effort and importance for the organization, many agencies (including the ones analyzed in this study) do not have detailed workload statistics for each enforcement output (e.g., number of person hours spent per case). In an aggregate analysis, one can logically presume that aggregation effects will typically attenuate workload differences between individual cases since they will tend to cancel out when summed up over the course of a fixed period.

14. It is true that budgets serve as a blunt instrument of political control (Bendor and Moe 1985, 1986; Moe 1987a). At the same time, these authors—and many others mentioned earlier—acknowledge the power and high value associated with the budgetary preferences of political principals and employ them as the foundations of their models. Even with this said, some may be skeptical of using the budgetary figures as representing the institutional behavior of political principals since it is an *ex post* method of administrative control. However, although some feel that "informal" *ex ante* methods of administrative control are more effective than "formal" *ex post* methods, because of the existence of multiple principals (McCubbins, Noll, and Weingast 1987, 1989), this claim has been challenged in recent work (Arnold 1987; Hill and Brazier 1991; Horn and Shepsle 1989; Robinson 1989). Kirst (1969) contends that these "informal" techniques have many of the same limitations as formal methods because of the existence of multiple principals. Therefore, the use of budgetary signals is at the very least just as valid as any alternative approach.

15. These points also hold true in formal models of agency-political relations (Banks and

Weingast 1992; Bendor and Moe 1985; Calvert, McCubbins, and Weingast 1989; McCubbins 1985; Miller and Moe 1983).

16. In my illustration, the elected officials (principals) are "employers" while the bureaucratic organization serves as the "subordinate." This terminology is consistent with the well-known principal-agent framework of analysis.

17. Personal interest may be primarily the result of possible electoral payoffs or partisanship loyalties, as some suggest (Fiorina 1974, 1977; Grier 1989; Hibbs 1977, 1987; Mayhew 1974; Tufte 1978; Woolley 1984, 1988), or the desire to make good public policy (Fenno 1973; Smith and Deering 1984). In addition, substantive policy area expertise and public interest may also play a role (Kingdon 1984).

18. Closer institutional proximity and long-term historical relations are typically synonymous; however, there are some exceptions to this general rule. For instance, both the Army Corps of Engineers and the Agricultural Research Service are executive agencies who have exhibited closer long-term historical relations with Congress than with presidents. I thank Ken Meier for bringing this point to my attention.

19. This does not mean that presidents cannot affect the behavior of independent regulatory commissions. Much of the empirical work on the subject convincingly demonstrates that presidents do, via various means, influence the behavior of these types of agencies (Moe 1982, 1985a; Wood and Waterman 1991).

20. MCs can possibly affect the behavior of executive agencies through more tangible means (such as oversight activity, appropriations, and so on) as has been demonstrated by a host of studies (Moe 1985a; Wood and Waterman 1991; Wood and Anderson 1993).

21. This line of argument is consistent with the theories of Barnard (1938) and Simon (1947) discussed in the preceding chapter.

22. These responses can either be positive (reciprocal) or negative (antagonistic). The former indicate policy congruence, the latter reveal policy divergence. For example, a positive response by an agency may reflect either sincere contentment or a goodwill gesture toward elected officials as a means of promoting better relations or mitigating recent tensions. Negative responses by an agency may reveal sincere displeasure toward political principals.

23. During this period, the literature generally acknowledges that Reagan was responding to direct congressional pressure, which was brought about by mass defections from the agency and the leaking of agency information to oversight committees by both current employees and those who defected (Vig and Kraft 1984; Wood 1988; Wood and Waterman 1991, 1993, 1994). This same body of literature also contends that, while environmental interest groups did not support her nomination, Burford passed with very little opposition in the Senate confirmation process, which at the time was controlled by the Republicans. In this instance, members of Congress and a large group of disillusioned EPA career bureaucrats combined to take effective joint action against the administration's radical environmental policy views.

24. Eisner and Meier (1990: 284) note that the Reagan antitrust record was essentially an extension of well-established trends of policy change dating back to 1972. However, Wood

and Anderson (1993) offer a "principal-agent" response to the policy change/institutional argument by claiming that the ratio of economists to attorneys was determined in a "top-down" manner from the executive branch—not within the agency as purported by Eisner and Meier (1990) and Eisner (1991, 1992). Furthermore, Wood and Anderson (1993) argue that political forces do affect both the level and the substance of antitrust division policy outputs.

25. This typology is distinct from the one proposed by Jeffrey Cohen (1992) in three ways. First, the focus of this classification scheme is not on the distribution of relative resources but rather on the nature of institutional influence (or lack thereof). In this study, institutional influence is a function in dynamic changes in the budgetary preferences of political preferences and policy outputs of administrative agencies. Second, the interaction between politicians and bureaucrats from Cohen's model does not consider the possibility of bidirectional causal relations. As a result, his relative resources model does not portray administrative politics as a dynamic system of interdependent governmental institutions. Finally, one cannot, using Cohen's typology, distinguish between the concepts of bureaucratic power (or influence) and autonomy.

26. See Wood (1988) and Wood and Waterman (1991, 1993), regarding the more moderate stance toward environmental policy following Ann Burford's resignation. In the area of monetary policy, Chappell, Havrilesky, and McGregor (1993) convincingly argue that the Reagan administration did an about-face with respect to the types of individuals appointed to the Board of Governors (BOG) of the Federal Reserve System following Reagan's first two years in office. Specifically, the Reagan administration appointed "supply-side" individuals from 1981–1983 who advocated less restrictive monetary policy than their "conventional" Republican BOG counterparts. "Conventional" tight-money Republicans were appointed to the BOG in the subsequent years of the Reagan administration.

27. The most notable political science applications of sophisticated reaction occur in the area of international relations (Goldstein and Freeman 1990, 1991; Williams and McGinnis 1988, 1992). See Krause (1997) for an application involving the dynamics of the commercial banking regulatory policy subsystem.

28. This suggests that policy actors/institutions will behave strategically by altering their future behavior in response to an innovation on the part of another actor/institution.

29. Taken intuitively, this definition translates into the notion that policy actors must be able to correct their mistakes in such a manner that their forecasts of the other policy actors' preferences will not be systematically incorrect. Thus, the behavior of institutional participants which is not driven by the predictable (past) behavior of others within the system could in fact be a function of a shock (surprise) from other government institutions during the current period.

30. In empirical settings, the information set represents all of the specified variables included in the model specification.

31. Generally, the use of retrospective information does not necessarily lead to rejecting rational expectations as long as such information does not improve the efficiency of fore-

casts via prediction error. However, within this particular test the phenomena of interest is not a measure of forecast error or a deviation from a long-run (equilibrium) path, but rather the observed variable itself. Therefore, the empirical definition listed in note 29 is consistent with this theoretical concept for the purposes of this study.

32. This definition of rational expectations acknowledges and encompasses the dilemmas set forth from the behavioralist tradition in organization theory, while suggesting that even with these information and cognitive constraints, policy actors may be able to alter their future behavior in a systematic manner following a policy innovation by fellow actors. In other words, behavioral relations should not always be perceived in only a lagged predictable ("lumbering") manner as much of the previous research maintains (Carpenter 1992, 1996; Cyert and March 1963; March and Simon 1958; Moe 1982, 1985a; Simon 1947; Wood and Waterman 1991, 1993).

33. Moe (1988, 1989, 1990) constitutes an exception to this observation; but although his work acknowledges the existence of such behaviors, it does not formulate hypotheses and corresponding statistical tests.

34. It is important to remember that the policy "surprise" often conveyed in formal models of administrative politics pertains to the formulation and adoption of specific administrative rules and procedures, not their intended policy (implementation) effects on agency behavior or preferences (Calvert, McCubbins, and Weingast 1989; Epstein and O'Halloran 1994; McCubbins, Noll, and Weingast 1987, 1989). For instance, Calvert, McCubbins, and Weingast's (1989: 498) view of a "policy surprise" reflects the distance between the agency's policy choice and the choice the elected officials were obtaining based on the nominee that they agreed on (i.e., $x - x^*_a$).

35. This argument is analogous to the one made by Suzuki (1991) in his comparison of adaptive and rational expectations with respect to the rationality of economic voting.

36. OMB budget formulation generally follows presidential wishes (Carpenter 1992; Padgett 1981).

37. In all fairness to Hammond and Knott (1993, 1996), they claim that their study examines only the various conditions under which the bureaucracy will or will not be autonomous, in a static sense. To some degree, the studies and arguments contained in this book complement one another, since Hammond and Knott's perspective is more micro-oriented than the broad dynamic macro-oriented approach presented here. One common point between the two frameworks is that they both are better suited than past research to capture the possibility that agency behavior may not always change in response to behavioral changes on the part of political principals.

38. This pluralist outcome may include pressure groups and/or the courts where applicable. For the purposes of this particular project, I have focused on only the agency, Congress, and the president since they are the key regular participants in my substantive case studies of the SEC and the Antitrust Division of the Department of Justice. These case studies are presented in chapter 3 respectively.

39. See Carpenter (1992) and Kettl (1993) who make valid criticisms regarding the

overutilization of discrete events as a means to explain bureaucratic behavior in empirical research on administrative politics.

40. A similar sentiment is echoed by Hammond and Knott (1993: 63), whose main purpose is to determine who controls the bureaucracy.

3. The Institutional Dynamics of Policy Administration in Practice

1. The FTC's role in antitrust regulation is not discussed here since it is not part of this project. Wood and Anderson (1993, n. 1) note that the vast proportion of antitrust enforcement responsibility lies with the Antitrust Division.

2. The role of the courts could be incorporated in this theoretical framework if deemed appropriate. Except for relatively infrequent (and discrete) landmark judicial decisions, both cases analyzed here—as well as previous research—recognize that the courts do not play a significant role in influencing the *aggregate* regulatory vigor displayed by administrative agencies. In these instances, courts may alter the types of cases undertaken by an administrative agency (Moe 1985a; Wood and Anderson 1993) but not necessarily reflect aggregate enforcement vigor exhibited by the agency. This latter task is clearly determined in a joint fashion by administrative and electoral institutions of democratic government. In simple terms, this study is not concerned with the incentives regarding individual case selection but rather is interested in viewing the comprehensive efforts at administering public policy via aggregate outputs and budgetary signals.

3. A majority of the qualitative and quantitative empirical analyses of policy administration is noncumulative, because different policy areas are investigated in diverse manners. Rather than add to the list of discordant research, this study examines policy areas that have come under much scrutiny by political scientists—as a way to demonstrate the oversimplified conceptualizations and conclusions drawn from past research.

4. There are definite limits of generalizability regarding the specific results of this study or any other analysis that only examines at most a handful of cases. It is generalizable, however, relative to past research (1) because of its long temporal resolution (forty-four years) and (2) because the results of past research involving these case studies have served as viable and accepted cases that have spurred further research. Moreover, very few singular studies in this area have focused on more than one case. For these reasons, the results obtained from this analysis are as generalizable as the vast majority of past research.

5. Scholars such as Seidman and Gilmour (1986) and Moe (1988, 1989) have noticed important differences in agency behavior directly related to agency administrative design. Moe (1988, 1989) posits that independent regulatory commissions will generally be more responsive to congressional wishes relative to presidential desires, and the opposite will occur for administrative organizations that take the form of an executive department or bureau.

6. One event that lends support for this contention occurred during the Bush administration with the well-noted disagreements between Treasury Secretary Nicholas Brady and SEC Chairman Richard Breeden over various issues such as agency budgets, enforcement activity, and full disclosure of CEOs' salaries. In the end, Breeden's view prevailed, not due to

the support of other administration officials, but rather because of the institutional autonomy the SEC processes by administrative design (interview with SEC official, June 1993).

7. For those interested, Khademian (1992) presents an excellent in-depth historical treatment of this policy area. Other fine treatments include Cary (1967), Karmel (1982), MacKay and Reid (1979), Ritchie (1980), Seligman (1982, 1985), and Shapiro (1984, 1985).

8. Demmler did not fit the popular view of a budget-maximizing bureaucrat (Niskanen 1971, 1975). Instead, Cathy Johnson (1992) contends that there may be instances where an agency will abandon its "imperialistic" nature by requesting fewer resources.

9. A congressional dominance interpretation of this phenomena would contend that MCs did not actually delegate authority to SEC expertise during this period, but rather that there was very little payoff for congressional involvement in securities regulation. Therefore, MCs did not choose to invest their time and political capital into this policy area (Weingast 1984).

10. This crisis transpired when antiquated methods for clearing and closing stock sales met large increases in trading volumes (Khademian 1992: 70; Loomis 1968; Sobel 1975: 290–91).

11. This delegation of congressional authority did not have an impact on SEC regulatory activity because, on one hand it gave the agency greater discretion (which could have been used for more or less stringent enforcement), yet it was also trying to promote greater competition via the deregulation of rates. Usually, the general policy intent underlying legislative action is pretty clear (even if the details are often vague). In this case, however, the SEC was basically given more freedom without any proscribed, politically clear direction to steer policy (i.e., more or less stringent enforcement).

12. This is interesting because of both administrations' keen interest in regulatory policy matters (e.g., the antitrust regulation of the Ford administration, and the commercial bank and airline deregulation of the Carter administration).

13. This phenomenon could be credited to non-instantaneous (i.e., gradual adjustment) change that took place at the SEC when Reagan (and his faithful appointee Shad) came in with sweeping regulatory changes quite different from the status quo at the agency during the Carter administration.

14. In an interview with Khademian, an SEC official confirms this point by stating that the agency has always been perceived as a lawyers' agency (1992: 105).

15. These points also hold true in formal models of agency-political relations (Banks and Weingast 1992; Bendor and Moe 1985; Calvert, McCubbins, and Weingast 1989; McCubbins 1985).

16. This ruling was boldly rejected in the 1945 *ALCOA v. United States* decision by Judge Learned Hand; however, its spirit was still influential in assessing market power (Shepherd 1985).

17. Some, such as Eisner (1991), Katzmann (1980), and Weaver (1977) view this internal bureaucratic change as a distinct, independent source of policy change. Others remain less convinced (Anderson 1986; Mueller 1986; Wood and Anderson 1993).

18. Wood and Anderson (1992, 1993) provide quantitative evidence to the contrary. This issue is not explored because this study is concerned with the general (aggregate) influence and the responsiveness of these institutions across time.

19. This was the consensus among those individuals at the Antitrust Division interviewed by the author during June 1993.

20. Based upon Khademian's account (1992), one could argue that much of the growth in SEC agency resources—compared to its past history, other agencies, and request-appropriation differential—was not for political purposes per se. Instead this increase in so-called congressional pecuniary investment was a means to meet the greater demand of increased securities activity during the late 1960s and early 1970s.

21. This study is not concerned with addressing the disaggregated portion of AD enforcement activity (e.g., percentage of horizontal restraint-litigations cases to total cases, etc.) since the purpose of this project is to examine how bureaucratic resources (controlled by political principals) affect various types of *aggregate* policy outputs (i.e., regulatory vigor) for a given administrative organization. This is not problematic since the vast majority of research on agency-political relationships is concerned with enforcement vigor and examines a variety of measures dealing with aggregate enforcement activity.

22. One notable example of presidential influence mentioned by Katzmann is the proposed merger case between pharmaceutical giants Parke-Davis and Warner-Lambert in 1970. In this instance, the White House (through Deputy Attorney General Richard Kleindienst) overruled the original decision made by Assistant Attorney General–Head of Antitrust Division Richard McClaren to halt these merger plans (Katzmann 1980: 197). It became apparent that a possible conflict of interest arose, in that two principal members—President Richard Nixon and Attorney General John Mitchell—had former legal ties with the law firm representing Warner-Lambert. This decision, in turn, received much publicity and was later referred to the FTC in order to diffuse the controversy.

4. An Empirical Investigation into the Institutional Dynamics of Regulatory Enforcement in a Democratic System

1. This internal bureaucratic policy change came in the form of the prominent role played by economic analysis in policy development and regulatory enforcement beginning in the early to mid-1970s.

2. Numerous studies on agency-political relations have employed a dynamic empirical methodology (Moe 1982; Ringquist 1995; Wood and Waterman 1991, 1993, 1994); however, none of these works contains theoretical or empirical models that allow for possible endogeneity or sophisticated responses of the president, Congress, and administrative agencies.

3. This point is also supported by the anecdotal evidence obtained from the interviews conducted for each case study.

4. A great deal of research in the political control vein has assumed that the agency is in a subordinate position. This tenuous assumption is relaxed by treating the agency as an

equal, a priori, before the model is tested. By treating the bureaucracy in this manner, this model does not preclude this institution as a subordinate entity to democratic institutions; however, it is not presumed to be one either.

5. Anne Khademian (1992: 138) echoes this sentiment by stating that SEC enforcement activities demonstrate its independence. Whether this is true in a general sense is a question to be empirically examined later in this section. This claim made by Khademian, however, suggests that to examine agency independence one must analyze enforcement behavior in relation to the behavior of political principals.

6. Past research and interviews I conducted at the SEC lead me to believe that agency professionalization in terms of economists vis-à-vis attorneys within the agency will have an infinitesimal effect on policy. Unlike the antitrust regulation case, securities regulation has been dominated by attorneys since its inception.

7. This is consistent with McCubbins and Schwartz's (1984) notion of "fire alarm" control.

8. The variables examined in the SEC models are listed in table B.1 in Appendix B. The courts are not included as an institutional participant, for reasons discussed in chapter 2.

9. An analysis of the SEC annual reports for each year during the sample period reveals that these measures were defined in the same manner throughout the sample period. Thus, variations in measures do not represent changes in the definition of policy outputs. Furthermore, SEC criminal actions and cases are not analyzed here since such measures are not appropriate for assessing regulatory enforcement activity (Shapiro 1984, 1985).

10. The membership of subcommittees was not available for the 1949–1954 period; therefore, these variables were calculated for the entire committee during this six-year interval.

11. Although it is widely agreed upon that congressional oversight variables do not generally have a lagged effect on agency behavior (especially using annual data), there is no consistent viewpoint on whether these types of variables have a lagged (one-year) impact on political resource decisions. Wood (1990) and Wood and Anderson (1993) lag these variables by one year, whereas Carpenter (1992) and Kiewiet and McCubbins (1988, 1991) do not. Preliminary analysis followed both perspectives. The results in terms of explanatory power and model specification adequacy revealed that the nonlagged oversight variables outperformed the lagged variables.

The use of the relative median ADA policy liberalism measure accounts for the relative liberalism (conservativeness) of the relevant congressional committees vis-à-vis the chamber. This operationalization has the added advantage of attenuating the effects of such measures that make it difficult to make interchamber and across time comparisons.

12. The people interviewed for this case study noted that real economic growth was a key environmental variable that affected their decision making. None of these individuals mentioned unemployment or inflation as economic factors affecting agency caseload, or the regulatory (budgetary) preferences of political principals.

13. The SEC models are void of intra-institutional features emanating from the agency since none exist. Specifically, Khademian (1992) convincingly asserts that agency profes-

sionalization (in terms of educational training) plays practically no role in determining agency behavior because the SEC places a premium on organizational solidarity. She adds that lawyers have always dominated the regulatory behavior of the agency. Unlike the AD case described by Eisner and Meier (1990), Khademian (1992) convincingly shows that the creation of an economic policy office during the Reagan administration played practically no role in affecting SEC regulatory behavior since (1) lawyers have always dominated the regulatory mission of the agency, and (2) the SEC places a heavy premium on organizational solidarity. An attempt to accurately measure the concept of internal bureaucratic professionalization proved fruitless, since an overwhelming majority of the "economists" within the agency were individuals without Ph.D. degrees in economics, whose main purpose was to gather agency statistics, not shape the policy direction of the agency via case selection or other forms of regulatory decision making (Anne Khademian, telephone conversation, August 4, 1995).

Furthermore, a measure of issue salience is not specified in any of these models. Although past studies have operationalized such a measure as an event count of the number of articles appearing in the *New York Times* (Meier 1994; Twombly 1992), or in the *Reader's Guide to Periodical Literature* (Wood and Anderson 1993), two major problems exist. First, the validity of these event counts may be questionable, since they are often calculated from a key word or words describing the policy area under study. This can have dire consequences, since many stories or articles concerning a given policy area may not have a plethora of key words. For instance, if one only counts news articles on securities regulation, one may miss such important related issues as "insider trading," commodities, or relevant documents on specific exchanges (e.g., NYSE, AMEX). Second, these event counts examine only the number of items found on a topic. This implies that each and every item is clamoring for increased enforcement or regulation. This is a tenuous assumption to make. For example, commercial bank regulation became a much more salient issue in the late 1970s and early 1980s, but a sizable proportion of articles were either calling for or supporting deregulatory efforts. Thus, the strategy undertaken in this study is to prefer no variable to a poorly operationalized one.

14. Moe (1982) and Kohlmeier (1969) argue that presidential preferences are the dominant force behind SEC behavior, whereas Weingast (1984) contends it is Congress. Because of the lack of unity in these claims and the dynamic systems emphasis on *theoretical induction*, it is inappropriate to discuss hypotheses as one normally does in a single-equation multiple regression framework.

15. This does not mean that presidents cannot affect the behavior of independent regulatory commissions. Much of the empirical work on the subject convincingly demonstrates that presidents do, via various means, influence the behavior of these types of administrative agencies (Moe 1982, 1985a; Wood and Waterman 1991, 1994).

16. Models with differenced data generally yield a poorer statistical fit. It should be noted that almost every previous empirical study encountered assumes that the data are stationary, without testing for this condition (exceptions include Carpenter 1992, 1996; Wood 1988). Violation of this statistical assumption allows for the possibility that past

findings are based upon invalid tests of statistical inference. Please see Appendix C for more details.

17. On the importance of proper model specification in political science research, please see Bartels (1991); Freeman, Williams, and Lin (1989); Freeman (1993); Granato (1992); Beck (1992); King (1989).

18. A result such as this is not entirely curious. Carpenter's (1992, 1996) examination of the FDA and FCC found that the partisan balance of the oversight committee for the House had a negative effect on presidential budgetary signals. This finding may also be the peculiar product of the SEC's particular involvement in administrative proceeding activities.

19. Khademian's contention is analogous to Moe's (1982) argument regarding presidential administrations in the area of economic regulation.

20. The contemporaneous correlation of the policy innovations between the presidential and congressional budgetary preference signal variables is quite high. If the variables are sensitive to their place in the causal ordering, then one should check to see which one relatively outperforms the other for any given ordering. Preliminary analysis (not presented here) of the decomposition of the forecast error variance for the VAR model revealed that, although these variables were sensitive to their ordering, the president variable performed relatively better in the first position and the congressional variable performed relatively better in the second position. This finding is consistent with our original causal ordering of the contemporaneous innovations. This ordering held true for each of the three equations in the SEC Administrative Proceedings model.

21. The differences in the range on the Y-axis of each impulse response graph reflects differences in each of these particular series. To be specific, when interpreting these graphs it is important to note that, although each shock is standardized, the impulse response is not, by definition.

22. Examples of institutional demands placed upon Congress within this context could be the stronger electoral imperative of MCs regarding specific policy behavior and the changing composition of this electoral institution.

23. This new equilibrium could be because of electoral changes, intra-institutional evolution, or some combination thereof. The significance attached to these possible explanations cannot be determined. At any rate, the essential lesson acquired from the dynamic analysis of policy innovations is that the political-bureaucratic system does indeed reequilibrate following a policy perturbation. This, in turn, reflects a natural equilibrating tendency among governmental institutions responsible for administering public policy.

24. This result is not surprising. Anecdotal evidence obtained from my interviews suggest it is quite possible. For instance, a senior career official at the SEC states that in 1989–1990 then SEC chair Richard Breeden (a Bush appointee) was in sharp conflict with the Bush administration's Secretary of the Treasury Nicholas Brady over disclosure regulations. The official added that Brady (even with administration backing) could not get the SEC (Breeden) to alter the agency's policy stance and interpretation, because of its institutional design, which grants it legislative and budgetary bypass authority from the White House (interview with author, June 1993).

25. The contemporaneous correlation of the policy innovations between the presidential and congressional preference variables is quite high (r = .60). Alternative causal ordering robustness checks were followed as in the previous model. Preliminary analysis (not presented here) of the decomposition of the forecast error variance for the VAR model revealed that, although these variables were sensitive to their ordering, the president variable performed better in the first position and the congressional variable performed better in the second position for both the presidential and congressional equations.

26. As the previous statistical results clearly show, presidential budgetary signals will affect congressional budgetary signals but not generally in an antagonistic manner.

27. The SEC enjoys both legislative and budgetary bypass authority. This means that the SEC can attempt to initiate legislation and draw up its budgetary requests without White House approval. This does not mean that the SEC completely ignores presidential preferences.

28. The contemporaneous correlation of the policy innovations between the presidential and congressional preference variables is quite high (r = .59). Alternative causal ordering robustness checks were followed as in the previous model. Preliminary analysis (not presented here) of the decomposition of the forecast error variance for the VAR model reveals that while these variables were sensitive to their ordering, the President variable performed relatively better in the first position while the Congressional variable performed relatively better in the second position for both the presidential and congressional equations. In none of the three equations were the variations of these budgetary-preference signals a direct function of their causal ordering.

29. This finding is corroborated by the results of the multivariate Granger exogeneity tests of lagged causal relations.

30. A similar corresponding finding is provided in the multivariate Granger exogeneity tests of lagged causal relations. The F-statistic in the congressional preference equation that has the largest value (and that is also the most significant) is presidential preferences.

31. This interpretation is quite reasonable. For instance, after eight years, innovations in SEC administrative proceedings and caseload activity explain almost 29 percent of the forecast error variance in presidential budgetary signals and about 37 percent for congressional budgetary signals. Furthermore, this finding is not a statistical artifact of the contemporaneous causal ordering. Preliminary analysis revealed that switching the order of the presidential and congressional variables still resulted in the same percentages of explained forecast error variance for the SEC as in the previously noted (final) VAR model.

32. This finding is especially impressive given that the SEC enforcement variables appear as the last system variable in the temporal sequence of the dynamic simulation analysis.

33. The proposed method of examining agency power inference (or lack thereof) is much more direct than the examination of other proxies of the same concept, most notably internal sources of agency professionalization and/or policy change or innovation (Eisner and Meier 1990; Eisner 1991, 1992).

34. A great deal of research in the political control vein has assumed that the agency is in a subordinate position. This tenuous assumption is relaxed in this model by treating the

agency as an equal, a priori, before the model is tested. Treating the bureaucracy in this manner is not to preclude it as a subordinate entity to democratic institutions; however, the effects of hierarchy are not being presumed either.

35. Each of the variables used in the AD models is listed in table B.2 in appendix B. The courts are not included as an institutional participant for reasons discussed in chapter 2.

36. The subcommittee membership for either chamber was not reported for the 1949–1954 period. Also, in 1981, Senate Judiciary Committee chair Strom Thurmond abolished the subcommittee on antitrust so as to prevent Charles Mathias from becoming subcommittee chair (Eisner and Meier 1990, 278 n. 11; Wood and Anderson 1993, 12 n. 9). In those instances in which subcommittee membership was not available, the relative median policy liberalism scores for the entire committee were calculated.

37. Once again, the results in terms of explanatory power and model specification adequacy revealed that the nonlagged oversight variables outperformed the lagged variables.

38. Wood and Anderson's (1993) graphical illustrations hint that litigation activities rose and investigations slightly fell during the Reagan administration. The anecdotal evidence garnered from my interviews indicates that the overall regulatory vitality of the Antitrust Division diminished during the Reagan administration. These modestly conflicting claims will be addressed through a statistical analysis of the data.

39. For an opposing (and skeptical) view regarding the impact of internal bureaucratic factors on antitrust enforcement behavior, see Wood and Anderson (1993).

40. In Eisner and Meier's (1990) research they examine how these internal bureaucratic factors will alter the *type* of enforcement activity pursued by the agency. The present study examines the effects of these variables on *aggregate* regulatory vigor. As a result, these findings cannot (and do not) attempt to answer this former issue directly. The results, however, will provide us with a clear indication of the manner in which these administrative forces influence aggregate AD enforcement behavior, and also of how they shape political principals' behavior toward the general enforcement of antitrust laws.

41. Industry concentration variables are irrelevant to this study since it examines antitrust enforcement activity in an aggregate fashion. Furthermore, research on the micro-analytic aspects of antitrust decision making reaches the same general conclusion: that AD enforcement behavior is not based on achieving a higher level of social welfare (Long, Schramm, and Tollison 1973; Siegfried 1975), nor is it related to market conditions within a given industry (Asch 1975).

42. The Hart-Scott-Rodino Antitrust Improvements Act was intended to require parties engaged in potentially sizable transactions to file a premerger application with both the Antitrust Division and the FTC. According to this act, a waiting period exists for merger participants in order to supply these agencies with ample time to facilitate their decision making. Opposition from either regulatory agency can prevent the merger from taking place.

43. This does not necessarily mean that a "more distant" political institution cannot affect the behavior of the administrative organization in question. The existing empirical work on the subject shows that Congress—through its final appropriation, which is treated

as being a shared tool of political control, and also through its oversight committees—does, via various means, influence the behavior of these types of agencies (Wood 1990; Wood and Waterman 1991; Wood and Anderson 1993).

44. The Reagan administration results, with respect to congressional budgetary signals and AD enforcement performance, hold in alternative VAR model specifications analyzed in preliminary analysis. The impact of the Reagan administration on presidential budgetary signals is, however, not robust across various preliminary models estimated.

45. These findings are consistent across the alternative model specifications conducted in the preliminary analysis.

46. These results do not hold in every version of this model. Please consult Note 20 in Appendix D for detailed information on the robustness of these results.

47. The F-block tests between the president and Congress in the AD Cases model hold in alternative model specifications analyzed in preliminary analysis. In the AD investigations model, the findings that indicate President $\rightarrow$ Congress and Congress $\rightarrow$ President holds in every instance. However, the lagged congressional signals on current congressional signals in the Investigations model are not robust across all preliminary VAR model specifications analyzed in Appendix D.

48. The F-block tests running from agency to president (AD $\rightarrow$ President) in the AD Cases model holds in alternative model specifications analyzed in preliminary analysis, save one instance. In the AD investigations model, the findings reveal that AD $\rightarrow$ Congress in every instance, while Congress $\rightarrow$ AD (p $\approx$ .09) in only one other alternative model specification (out of a possible five) besides the one presented here. Therefore, these findings are much more robust and convincing concerning the *bureaucratic influence* hypothesis than they are for the *mutual adaptation* hypothesis.

49. The positive president-AD contemporaneous innovation results hold in every version of this model. These correlation coefficients range between .11 and .31 across the alternative specifications in the AD Investigations model and are statistically significant at conventional levels in three out of five instances. These values range between .20 and .30 for the AD Cases model where it fails to obtain statistical significance at conventional levels in only one particular instance. Please consult Appendix D for detailed information on the robustness of these VAR model specifications.

50. The positive president-AD contemporaneous innovation results hold in every version of this model. These correlation coefficients range between .03 and .19 across the alternative specifications in the AD Investigations model and fail to obtain statistical significance at conventional levels in each instance. These values range between .08 and .18 for the AD Cases model where it also fails to obtain statistical significance at conventional levels in each instance. Please consult Appendix D for detailed information on the robustness of these VAR model specifications.

51. The negative congressional-AD contemporaneous innovation results hold in every version of this model. These correlation coefficients range between −.44 and −.61 across each of the alternative specifications in the AD Investigations model, and are statistically significant in every instance. These values range between −.16 and −.29 for the AD Cases

model where it fails to obtain statistical significance at conventional levels except in one instance. Please consult Appendix D for detailed information on the robustness of these VAR model specifications.

52. These results are robust to alternative variable orderings.

53. These results are robust to alternative variable orderings.

54. These results are not sensitive to alternative variable orderings, and are consistent across alternative model specifications.

55. These results are sensitive to switching variable orderings between the Congress and AD variables. However, switching the order of these variables still displays strong support for this finding (nearly 60% of the forecast error variance in AD investigations activity is the result of its own innovations). Furthermore, this particular set of results is consistent across alternative model specifications, save one instance where most of the congressional appropriation signals' series forecast error variance is not explained by presidential innovations, but instead by congressional innovations by a sizeable amount. The President-Congress-Agency ordering is employed here for substantive and theoretical reasons described earlier in this chapter.

56. This is consistent with conventional wisdom on executive-legislative relations on budgetary matters (Davis, Dempster, and Wildavsky 1974; Kiewiet and McCubbins 1988, 1991; Wildavsky 1964).

57. The findings generated from this study do indicate that Congress and the president influence SEC behavior to some limited extent. However, neither of these institutions is the sole preeminent force explaining administrative behavior.

58. These works ardently claim that internal bureaucratic factors—such as creation of a policy office or the balance between economists and attorneys—play a large role in determining the type of antitrust cases pursued by the Antitrust Division. Examination of the models tested in this study reveals modest support at best for the notion that internal bureaucratic factors impact AD aggregate regulatory vigor.

59. This result is, however, not robust across various alternative VAR models of antitrust investigatory activity as was noted earlier in this chapter. Specifically, in some instances, there is only evidence of *bureaucratic influence.* Therefore, in the AD Investigations model there seems to exist relatively greater empirical evidence that AD behavior influences congressional appropriation signals, than vice-versa.

5. Democratic Governance in the Modern Administrative State

1. This assertion is also made by Eisner (1991, 45–46) in his analysis of the AD role in antitrust regulation.

2. For an opposing viewpoint see Carpenter (1992, 1996), Moe (1982, 1985a), Wood (1990), Wood and Anderson (1993).

3. Not all research is subject to this problem (Moe 1982, 1985a; Weingast and Moran 1983; Weingast 1984).

4. Bendor and Moe (1985: 772) do state that future research needs to explore more com-

plex forms of dynamic adaptive behavior. This study has attempted to do so by investigating unanticipated responses to shocks in the Presidential-Congressional-Agency system.

5. In all fairness, static models tend to be more tractable than dynamic models because of the former's greater degree of simplification. Tractability is an important consideration, especially in formal analysis of such institutions.

6. One such example is Meier, Wrinkle, and Polinard's (1995) empirical investigation of political control over U.S. agricultural policy.

7. This point is further substantiated by the fact that the contemporaneous correlation of the innovations between the agency and political institutions is generally larger in the AD models than in the SEC models.

8. Political institutions may (and do) influence bureaucratic behavior through different patterns of behavior, transmitted in an alternative form not envisioned by these conventional principal-agent models. These issues need further exploration in future research.

9. Classic public bureaucracy works by Herbert Kaufman (1981) and James Q. Wilson (1989) echo this sentiment. Both works convincingly argue that while administrative agencies seek discretionary authority, they also possess a strong interest in maintaining or enhancing their reputation with elected officials.

10. For example, Bendor and Moe (1985) and Wood and Waterman (1993, 1994) use this terminology.

11. A formal theoretical model was not applicable to this project for two reasons. First, the mathematical articulation of this framework would have invariably resulted in an intractable model because of the simultaneous incorporation of heterogeneity, behavioral complexity, imperfect information, and dynamic evolution. Second, a formal version of this theoretical model would be contradictory (and counterproductive) since this analysis sets forth a framework that relaxes many of the encumbering assumptions found in existing research. I leave an attempt to address these issues for future research by students of bureaucratic politics.

12. Kettl (1993: 408) supports this sentiment by stating that the accumulation of knowledge in public administration research has not been evident compared to other fields within political science, which have yielded integrated disparate approaches to theoretical issues as a means of theory building.

13. This declaration is at the center of Paul Appleby's classic books on politics and administration (1945, 1949).

Appendix B

1. Budgetary resources and agency enforcement activities appear to reflect institutional behavior, whether these tangible items appear in the form of signals (Bendor and Moe 1985; Carpenter 1992; Weingast and Moran 1983) or as substantive behavior of these institutions (Downs 1967; Lewis-Beck 1979; Meier 1987; Quirk 1981; Seidman and Gilmour 1986; Weingast 1984; Wilson 1989; Yates 1982). In addition, budgets and agency output serve as the foundation of analysis for many positive theories of administrative politics (e.g., Banks

1989; Banks and Weingast 1992; Bendor and Moe 1985; Miller and Moe 1983; Niskanen 1971).

2. Although there are many different instruments that politicians can use to influence bureaucratic behavior (e.g., administrative design, oversight activity, executive orders, etc.), agency budgets are analyzed for the purposes of this study. It is also true that administrative outputs serve as only one dimension (or indicator) of agency policy and therefore cannot universally describe all aspects of bureaucratic agency-political institution relationships.

3. It is true that administrative policy outputs describe only a significant portion and not all aspects of regulatory behavior (Gormley 1989; Ringquist 1995; Wood and Anderson 1993). A vast majority of prior empirical research, however, bases its conclusions on such data. For the purposes of this study, personal interviews of agency personnel at the SEC and relevant staff at OMB, CBO, and on congressional committees generally concur that bureaucratic outputs are an accurate, *albeit imperfect*, reflection of agency regulatory performance (Krause 1994).

4. In other words, some enforcement actions involve much greater effort and are more important than others. Many agencies (including the SEC) do not have detailed workload statistics for each enforcement output (e.g., number of employee hours spent per case). However, as argued earlier in chapter 2 (note 13), it is extremely likely that aggregation effects among individual cases will cancel out such workload differences.

5. This individual informed me that these types of finely detailed measures are not kept by the SEC; therefore, the agency and its political principals have no way to gauge such factors.

Appendix C

1. There are a few examples where students of administrative politics have modeled agency behavior in a systems fashion. Terry Moe's (1985a) classic study of agency-political relations at the National Labor Relations Board (NLRB) examines endogeneity in terms of agency decision making. Moe's approach, however, only captures the "systems" aspect of the agency decision-making process, while not relating it to the larger political environment. In a major contribution to the subject of regulatory federalism, B. Dan Wood (1992) sets forth an elegant, two-tiered (hierarchical) principal-agent model of clean air regulatory enforcement in a federal system. Wood's "systems" model of federal policy implementation acknowledges this endogeneity from an intergovernmental dimension by incorporating mutual interdependence between national and subnational bureaucratic outputs but does not relate it to political principals. Neither Moe's nor Wood's basis for this causal uncertainty, however, deals with political principals. As a result, there is a substantial difference in the theory and empirical modeling underlying the dynamic systems model of administrative politics proposed in this book and those proposed by Moe and Wood, because the latter studies do not treat the president, Congress, and the bureaucracy as an *endogenous* system of institutional participants.

2. This modeling approach is also consistent with the prevailing view of administrative

politics that the policy model of bureaucratic implementation involves the interaction between government agencies and other democratic institutions (Meier 1987; Rourke 1984).

3. For more information on this concept and other concepts germane to VAR modeling, please see political science applications (such as Williams and McGinnis 1988; Freeman, Williams, and Lin 1989; Freeman et al. 1998; Goldstein and Freeman 1991), or economic treatments (such as Enders 1995; Hamilton 1994; Litterman 1984; Litterman and Weiss 1985; Sims 1980, 1981, 1982, 1986, 1987, 1988; Sims, Stock, and Watson 1990; Runkle 1987a, 1987b).

4. A variable (y_t) "Granger causes" another variable (x_t) if, by incorporating the past history of the former variable (y_t), one can improve a prediction of the variable (x_t) based only upon the past history of this variable (x_t) (Granger 1969; Freeman 1983; Wood 1992).

5. These exogeneity tests are rather powerful, though there is always a chance for mistaken inference (Freeman, Williams, and Lin 1989). In the nonstationary noncointegrated case, these tests provide information on *strict* exogeneity (Granato and Smith 1994). Engle, Hendry, and Richard (1983) contend that *weak* exogeneity is only necessary for the estimation of certain types of structural models. By the same token, however, this implies that weak exogeneity will not always (and conclusively) be sufficient for properly estimating all structural models. In situations where weak exogeneity is not sufficient for structural model estimation, this deficiency will lead to erroneous results and causal inferences, especially if (a) multiple competing theories exist, and/or (b) the nature of the autoregressive process is not known with precision. To be conservative, the concept of strict exogeneity is central to this study.

6. In this discussion, nonstochastic variables are assumed to have a *deterministic* nature (i.e., none of these variables ever appear on the left-hand side of any equation). The concept of exogeneity and how it relates to this study will be discussed throughout this section. Those interested in the meaning of econometric exogeneity can refer to Engle, Hendry, and Richard (1983), Freeman (1983), Freeman, Williams, and Lin (1989), and Granger (1969).

7. This is verified by testing each series for the existence of nonstationarity in the time series (i.e., unit roots that may lead to possible cointegration within the *endogenous* portion of the model) by variants of the Dickey-Fuller unit root test (see appendix D for the results of these tests). From past intuition and experience, it is likely that the endogenous variables in the VAR system will probably suffer from this problem since budgetary and appropriations data tend to be nonstationary time series. The use of logged-differenced series in the endogenous portion of the VAR model will lead to conservative estimates for both the endogenous and the deterministic effects in these VAR models. If the results of these tests reveal that the problem of cointegration exists, then the long-run dynamics of political-bureaucratic equilibrium could be addressed via an error correction approach (Beck 1987; Durr 1992a, 1992b; Engle and Granger 1987; Granger and Newbold 1986; Ostrom and Smith 1993), although this is a source of some controversy in VAR modeling (Freeman 1993; Freeman et al. 1998; Sims, Stock, and Watson 1990; Williams 1993).

8. Williams and McGinnis (1992: 295) note that decision rules of actors (institutions) may be temporally unstable. Goldstein and Freeman (1990) acknowledge (and live with) this form of model instability. Both sets of authors imply that only *permanent*—not *tempo-*

rary—instability in the model's parameters has deleterious consequences for the results of the model. According to Williams and McGinnis (1992), using past information produces a dynamic model that is more realistic than one trying to account for changing decision rules, which themselves change in the future. This line of argument is supported by Litterman's (1980) findings, which suggest that correcting for instability in VAR estimates actually results in poorer forecasts.

9. Currently, there is no way of correcting this dilemma within the context of exogeneity tests. However, this should not have deleterious consequences since the F-block tests do not take into account the impact of contemporaneous policy innovations (Freeman, Williams, and Lin 1989). This makes it necessary for VAR modelers to complement these exogeneity tests with a dynamic MAR exercise. Such a result may occur when a pair of institutions are connected through contemporaneous response to shocks that may in certain instances be indicative of rational expectations (Freeman, Williams, and Lin 1989; Krause 1997; Williams and McGinnis 1988).

10. The VAR representation is not theoretically parsimonious; therefore, it is difficult to ascertain the significance of individual *endogenous* variables in the system (Sims 1980; Hsaio 1981; Freeman, Williams, and Lin 1989). The individual regression coefficients for these variables are not efficient because of the overparameterized nature of VAR models and the inclusion of unnecessary "blocks" of right-hand-side variables (Freeman, Williams, and Lin 1989). However, the efficiency of the t-tests on the deterministic variables should not pose a problem, since these variables are strictly exogenous to the VAR system.

11. Empirically, for this particular empirical test policy actors may possess rational expectations when the following conditions exist: (a) neither series (variable) "Granger causes" the other, and (b) the contemporaneous errors of these equations are significantly correlated (Williams and McGinnis 1988; but see Goldstein and Freeman 1991 for a modified viewpoint).

12. The method used here to analyze the MAR simulation exercise is Choleski factorization. This method factors the covariance matrix of the policy innovations into a triangular matrix, which produces an ordered chain of innovations. For the purposes of this study, this ordered chain of innovations means that the first variable (president) influences all others contemporaneously, the second variable (Congress) affects all but the first variable contemporaneously, and the third variable (SEC or AD) alters neither the first (president) nor the second (Congress) contemporaneously. Brady and Bartels (1993: 126–27) claim unfairly that by using Choleski factorization (nonstructural VAR), such an ordering is "letting theory in the back door." The contemporaneous assumptions inherent in VAR models are often based, however, on the temporal sequence realities of political processes (see Williams and McGinnis 1992: 295). Furthermore, this type of factorization does not necessarily eliminate the influence of lower ordered variables, since both the MAR innovation accounting exercise and the decomposition of the forecast error variance for each equation is analyzed over not one (contemporaneous) period, but over a lengthy time horizon (eight periods in this study).

13. In addition, VAR analysts use robustness checks (i.e., alternative orderings) in instances when the contemporaneous correlation between any two variables is high, so as to make sure that the correct contemporaneous ordering of the innovations is selected. The recent attempts at more theoretically informed means to analyze VAR models—often termed structural (decompositions) VARs (Bernanke 1986)—also make certain restrictions on behavioral relations by placing their own "theoretically implied" a priori restrictions on the variance-covariance matrix of the innovations, producing results that are rather sensitive to these restrictions as well as to model specification choices (see Bernanke and Blinder 1992; Freeman 1993: 8, n. 13; Hamilton 1994: 324–36). For these purposes an unrestricted VAR approach is preferable. At least in this sense, these "structural" VARs are subject to similar criticisms concerning the role of theory in the VAR approach made by Brady and Bartels (1993), Cooley and LeRoy (1985), Leamer (1985), Runkle (1987a, 1987b), and others who criticize the use of unrestricted (nonstructural) VAR models.

14. The term "orthogonalization" refers to the assumption that the shocks in the first sequential variable in the VAR model have an immediate impact on all other variables in the system; the shocks in the second sequential variable have an immediate impact on all variables in the system except for the first sequential variable; and so on, until finally the last sequential variable in the model has only an immediate impact on itself (Freeman, Williams, and Lin 1989). The orthogonalization process for a system of equations may be sensitive to the ordering of the variables. In these instances, a theoretically based a priori assumption about the structure of the MAR process must be made (Sims 1981; Litterman 1984; Freeman, Williams, and Lin 1989).

15. Relating to equation C-1, v_t represents a *"policy innovation"* in the sense that this represents the proportion of change in each of the endogenous VAR variables that cannot be predicted using historical values of these same variables and the deterministic variables specified in the VAR model.

16. The results of this simulation exercise should be interpreted with caution since it is based upon a reduced form, not a structural equation (Freeman, Williams, and Lin 1989).

17. The cointegrating regression is a two-stage procedure. If one wishes to implement an ADF(1) cointegration test assuming a random walk with a deterministic trend as the null hypothesis, the first stage entails estimating a conventional regression model with ordinary least squares (OLS) in the following form:

$$Y_t = \alpha + \beta X_t + \delta T + u_t$$

where Y_t is the dependent series, X_t is a vector of independent variables, T is a time trend variable, and u_t is an independently and identically distributed error term. The second stage involves estimating the residuals from the first stage in first difference form:

$$\Delta u_1 = \alpha + \lambda u_{t-1} + \eta(\Delta u_{t-1}) + v_t$$

where α, λ, and η are estimated parameters, Δu_t is the first differenced residuals from the first stage regression, u_{t-1} is the lagged (one period) residual term, (Δu_{t-1}) is the first difference of the lagged (one period) residual term, and v_t constitutes a noise term. If the test statistic is significant, then one can conclude that Y_t and X_t are first-order cointegrated time series, $C(1,1)$.

18. The Johansen (1988, 1991) system cointegration procedure can be viewed compactly as:

$$\Delta x_t = A_0 + \sum_{i=1}^{n} A_i\, x_{t\text{-}i} - x_{t\text{-}i} + \epsilon_t$$

$$= A_0 + (\sum_{i=1}^{n} A_i - I)x_{t-1} + \epsilon_t$$

$$= A_0 + \pi x_{t-1} + \epsilon_t$$

where x_t and ϵ_t are n x 1 vectors of variables and residual terms, A_0 is n x 1 vector of constants to allow for drift, A_1 is an n x n matrix of parameters associated with the vector of variables and corresponding i lags, I is an n x n identity matrix, and π is $(A - I)$. The rank of π is equal to the number of cointegrating vectors (r).

The test statistic for determining the appropriate cointegrating rank is the Maximum Eigenvalue statistic (λ_{Max}):

$$\lambda_{Max}(r) = -T \ln (1 - \hat{\lambda}_{ir+1})$$

where T equals the number of usable observations, $\hat{\lambda}$ is the estimated values of the eigenvalues (i.e., characteristic roots) obtained from the estimated π matrix of parameters, and r equals the cointegrating rank.

19. The calculation of the Q-statistic is limited to six lags, since the number of lags taken into account should not exceed the square root of the total sample size (Hosking 1980). Lag lengths that exceed this criterion will result in a significant loss in statistical power. The effective sample size for the models presented here is either 38 (SEC models) or 37 (AD models), depending on the number of lags included in each VAR model.

20. The recursive residuals test statistic is given by the following equation:

$$w_t = \frac{y_t - x'_t\, b_{t\text{-}1}}{(1 + x'(X'_{t\text{-}1} X_{t\text{-}1})^{-1} x_t)^{1/2}}$$

where $w_t \sim N(0, \sigma^2)$ and w_t and w_s are independent of one another. The CUSUM test is a cumulated sum plot based upon recursive residuals. Its formula is given by the following equation:

$$W_t = \sum w_t / s$$

where w_t is the recursive residuals and **s** is the standard error of regression fitted to all n sample points. The results of these tests can be obtained by contacting the author.

21. VAR models are estimated via ordinary least squares (OLS). OLS estimation is appropriate since each of the same (endogenous) variables appears in the right-hand side for each equation (Sims 1980; Goldstein and Freeman 1991; Theil 1971; Williams and McGinnis 1988).

Appendix D

1. The Augmented Dickey-Fuller (ADF) tests are employed since the error term of each series is not independent (Cromwell, Labys, and Terreza 1994; Dickey and Fuller 1979; Enders 1995; Hamilton 1994). The ADF(1) test includes a lagged first-difference term as an independent variable in this unit root test procedure.

2. Additional tests were performed for cointegration just between the president's budget request and congressional appropriations for each respective agency. Both the Engle-Granger two-step method of performing an Augmented Dickey-Fuller test on the residuals from the cointegrating regression and the Johansen cointegration test procedure indicated that these cointegration tests failed to reject the hypothesis of non-cointegration at conventional significance levels.

3. The results of the Engle and Granger cointegration tests are substantively identical in the less powerful versions of this test.

4. According to Hamilton (1994: 652), an appropriately modeled VAR in differences will improve the small-sample properties of the statistical model—an important point to consider since I am working with small sample sizes in this study. These diagnostics clearly indicate that the appropriate specification is a VAR in differences (not a VAR in levels or a Vector Error Correction Modeling approach [VECM]). Moreover, the recent time series econometric literature emphasizes the importance of not analyzing nonstationary—e.g., I(1)—time series in levels within a VAR framework (Cromwell, Labys, and Terreza 1994; Engle and Granger 1987; Hamilton 1994; Sims, Stock, and Watson 1993; Toda and Phillips 1993).

5. Within the theoretical framework presented here the opposite may also hold true. In other words, the agency can emit signals of its own through its regulatory enforcement behavior to political principals.   .

6. This method of computing annual percentage changes has a number of advantages. First, the use of natural logs allows one to express relations between variables as proportional changes. For example, instead of stating that a one *unit* change in presidential budgetary requests has Z *unit* change on the total number of administrative proceedings initiated in a given year, one can state that a one *percent* change in the former leads to a Z *percent* change in the latter. Second, using a baseline (denominator value) of X_{t-1} will overestimate changes in X, while a baseline employing X_t will underestimate changes when there is a large change from one year to another. The use of natural logs is a nice middle ground, since one is not dividing through the previous or current value of the variable under investigation.

7. These results also held true in 2 preliminary analyses that calculated the annual percentage change of these variables in nonlogarithmic form.

8. Goldstein and Freeman (1990) treat periods of temporary instability as part of their sample period. They define significant structural change as a *permanent* break (or shift) in model stability. The temporary instability found in this analysis is not nearly as severe as the Goldstein and Freeman (1990) case since it only lasts for a single year (n = 1 period, or about 2 percent of the sample period—not reported here) as opposed to a five-and-a-half-year temporary break (n = 66 periods, or about 22 percent of their sample period). As a result,

the relatively meager nature of temporary parameter instability found in this study allows one to presume it most unlikely that this should pose a problem with the data analysis presented here.

9. A finding of a *permanent* structural break (or change) would be represented by a residual plot that went beyond the 5 percent–level confidence bands without returning for the duration of the sample period.

10. The Wald F-test for exclusion of real GNP growth and 1987 Stock Market Crash event variables for the President equation is: F-statistic = .58 (p = .57), for the Congress equation: F-statistic = .31 (p = .74), and for the SEC equation: F-statistic = .65 (p = .53).

11. The Wald F-tests for exclusion of real GNP growth and House subcommittee policy liberalism variables for the President equation is: F-statistic = .11 (p = .90), for the Congress equation: F-statistic = 1.98 (p = .17), and for the SEC equation: F-statistic = 1.38 (p = .28).

12. The Wald F-tests for exclusion of the House subcommittee policy liberalism and 1987 Stock Market Crash event variables for the President equation is: F-statistic = .44 (p = .65), for the Congress equation: F-statistic = 1.25 (p = .31), and for the SEC equation: F-statistic = .07 (p = .93).

13. The AD cases variable exhibits a significant ADF coefficient at the 5 percent level when both a constant and a trend term are included. Inspection of the correlogram revealed that this series reflects a near-stationary time series process (DeBoef and Granato 1997). Given both this condition and the failure to reject the unit root hypothesis in the other two variants of this test, this variable is also transformed into log first-difference percentage form in order to ensure stationarity.

14. The results of the Engle and Granger cointegration tests were substantively identical in the less powerful versions of this test.

15. Preliminary analysis revealed that a VAR(4) model suffered from a serial correlation problem in the Antitrust Division equation (Antitrust Division Cases model), while the same VAR order suffered from the same problem in the Congress equation (Antitrust Investigations model).

16. Although congressional oversight committee preferences are considered noteworthy explanatory factors in explaining administrative behavior in the area of antitrust regulation (Wood and Anderson 1993), this variable's exclusion from this antitrust model specification is not astonishing given the qualitative evidence to the contrary. For instance, Eisner (1991: 43) purports that congressional oversight in antitrust regulation is ineffectual because it is not a top congressional priority relative to legislative activity and constituency service (Dodd and Schott 1979; Fiorina 1977; Ogul 1976; Scher 1963; but see Aberbach 1990 for an opposing viewpoint on this general issue). The interviews conducted for this study lend convincing anecdotal support for this former position. A top official at the Antitrust Division believes that congressional oversight activity plays an impotent and intermittent role in affecting the agency's enforcement behavior. This sentiment was echoed by a top staff member on the committee on appropriations for the House Judiciary Committee who insists that "most oversight committees do not have as close of a relationship with bureaucratic agencies compared to appropriations committees" (interview with author, June 1993).

17. The Wald F-tests for exclusion of these deterministic variables are F-statistic = .67 (p = .66) for the President equation, F-statistic = .92 (p = .50) for the Congress equation, F-statistic = .85 (p = .54) for the AD equation.

18. Alternative formulations of the fully specified VAR model were explored. The best rival specifications included the following deterministic variables: (a) economist to attorney ratio, Reagan administration dummy, unemployment rate, and Hart-Scott-Rodino Antitrust Improvements Act dummy; and (b) Reagan administration and unemployment rate. The former model specification failed the Ramsey RESET test at least once in each equation (in the President and Congress equations - p < .05). The latter model specification suffered from omitted variables problem in the President equation as well as a marginally significant first-order Ramsey RESET test (p = .06) in the AD equation. Therefore, a decision was to use the model appearing in the presentation of the statistical results since it was the best specification that could be obtained and performs relatively better than these alternative models. In terms of the statistical results, the reported VAR Antitrust Cases model presented in chapter 4 is substantively very similar to these two alternative models in terms of the general pattern of impulse responses, decomposition of the forecast error variance with only a couple of exceptions. First, only lagged presidential and congressional budgetary signals are temporally prior to current presidential request signals in model (b). Specifically, AD enforcement signals miss obtaining a statistically significant impact on presidential budgetary signals to the AD (p = .14) in this model. Second, the contemporaneous correlation of the innovations between the President and Congress is marginally significant (p < .10) in model (b), and the same goes for Congress and AD in model (a). Also, the addition of the economist to attorney ratio to the President equation in the VAR system in model (a) drops the significance of the Hart-Scott-Rodino dummy from p < .01 to p = .09. However, the reported model's results provide a better fit to the data for the President equation.

19. The Wald F-tests for exclusion of these determinist variables are F-statistic = 2.50 (p = .07) for the President equation, F-statistic = 2.40 (p = .08) for the Congress equation, F-statistic = .83 (p = .57) for the AD equation.

20. The EPO trend (deterministic) variable remained the same sign and obtained statistical significance in both the President and Congress equations for four out of five instances, besides the model specification reported in chapter 4. However, the economist to attorney ratio variable is significant in the Congress equation in only one out of five variants of the Antitrust Investigations model.

21. The alternative analyses of the Antitrust Investigations model reveal that the impulse responses and decomposition of the forecast variance for each series in the system are substantively consistent across all model specifications, including the ones reported here.

Bibliography

Aberbach, Joel D. 1990. *Keeping a Watchful Eye: The Politics of Congressional Oversight.* Washington, D.C.: Brookings Institution.

Aberbach, Joel D., and Bert A. Rockman. 1976. "Clashing Beliefs within the Bureaucracy: The Nixon Administration Bureaucracy." *American Political Science Review* 70: 456–68.

Addlyston Pipe and Steel Company v. United States [1899].

Akaike, H. 1974. "A New Look at the Statistical Identification Model." *IEEE: Trans. Auto. Control* 19: 716–23.

ALCOA v. United States [1945].

Allison, Graham. 1971. *Essence of a Decision: Explaining the Cuban Missile Crisis.* Boston: Little, Brown.

Amacher, Ryan C., Richard S. Higgins, William F. Shugart, and Robert D. Tollison. 1985. "The Behavior of Regulatory Activity over the Business Cycle: An Empirical Test." *Economic Inquiry* 23: 7–20.

Amemiya, Takeshi. 1985. *Advanced Econometrics.* Cambridge, Mass.: Harvard University Press.

American Tobacco Corporation v. United States [1911].

Anderson, James E. 1986. "The Reagan Administration, Antitrust Action, and Policy Change." Paper presented at the annual meeting of the Midwest Political Science Association Meetings, Chicago, Illinois. April.

———. 1990. *Public Policymaking.* Boston: Houghton Mifflin.

Appleby, Paul H. 1945. *Big Democracy.* New York: Alfred Knopf.

———. 1949. *Policy and Administration.* Tuscaloosa: University of Alabama Press.

Arnold, Perri E. 1986. *Making the Managerial Presidency: Comprehensive Reorganization Planning, 1905–1980.* Princeton, N.J.: Princeton University Press.

Arnold, R. Douglas. 1987. "Political Control of Administrative Officials." *Journal of Law, Economics, and Organization* 3: 279–86.

Arrow, Kenneth. 1985. "The Economics of Agency." In *Principals and Agents: The Structure of Business,* ed. John Pratt and Richard J. Zeckhauser. Cambridge, Mass.: Harvard University Press.

Asch, Peter. 1975. "The Determinants and Effects of Antitrust Activity." *Journal of Law and Economics* 18: 571–81.

Austen-Smith, David. 1987. "Sophisticated Sincerity: Voting over Endogenous Agendas." *American Political Science Review* 81: 1323–29.

Banks, Jeffrey S., and Barry R. Weingast. 1992. "The Political Control of Bureaucracies under Asymmetric Information." *American Journal of Political Science* 36: 509–24.

Barnard, Chester I. 1938. *The Functions of the Executive.* Cambridge, Mass.: Harvard University Press.

Bartels, Larry M. 1991. "Instrumental and 'Quasi-Instrumental' Variables." *American Journal of Political Science* 35: 777–800.

Baruch, Hurd. 1971. *Wall Street: Security Risk.* Washington, D.C.: Acropolis Books.

Beck, Nathaniel. 1987. "Alternative Dynamic Specifications of Popularity Functions." Paper presented at the annual meeting of the Political Methodology Group, Durham, North Carolina. August.

———. 1992. "Comparing Dynamic Specifications: The Case of Presidential Approval." *Political Analysis* 3: 51–87.

Bendor, Jonathan, and Terry M. Moe. 1985. "An Adaptive Model of Bureaucratic Politics." *American Political Science Review* 79: 755–74.

———. 1986. "Agenda Control, Committee Capture, and the Dynamics of Institutional Politics." *American Political Science Review* 80: 1187–207.

Bendor, Jonathan, Serge Taylor, and Roland Van Gaalen. 1985. "Bureaucratic Expertise versus Legislative Authority: A Model of Deception and Monitoring in Budgeting." *American Political Science Review* 79: 1041–60.

———. 1987. "Politicians, Bureaucrats, and Asymmetric Information." *American Journal of Political Science* 31: 796–828.

Bernanke, Ben S. 1986. "Alternative Explanations of the Money-Income Correlation." *Carnegie-Rochester Conference Series on Public Policy* 25: 49–100.

Bernanke, Ben S., and Alan S. Blinder. 1992. "The Federal Funds Rate and the Channels of Monetary Policy." *American Economic Review* 82: 901–21.

Bond, Jon R., and Richard Fleisher. 1990. *The President in the Legislative Arena.* Chicago: University of Chicago Press.

Bork, Robert H. 1978. *The Antitrust Paradox: A Policy at War with Itself.* New York: Basic Books.

Brady, Henry E., and Larry M. Bartels. 1993. "The State of Quantitative Political Methodology." In *Political Science: The State of the Discipline,* ed. Ada Finifter. 2d edition. Washington, D.C.: American Political Science Association.

Breton, Albert, and Ronald Wintrobe. 1975. "The Equilibrium Size of a Budget-Maximizing Bureau: A Note on Niskanen's Theory of Bureaucracy." *Journal of Political Economy* 82: 195–207.

Bryner, Gary C. 1987. *Bureaucratic Discretion: Law and Policy in Federal Regulatory Agencies.* New York: Pergamon Press.

Calvert, Randall, Matthew McCubbins, and Barry Weingast. 1989. "A Theory of Political Control of Agency Discretion." *American Journal of Political Science* 33: 588–610.

Calvert, Randall, Mark J. Moran, and Barry R. Weingast. 1987. "Congressional Influence over Policymaking: The Case of the FTC." In *Congress: Structure and Policy,* ed. Matthew D. McCubbins and Terry Sullivan. New York: Cambridge University Press.

Carpenter, Daniel P. 1992. "Presidential Budgetary Influence in Federal Regulation: The Phenomena of Loose Control." Paper presented at the annual meetings of the Midwest Political Science Association, Chicago, Illinois. April.

———. 1996. "Adaptive Signal Processing, Hierarchy, and Budgetary Control in Federal Regulation." *American Political Science Review* 90: 283–302.

Cary, William L. 1967. *Politics and the Regulatory Agencies.* New York: McGraw-Hill.

Chappell, Henry W. Jr., Thomas M. Havrilesky, and Rob Roy McGregor. 1993. "Partisan Monetary Policies: Presidential Influence Through the Power of Appointment." *Quarterly Journal of Economics* 108: 185–218.

Clarkson, Kenneth W., and Timothy J. Muris. 1981. *The Federal Trade Commission Since 1970.* Cambridge, England: Cambridge University Press.

Cohen, Jeffrey E. 1985. "Presidential Control of Independent Regulatory Commissions Through Appointment: The Case of the ICC." *Administration and Society* 17: 61–70.

———. 1992. *The Politics of Telecommunications Regulation: The States and Divestiture of AT&T.* Armonk, N.Y.: M. E. Sharpe.

Cohen, Michael D., and Robert Axelrod. 1984. "Coping with Complexity: The Adaptive Value of Changing Utility." *American Economic Review* 74: 30–42.

Cohodas, Nadine. 1986. "Reagan Seeks Relaxation of Antitrust Laws." *Congressional Weekly Report* 44: 187–92.

Cole, Richard L., and David A. Caputo. 1979. "Presidential Control of the Senior Civil Service: Assessing the Strategies of the Nixon Years." *American Political Science Review* 73: 399–413.

Congressional Quarterly Almanac. 1970. Washington, D.C.: Congressional Quarterly Press.

Cooley, Thomas F., and Stephen F. LeRoy. 1985. "Atheoretical Macroeconomics: A Critique." *Journal of Monetary Economics* 16: 283–308.

Cooper, Joseph, and William F. West 1988. "Presidential Power and Republican Government: The Theory and Practice of OMB Review of Agency Rules." *Journal of Politics* 50: 864–95.

Cox, James, Gregory Hager, and David Lowery. 1993. "Regime Change in Presidential and Congressional Budgeting: Role Discontinuity or Role Evolution." *American Journal of Political Science* 37: 88–118.

Cromwell, Jeff B., Walter C. Labys, and Michel Terraza. 1994. *Univariate Tests for Time Series Models.* Beverly Hills, Calif.: Sage Publications.

Crozier, Michel. 1964. *The Bureaucratic Phenomenon.* Chicago: University of Chicago Press.

Cyert, Richard M., and James G. March. 1963. *A Behavioral Theory of the Firm.* Englewood Cliffs, N.J.: Prentice-Hall.

Dahl, Robert A., and Charles E. Lindblom. 1953. *Politics, Economics, and Welfare.* New York: Harper and Row.

Davidson, J., David Hendry, F. Srba, and S. Yeo. 1978. "Econometric Modeling of the Aggregate Time-Series Relationship Between Consumers' Expenditure and Income in the United Kingdom." *Economic Journal* 8: 661–92.

Davis, Otto A., M. A. H. Dempster, and Aaron Wildavsky. 1966. "A Theory of the Budgetary Process." *American Political Science Review* 60: 529–47.

———. 1971. "On the Process of Budgeting II: An Empirical Study of Congressional Appropriations." In *Studies in Budgeting,* ed. R. F. Byrne, A. Charnes, W. W. Cooper, O. A. Davis, and D. Gilford, chap. 9. Amsterdam: North-Holland.

Derthick, Martha, and Paul J. Quirk. 1985a. *The Politics of Deregulation.* Washington, D.C.: Brookings Institution.

DeBoef, Suzanna, and Jim Granato. 1997. "Near-Integrated Data and the Analysis of Political Relationships." *American Journal of Political Science* 41: 619–40.

———. 1974. "Toward a Predictive Theory of the Federal Budgetary Process." *British Journal of Political Science* 4: 419–1452.

———. 1985b. "Why Regulators Chose to Deregulate." In *Regulatory Policy and the Social Sciences,* ed. Roger G. Noll. Berkeley and Los Angeles: University of California Press.

Dewey, Donald J. 1990. *The Antitrust Experiment in America.* New York: Columbia University Press.

Dickey, David A., and Wayne A. Fuller. 1979. "Distribution of the Estimators for Autoregressive Series with a Unit Root." *Journal of the American Statistical Association* 74: 427–31.

Dodd, Lawrence C., and Richard L. Schott. 1979. *Congress and the Administrative State.* New York: John Wiley and Sons.

Downs, Anthony. 1967. *Inside Bureaucracy.* Boston: Little, Brown.

Durant, Robert F. 1992. *The Administrative Presidency Revisited: Public Lands, the BLM, and the Reagan Revolution.* Albany, N.Y.: State University of New York Press.

Durr, Robert H. 1992a. "An Essay on Cointegration and Error Correction Models." *Political Analysis* 4: 185–228.

———. 1992b. "What Moves Policy Sentiment?" *American Political Science Review* 87: 158–70.

Dye, Thomas R. 1966. *Politics, Economics, and Public Policy.* Chicago: Rand McNally.

Eads, George C., and Michael Fix, eds. 1984. *Relief or Reform? Reagan's Regulatory Dilemma.* Washington, D.C.: Urban Institute.

Eavey, Cheryl L., and Gary J. Miller. 1984. "Bureaucratic Agenda Control: Imposition or Bargaining." *American Political Science Review* 78: 719–33.

Eisner, Marc A. 1991. *Antitrust and the Triumph of Economics: Institutions, Expertise, and Policy Change.* Chapel Hill: University of North Carolina Press.

———. 1992. "Agency Professionalization and Policy Change: The Case of the Federal Trade Commission." Paper presented at the annual meetings of the Midwest Political Science Association, Chicago, Illinois. April.

Eisner, Marc A., and Kenneth J. Meier. 1990. "Presidential Control Versus Bureaucratic Power: Explaining the Reagan Revolution in Antitrust." *American Journal of Political Science* 34: 269–87.

Eisner, Marc A., Jeffrey S. Worsham, and Evan J. Ringquist. 1993. "Professionalization, Political Control, and Regulatory Policy Change." Paper presented at the annual meetings of
the American Political Science Association, Washington, D.C. September.

Enders, Walter. 1995. *Applied Econometric Time Series.* New York: John Wiley and Sons.

Engle, Robert F. 1982. "Autoregressive Conditional Heteroskedasticity with Estimates of the
Variance of United Kingdom Inflation." *Econometrica* 50: 987–1008.

Engle, Robert F., and Clive W. J. Granger. 1987. "Co-integration and Error Correction: Representation, Estimation, and Testing." *Econometrica* 55: 251–76.

Engle, Robert F., David F. Hendry, Jean-François Richard. 1983. "Exogeneity." *Econometrica*
51: 277–304.

Epstein, David, and Sharyn O'Halloran. 1994. "Administrative Procedures, Information,
and Agency Discretion." *American Journal of Political Science* 38: 697–722.

Faith, Roger L., Donald R. Leavens, and Robert D. Tollison. 1982. "Antitrust Pork Barrel."
Journal of Law and Economics 15: 329–42.

Feldman, Martha S. 1989. *Order Without Design: Information Production and Policy Making.*
Stanford, Calif.: Stanford University Press.

Fenno, Richard. 1973. *Congressmen in Committees.* Boston: Little, Brown.

Fiorina, Morris P. 1974. *Representatives, Roll Calls, and Constituencies.* Lexington, Mass.:
Heath.

———. 1977. *Congress: Keystone of the Washington Establishment.* New Haven: Yale University
Press.

———. 1981. "Congressional Control of the Bureaucracy: A Mismatch of Incentives and Capabilities." In *Congress Reconsidered,* ed. Lawrence Dodd and Bruce Oppenheimer. Washington, D.C.: Congressional Quarterly Press.

———. 1982. "Legislative Choice of Regulatory Reforms: Legal Process or Administrative
Process." *Public Choice* 39: 33–66.

Freeman, J. Leiper. 1965. *The Political Process: Executive Bureau–Legislative Committee Relations.* New York: Random House.

Freeman, John R. 1983. "Granger Causality and the Time Series Analysis of Political Relationships." *American Journal of Political Science* 27: 327–58.

———. 1990. "Systematic Sampling, Temporal Aggregation, and the Study of Political Relationships." In *Political Analysis,* ed. James A. Stimson. Ann Arbor: University of Michigan Press.

———. 1993. "The Searchers I: Specification Uncertainty in the Study of Macro Politics."
Paper presented at the annual meetings of the American Political Science Association,
Washington, D.C. September.

Freeman, John R., John T. Williams, and Tse-min Lin. 1989. "Vector Autoregression and the
Study of Politics." *American Journal of Political Science* 33: 842–77.

Freeman, John R., Daniel Houser, Paul M. Kellstedt, and John T. Williams. 1998. "Long-
Memoried Processes, Unit Roots, and Causal Inference in Political Science." *American
Journal of Political Science* 42: 1289–1327.

Gaus, John. 1950. "Trends in the Theory of Public Administration." *Public Administration
Review* 10: 161–68.

Gerston, Larry N., Cynthia Fraleigh, and Robert Schwab. 1988. *The Deregulated Society.* Pacific Grove, Calif.: Brooks/Cole.

Geweke, John. 1989. "Bayesian Inference in Econometric Models Using Monte Carlo Integration." *Econometrica* 57: 1319–39.

Gildea, John A. 1990. "A Theory of Open Market Committee Voting Behavior." In *The Political Economy of American Monetary Policy*, ed. Thomas Mayer. Cambridge, England: Cambridge University Press.

Goldstein, Joshua S., and John R. Freeman. 1990. *Three-way Street: Strategic Reciprocity in World Politics.* Chicago: University of Chicago Press.

———. 1991. "U.S.-Soviet-Chinese Relations: Routine, Reciprocity, or Rational Expectations?" *American Political Science Review* 85: 17–35.

Goodnow, Frank J. 1900. *Politics and Administration.* New York: Macmillan.

Gorinson, Stanley M. 1985. "Antitrust Division Reorganized." *Antitrust* 7 (October): 18–19.

Gormley, William T. 1989. *Taming the Bureaucracy: Muscles, Prayers, and Other Strategies.* Princeton, N.J.: Princeton University Press.

Granato, Jim. 1992. "An Agenda for Econometric Model Building." *Political Analysis* 3: 123–54.

Granato, Jim, and Renee M. Smith. 1994. "Exogeneity, Inference, and Granger Causality: Part 1, The Stationary Case." *The Political Methodologist* 5(2): 24–28.

Granger, Clive W. J. 1969. "Some Recent Developments in a Concept of Causality." *Econometrica* 37: 424–38.

Granger, Clive W. J., and Paul Newbold. 1986. *Forecasting Economic Time Series.* 2d edition. Orlando: Academic Press.

Grier, Kevin. 1989. "On the Existence of a Political Monetary Cycle." *American Journal of Political Science* 33: 376–89.

———. 1991. "Congressional Influence on U.S. Monetary Policy: An Empirical Test." *Journal of Monetary Economics* 28(2): 201–20.

Gujarati, Damodar. 1984. *Government and Business.* New York: McGraw-Hill.

Gulick, Luther, and Lyndall Urwick, eds. 1937. *Papers on the Science of Administration.* New York: Columbia University Press.

Hamilton, James D. 1994. *Time Series Analysis.* Princeton, N.J.: Princeton University Press.

Hammersley, J. M., and D. C. Handscomb. 1964. *Monte Carlo Methods.* London: Chapman and Hall.

Hammond, Thomas H. 1984. "Agenda Control, Organizational Structure, and Bureaucratic Politics." *American Journal of Political Science* 28: 379–420.

Hammond, Thomas H., and Jack H. Knott. 1988. "The Deregulatory Snowball: Explaining Deregulation in the Financial Industry." *Journal of Politics* 50: 3–30.

———. 1993. "Presidential Power, Congressional Dominance, and Bureaucratic Autonomy in a Model of Multi-Institutional Policymaking." Paper presented at the annual meetings of the American Political Science Association, Washington, D.C. September.

———. 1996. "Who Controls the Bureaucracy? Presidential Power, Congressional Dominance, Legal Constraints, and Bureaucratic Autonomy in a Model of Multi-Institutional Policymaking." *Journal of Law, Economics, and Organization* 12: 119–66.

Hansen, Lars R., and Thomas J. Sargent. 1980. "Formulating and Estimating Dynamic Linear Rational Expectations Models." *Journal of Economic Dynamics and Control* 2: 7–46.

Heclo, Hugh. 1977. *A Government of Strangers: Executive Politics in Washington.* Washington, D.C.: Brookings Institution.

Hedge, David M., and Michael J. Scicchitano. 1994. "Regulating in Space and Time: The Case of Regulatory Federalism." *Journal of Politics* 56: 134–53.

Hendry, David F., Duo Qin, and Carlo Favero. 1989. *Lectures on Econometric Methodology.* Oxford: Oxford University Press.

Hibbs, Douglas A. 1977. "Political Parties and Macroeconomic Policy." *American Political Science Review* 71: 1467–87.

———. 1987. *The American Political Economy: Macroeconomics and Electoral Politics.* Cambridge, Mass.: Harvard University Press.

Hill, Jeffrey S., and James E. Brazier. 1991. "Constraining Administrative Decisions: A Critical Examination of the Structure and Process Hypothesis." *Journal of Law, Economics, and Organization* 7: 373–400.

Hofstadter, Richard. 1991. "What Happened to the Antitrust Movement." In *The Political Economy of the Sherman Act: The First One Hundred Years,* ed. E. Thomas Sullivan. New York: Oxford University Press.

Horn, Murray J., and Kenneth A. Shepsle. 1989. "Commentary on 'Administrative Arrangements and the Political Control of Agencies': Administrative Process and Organizational Form as Legislative Responses to Agency Costs." *Virginia Law Review* 75: 499–508.

Hosking, J. R. M. 1980. "The Multivariate Portmanteau Statistic." *Journal of American Statistical Association* 75: 369–72.

Hsiao, Cheng, 1981. "Autoregressive Modeling and Money-Income Causality Detection." *Journal of Monetary Economics* 7: 85–106.

Hult, Karen. 1987. *Agency Merger and Bureaucratic Design.* Pittsburgh, Pa.: University of Pittsburgh Press.

Inder, Brett. 1993. "Estimating Long-Run Relationships in Economics: A Comparison of Different Approaches." *Journal of Econometrics* 57: 53–68.

Johansen, Soren. 1988. "Statistical Analysis of Cointegration Vectors." *Journal of Economic Dynamics and Control* 12: 231–54.

———. 1991. "Estimation and Hypothesis Testing of Cointegration Vectors in Gaussian Vector Autoregressive Models." *Econometrica* 59: 1551–80.

Johansen, Soren, and Katarina Juselius. 1990. "Maximum Likelihood Estimation and Inference on Cointegration—with Applications to the Demand for Money." *Oxford Bulletin of Economics and Statistics* 52: 169–210.

Johnson, Cathy M. 1992. *The Dynamics of Conflict Between Bureaucrats and Legislators.* Armonk, N.Y.: M. E. Sharpe.

Jones, Charles O. 1984. *An Introduction to the Study of Public Policy.* Monterey, Calif.: Brooks/Cole.

Judge, George G., R. Carter Hill, W. E. Griffiths, Helmut Lutkepohl, and Tsoung-Chao Lee. 1985. *The Theory and Practice of Econometrics.* New York: John Wiley and Sons.

———. 1988. *Introduction to the Theory and Practice of Econometrics.* New York: John Wiley and Sons.

Kamlet, Mark S., and David C. Mowery. 1980. "The Budgetary Base in Federal Resource Allocation." *American Journal of Political Science* 24: 804–21.

Karmel, Roberta S. 1982. *Regulation by Prosecution: The Securities and Exchange Commission vs. Corporate America.* New York: Simon and Schuster.

Katzmann, Robert A. 1980. *Regulatory Bureaucracy: The Federal Trade Commission and Antitrust Policy.* Cambridge, Mass.: MIT Press.

Kaufman, Herbert. 1956. "Emerging Conflicts in the Doctrines of Public Administration." *American Political Science Review* 50: 1057–73.

———. 1981. *The Administrative Behavior of Federal Bureau Chiefs.* Washington, D.C.: Brookings Institution.

Kelman, Steven A. 1980. "Occupational and Safety and Health Administration." In *The Politics of Regulation,* ed. James Q. Wilson. New York: Basic Books.

Kettl, Donald F. 1993. "Public Administration: The State of the Field." In *Political Science: The State of the Discipline II,* ed. Ada W. Finifter. Washington, D.C.: American Political Science Association.

Khademian, Anne M. 1992. *The SEC and Capital Market Regulation: The Politics of Expertise.* Pittsburgh, Pa.: University of Pittsburgh Press.

Kiewiet, D. Roderick, and Matthew D. McCubbins. 1985. "Congressional Appropriations and the Electoral Connection." *Journal of Politics* 47: 59–82.

———. 1988. "Presidential Influence on Congressional Appropriation Decisions." *American Journal of Political Science* 32: 713–36.

———. 1991. *The Logic of Delegation: Congressional Parties and the Appropriations Process.* Chicago: University of Chicago Press.

King, Gary. 1989. *Unifying Political Methodology: The Likelihood Theory of Statistical Inference.* Cambridge, England: Cambridge University Press.

Kingdon, John. 1984. *Agendas, Alternatives and Public Policies.* Boston: Little, Brown.

Kirst, Michael W. 1969. *Government Without Passing Laws.* Chapel Hill: University of North Carolina Press.

Kloek, Teu, and Herman K. Van Dijk. 1978. "Bayesian Estimates of Equation System Parameters: An Application of Integration by Monte Carlo." *Econometrica* 46: 1–20.

Knott, Jack H., and Gary J. Miller. 1987. *Reforming Bureaucracy: The Politics of Institutional Choice.* Englewood Cliffs, N.J.: Prentice-Hall.

Kohlmeier, Louis M. 1969. *The Regulators.* New York: Harper and Row.

Krause, George A. 1994. *Politicians, Bureaucrats, and the Institutional Dynamics of Economic Regulation.* Ph.D. dissertation. West Virginia University. Morgantown, W. Va.

———. 1996. "The Institutional Dynamics of Policy Administration: Bureaucratic Influence over Securities Regulation." *American Journal of Political Science* 40: 1083–121.

———. 1997. "Policy Preference Formation and Subsystem Behaviour: The Case of Commercial Bank Regulation." *British Journal of Political Science* 25: 525–50.

———. 1998. "Uncertainty, Information Processing, and Organizational Response: A Positive Theory of Risk-Bearing Behavior in Public Bureaucracies." Paper presented at the annual meetings of the Midwest Political Science Association, Chicago, Illinois. April.

Leamer, Edward E. 1985. "Vector Autoregressions for Causal Inference?" *Carnegie-Rochester Conference Series on Public Policy* 22: 255–304.

Lewis-Beck, Michael S. 1979. "Maintaining Economic Competition: The Causes and Consequences of Antitrust." *The Journal of Politics* 41: 169–91.

Light, Paul C. 1991. *The President's Agenda: Domestic Policy Choice from Kennedy to Reagan.* 2d edition. Baltimore, Md.: Johns Hopkins University Press.

Lindblom, Charles E. 1959. "The Science of 'Muddling Through'." *Public Administration Review* 19: 79–88.

Lipsky, Michael. 1980. *Street-Level Bureaucracy: Dilemmas of the Individual in Public Service.* Beverly Hills, Calif.: Sage Publications.

Litterman, Robert B. 1980. *Techniques for Forecasting with Vector Autoregressions.* Ph.D. dissertation. University of Minnesota. Minneapolis, Minn.

———. 1984. *Specifying Vector Autoregressions for Macroeconomic Forecasting.* Staff Report 92. Minneapolis: Federal Reserve Bank of Minneapolis.

Litterman, Robert B., and Lawrence Weiss. 1985. "Money, Real Interest Rates, and Output: A Reinterpretation of Postwar U.S. Data." *Econometrica* 53: 129–56.

Long, Norton E. 1952. "Bureaucracy and Constitutionalism." *American Political Science Review* 46: 808–18.

Long, William F., Richard Schramm, and Robert Tollison. 1973. "The Economic Determinants of Antitrust Policy." *Journal of Law and Economics* 16: 351–64.

Loomis, Carol. 1968. "Big Board, Big Volume, Big Trouble." *Fortune* 77 (May): 146.

Lowi, Theodore J. 1969. *The End of Liberalism.* New York: Norton.

Lucas, Robert E. Jr., and Thomas J. Sargent, eds. 1981. *Rational Expectations and Econometric Practice.* Minneapolis: University of Minnesota Press.

Lutkepohl, Helmut. 1982. "Non-Causality due to Omitted Variables." *Journal of Econometrics* 19: 367–78.

———. 1990. "Asymptotic Distributions of Impulse Response Functions and Forecast Error Variance Decompositions of Vector Autoregressive Models." *Review of Economics and Statistics* 72: 116–25.

MacKay, Robert R., and Joseph D. Reid Jr. 1979. "On Understanding the Birth and Evolution of the Securities and Exchange Commission." In *Regulatory Change in an Atmosphere of Crisis: Current Implications of the Roosevelt Years,* ed. Gary M. Walton. New York: Academic Press.

MacKinnon, Dennis. 1990. "Critical Values for Cointegration Tests." Working paper, University of California, San Diego. January.

March, James G., and Johan P. Olsen. 1976. *Ambiguity and Choice in Organizations.* Bergen, Norway: Universitesforlaget.

———. 1984. "The New Institutionalism: Organizational Factors in Political Life." *American Political Science Review* 78: 734–49.

———. 1989. *Rediscovering Institutions: The Organizational Basis of Politics.* New York: Free Press.

March, James G., and Herbert A. Simon. 1958. *Organizations.* New York: Free Press.

Marcus, Alfred E. 1980. "Environmental Protection Agency." In *The Politics of Regulation,* ed. James Q. Wilson. New York: Free Press.

Mayhew, David. 1974. *Congress: The Electoral Connection.* New Haven: Yale University Press.

Mazmanian, Daniel A., and Paul A. Sabatier. 1983. *Implementation and Public Policy.* Glenview, Ill.: Scott, Foresman.

McCraw, Thomas K. 1984. *The Prophets of Regulation.* Cambridge, Mass.: Harvard University Press.

McCubbins, Matthew D. 1985. "Legislative Design of Regulatory Structure." *American Journal of Political Science* 29: 721–48.

McCubbins, Matthew D., Roger G. Noll, and Barry R. Weingast. 1987. "Administrative Procedures as Instruments of Political Control." *Journal of Law, Economics, and Organization* 3: 243–77.

———. 1989. "Structure and Process as Solutions to the Politicians Principal-Agency Problem." *Virginia Law Review* 74: 431–82.

McCubbins, Matthew D., and Talbot Page. 1987. "A Theory of Congressional Delegation." In *Congress: Structure and Policy,* ed. Matthew D. McCubbins and Terry Sullivan. New York: Cambridge University Press.

McCubbins, Matthew D., and Thomas Schwartz. 1984. "Congressional Oversight Overlooked: Police Patrols Versus Fire Alarms." *American Journal of Political Science* 28: 165–79.

Meier, Kenneth J. 1980. "Executive Reorganization of Government." *American Journal of Political Science* 24: 396–412.

———. 1985. *Regulation: Politics, Bureaucracy, and Economics.* New York: St. Martin's Press.

———. 1987. *Politics and the Bureaucracy: Policymaking in the Fourth Branch of Government.* 2d edition. Monterey, Calif.: Brooks/Cole.

———. 1993a. *Politics and the Bureaucracy: Policymaking in the Fourth Branch of Government.* 3d edition. Monterey, Calif.: Brooks/Cole.

———. 1993b. "Public Administration Theory and Applied Economics: Some Intemperate Remarks." *Administration and Politics: The Newsletter for the Section on Public Administration of the American Political Science Association* 3: 4–6.

———. 1994. *The Politics of Sin: Drugs, Alcohol, and Public Policy.* Armonk, N.Y.: M. E. Sharpe.

Meier, Kenneth J., J. L. Polinard, and Robert Wrinkle. 1995. "Politics, Bureaucracy, and Agricultural Policy: An Alternative View of Political Control." *American Politics Quarterly* 22: 427–60.

Miller, Gary J. 1992. *Managerial Dilemmas: The Political Economy of Hierarchy.* New York: Cambridge University Press.

Miller, Gary J., and Terry M. Moe. 1983. "Bureaucrats, Legislators, and the Size of Government." *American Political Science Review* 77: 297–322.

Mishkin, Frederic S. 1983. *A Rational Expectations Approach to Macroeconometrics.* Chicago: University of Chicago Press.

Mitnick, Barry M. 1980. *The Political Economy of Regulation.* New York: Columbia University Press.

Moe, Terry M. 1982. "Regulatory Performance and Presidential Administration." *American Journal of Political Science* 26: 197–224.

———. 1984. "The New Economics of Organization." *American Journal of Political Science* 28: 739–77.

———. 1985a. "Control and Feedback in Economic Regulation: The Case of the NLRB." *American Political Science Review* 79: 1094–116.

———. 1985b. "The Politicized Presidency." In *New Directions in American Politics,* ed. John E. Chubb and Paul E. Peterson. Washington, D.C.: Brookings Institution.

———. 1987a. "An Assessment of the Positive Theory of 'Congressional Dominance'." *Legislative Studies Quarterly* 12: 475–520.

———. 1987b. "Interests, Institutions, and Positive Theory: The Politics of the NLRB." In *Studies in American Political Development,* ed. Karen Orren and Stephen Skowronek, vol. 2, pp. 236–99.

———. 1988. "The Politics of Structural Choice: Toward a Theory of Public Bureaucracy." Paper presented at the annual meetings of the American Political Science Association, Washington, D.C. September.

———. 1989. "The Politics of Bureaucratic Structure." In *Can Government Govern?* ed. John E. Chubb and Paul Peterson. Washington, D.C.: Brookings Institution.

———. 1990. "The Politics of Structural Choice: Toward a Theory of Public Bureaucracy." In *Organization Theory from Chester Barnard to Present and Beyond,* ed. Oliver E. Williamson. New York: Oxford University Press.

———. 1993. "Presidents, Institutions, and Theory." In *Researching the Presidency: Vital Questions, New Approaches,* ed. George C. Edwards III, John H. Kessel, and Bert A. Rockman. Pittsburgh, Pa.: University of Pittsburgh Press.

Mosher, Frederick C. 1968. *Democracy in the Public Service.* New York: Oxford University Press.

Mueller, Willard F. 1986. "A New Attack on Antitrust: The Chicago Case." *Antitrust Law and Economics Review* 18: 29–66.

Muth, John F. 1961. "Rational Expectations and the Theory of Price Movements." *Econometrica* 29: 315–35.

Nathan, Richard. 1983. *The Administrative Presidency.* 1st edition. New York: John Wiley and Sons.

———. 1986. *The Administrative Presidency.* 2d edition. New York: John Wiley and Sons.

Nelson, William E. 1982. *The Roots of American Bureaucracy, 1830–1900.* Cambridge, Mass.: Harvard University Press.

Neustadt, Richard E. 1960. *Presidential Power: The Politics of Leadership.* New York: John Wiley and Sons.

Nickelburg, Gerald. 1985. "Small-Sample Properties of Dimensionality Statistics for Fitting VAR Models to Aggregate Economic Data: A Monte Carlo Study." *Journal of Econometrics* 28: 183–92.

Niskanen, William A. 1971. *Bureaucracy and Representative Government.* Chicago: Aldine-Atherton.

————. 1975. "Bureaucrats and Politicians." *Journal of Law and Economics* 18: 617–43.

Noll, Roger G. 1971. *Reforming Regulation.* Washington, D.C.: Brookings Institution.

Northern Securities Company v. United States [1904].

Ogul, Morris. 1976. *Congress Oversees the Bureaucracy.* Pittsburgh, Pa.: University of Pittsburgh Press.

O'Loughlin, Michael G. 1990. "What is Bureaucratic Accountability and How Can We Measure It?" *Administration and Society* 22: 275–303.

Ostrom, Charles T. Jr., and Renee Smith. 1993. "Error Correction, Attitude Persistence, and Executive Rewards and Punishment: A Behavioral Theory of Presidential Approval." *Political Analysis* 4: 127–83.

Padgett, John. 1980. "Bounded Rationality in Budgetary Research." *American Political Science Review* 74: 354–72.

————. 1981. "Hierarchy and Ecological Control in Federal Budgetary Decision Making." *American Journal of Sociology* 87: 75–129.

Perrow, Charles. 1986. *Complex Organizations: A Critical Analysis.* New York: Random House.

Peterson, Mark A. 1991. *Legislating Together: The White House and Capital Hill from Eisenhower to Reagan.* Cambridge, Mass.: Harvard University Press.

Pfiffner, James P. 1988. *The Strategic Presidency: Hitting the Ground Running.* Chicago: Dorsey Press.

Phillips, P. C. B. 1988. "Reflections on Econometric Methodology." *Economic Record* 64: 344–59.

Posner, Richard A. 1970. "A Statistical Study of Law Enforcement." *Journal of Law and Economics* 13: 365–419.

————. 1976. *Antitrust Law: An Economic Perspective.* Chicago: University of Chicago Press.

————. 1979. "The Chicago School of Antitrust Analysis." *University of Pennsylvania Law Review* 127: 48–105.

Pressman, Jeffrey L., and Aaron Wildavsky. 1973. *Implementation.* Berkeley and Los Angeles: University of California Press.

Quirk, Paul J. 1981. *Industry Influence in Federal Regulatory Agencies.* Princeton, N.J.: Princeton University Press.

————. 1988. "In Defense of the Politics of Ideas." *Journal of Politics* 50: 31–41.

Ramsey, James B. 1969. "Tests of Specification Error in the General Linear Model." *Journal of the Royal Statistical Society, B.* 31: 250–71.

Reagan, Michael D. 1987. *Regulation: The Politics of Policy.* Boston: Little, Brown.

Redford, Emmette S. 1969. *Democracy in the Administrative State.* New York: Oxford University Press.

Reimers, Hans-Eggert. 1992. "Comparisons of Tests for Multivariate Cointegration." *Statistical Papers* 33: 335–59.

Ringquist, Evan J. 1995. "Political Control and Policy Impact in EPA's Office of Water Quality." *American Journal of Political Science* 39: 336–63.

Ringquist, Evan J., Jeffrey Worsham, and Marc A. Eisner. 1994. "Double Agents—Who Is Working for Whom? Building a More Realistically Grounded Theory of Political Control of the Bureaucracy." Paper presented at the annual meetings of the Midwest Political Science Association, Chicago, Illinois. April.

Ripley, Randall B., and Grace A. Franklin. 1991. *Congress, the Bureaucracy, and Public Policy.* Homewood, Ill.: Dorsey Press.

Ritchie, Donald A. 1980. *James M. Landis: Dean of the Regulators.* Cambridge, Mass.: Harvard University Press.

Robinson, Glen O. 1989. "Commentary on 'Administrative Arrangements and the Political Control of Agencies': Political Uses of Structure and Processes." *Virginia Law Review* 75: 483–98.

Rockman, Bert A., and Kent R. Weaver. 1993. *Do Institutions Matter? Government Capabilities in the United States and Abroad.* Washington, D.C.: Brookings Institution.

Romer, Thomas, and Howard Rosenthal. 1978. "Political Resource Allocation, Controlled Agendas and the Status Quo." *Public Choice* 33: 27–44.

Ross, Stephen. 1973. "The Economic Theory of Agency: The Principal's Problem." *American Economic Review* 63: 134–39.

Rothenberg, Lawrence. 1994. *Regulations, Organizations, and Politics: Motor Freight Policy at the Interstate Commerce Commission.* Ann Arbor: University of Michigan Press.

Rourke, Francis E. 1984. *Bureaucracy, Politics, and Public Policy.* Boston: Little, Brown.

Runkle, David E. 1987a. "Vector Autoregressions and Reality." *Journal of Economics and Business Statistics* 5: 437–42.

———. 1987b. "Reply." *Journal of Economics and Business Statistics* 5: 454.

Rushefsky, Mark. 1990. *Public Policy in the United States: Toward the Twenty-First Century.* Monterey, Calif.: Brooks/Cole.

Sargent, Thomas J. 1984. "Autoregressions, Expectations, and Advice." *American Economic Review* 74: 408–15.

Scher, Seymour. 1963. "Conditions for Legislative Control." *Journal of Politics* 25: 526–51.

Schick, Allen. 1971. "Toward the Cybernetic State." In *Public Administration in a Time of Turbulence,* ed. Dwight Waldo. Scranton, Pa.: Chandler Publishing.

Scholz, John T., and Feng Heng Wei. 1986. "Regulatory Enforcement in a Federalist System." *American Political Science Review* 80: 1249–70.

Scholz, John T., Jim Twombly, and Barbara Headrick. 1991. "Home Style Political Controls over Federal Bureaucracy: OSHA Enforcement at the County Level." *American Political Science Review* 85: 829–51.

Schwartz, Bernard, ed. 1973. *The Economic Regulation of Business and Industry: A Legislative History of U.S. Regulatory Industry.* New York: Chelsea House.

Schwarz, Gideon. 1978. "Estimating the Dimension of a Model." *Annals of Statistics* 6: 461–64.

Seidman, Harold, and Robert Gilmour. 1986. *Politics, Position, and Power.* New York: Oxford University Press.

Seligman, Joel. 1982. *The Transformation of Wall Street: A History of the Securities and Exchange Commission and Modern Corporate Finance.* Boston: Houghton Mifflin.

———. 1985. *The SEC and the Future of Finance.* New York: Praeger.

Shapiro, Susan P. 1984. *Wayward Capitalists: Target of the Securities and Exchange Commission.* New Haven, Conn.: Yale University Press.

———. 1985. "The Road Not Taken: The Elusive Path to Criminal Prosecution for White-Collar Offenders." *Law and Society Review* 19: 179–217.

Shaw, Graham K. 1984. *Rational Expectations: An Elementary Exposition.* New York: St. Martin's Press.

Shepherd, William G. 1985. *Public Policies Towards Business.* Homewood, Ill.: Richard D. Irwin Publishing.

Shepsle, Kenneth A., and Barry R. Weingast. 1984. "The Institutional Foundations of Committee Power." *American Political Science Review* 81: 85–104.

Shugart, William F. II. 1987. "Don't Revise the Clayton Act, Scrap It!" *Cato Journal* 6: 925–32.

———. 1990. *Antitrust Policy and Interest Group Politics.* New York: Quorum Books.

Siegfried, John J. 1975. "The Determinants of Antitrust Activity." *Journal of Law and Economics* 18: 559–74.

Simon, Herbert A. 1947. *Administrative Behavior.* New York: Macmillan.

———. 1955. "A Behavioral Model of Rational Choice." *Quarterly Journal of Economics* 69: 99–118.

Simon, Herbert A., Donald W. Smithburg, and Victor A. Thompson. 1950. *Public Administration.* New York: Knopf.

Sims, Christopher A. 1980. "Macroeconomics and Reality." *Econometrica* 48: 1–48.

———. 1981. "An Autoregressive Index Model for the U.S., 1948–1975." In *Large-Scale Macroeconomic Models: Theory and Practice,* ed. Jan Kmenta and James B. Ramsey. New York: North-Holland.

———. 1982. "Policy Analysis with Econometric Models." *Brookings Papers on Economic Activity* 1: 107–52.

———. 1986. "Are Forecasting Models Usable for Policy Analysis?" *Federal Reserve Bank of Minneapolis Quarterly Review* 10: 2–16.

———. 1987. "Comment [on Runkle]." *Journal of Economics and Business Statistics* 5: 443–49.

———. 1988. "Bayesian Skepticism on Unit Root Econometrics." *Journal of Economic Dynamics and Control* 12: 463–74.

Sims, Christopher A., James H. Stock, and Mark W. Watson. 1990. "Inference in Linear Time Series Models with Some Unit Roots." *Econometrica* 58: 113–44.

Skocpol, Theda. 1992. *Protecting Soldiers and Mothers: The Political Origins of Social Policy in the United States.* Cambridge, Mass.: Harvard University Press.

Skowronek, Stephen. 1982. *Building a New American State: The Expansion of National Administrative Capabilities, 1877–1920.* Cambridge, England: Cambridge University Press.

Smith, Steven S., and Christopher Deering. 1984. *Committees in Congress.* Washington, D.C.: Congressional Quarterly Press.

Sobel, Robert. 1975. *N.Y.S.E.: A History of the New York Stock Exchange, 1935–1975.* New York: Weybright and Talley.

Standard Oil v. United States [1911].

Stewart, Joseph Jr., and Jane S. Cromartie. 1982. "Partisan Presidential Change and Regulatory Policy: The Case of the FTC and Deceptive Practices Enforcement." *Presidential Studies Quarterly* 12: 568–73.

Stigler, George J. 1971. "The Theory of Economic Regulation." *Bell Journal of Economics* 2(1): 3–21.

Straussman, Jeffrey. 1986. "Courts and Public Purse Strings: Have Portraits of Budgeting Missed Something?" *Public Administration Review* 46: 345–51.

Sullivan, E. Thomas. 1986. "The Antitrust Division as a Regulatory Agency: An Enforcement Policy in Transition." *Washington University Law Quarterly* 64: 997–1055.

Suzuki, Motoshi. 1991. "The Rationality of Economic Voting and the Macroeconomic Regime." *American Journal of Political Science* 35: 624–42.

Theil, Henri A. 1971. *Principles of Econometrics.* New York: John Wiley and Sons.

Thompson, Frank J., and Michael J. Scicchitano. 1985. "State Implementation Effort and Federal Regulatory Policy: The Case of Occupational Safety and Health." *Journal of Politics* 47: 686–703.

Toda, H., and Peter C. B. Phillips. 1993. "Vector Autoregressions and Causality." *Econometrica* 61: 1367–93.

Truman, David B. 1951. *The Governmental Process.* New York: Alfred Knopf.

Tufte, Edward R. 1978. *Political Control of the Economy.* Princeton, N.J.: Princeton University Press.

Tullock, Gordon. 1965. *The Politics of the Bureaucracy.* Washington, D.C.: Public Affairs Press.

Twombly, Jim. 1992. "Symbolic Reassurance and Substantive Response to Political Conditions by OSHA." Paper presented at the annual meetings of the Midwest Political Science Association, Chicago, Illinois. April.

United States Steel Corporation v. United States [1920].

United States v. General Dynamics [1974].

United States v. Marine Bancorporation [1974].

Van Dijk, Herman K., Teun Kloek, and C. Guus-E Boender. 1985. "Posterior Moments Computed by Mixed Integration." *Journal of Econometrics* 29: 3–18.

Vig, Norman J., and Michael E. Kraft. 1984. *Environmental Policy in the 1980's.* Washington, D.C.: Congressional Quarterly Press.

Waldo, Dwight. 1984. *The Administrative State: A Study of the Political Theory of American Public Administration.* New York: Ronald Press.

———. 1990. "A Theory of Public Administration Means in Our Time a Theory of Politics Also." In *Public Administration: The State of the Discipline,* ed. Naomi B. Lynn and Aaron Wildavsky. Chatham, N.J.: Chatham House Publishers.

Waterman, Richard W. 1989. *Presidential Influence and the Administrative State.* Knoxville: University of Tennessee Press.

Waterman, Richard W., and Kenneth J. Meier. 1998. "Principal-Agent Models: An Expansion?" *Journal of Public Administration Research and Theory* 8: 173–202.

Waterman, Richard W., Amelia Rouse, and Robert Wright. 1998. "The Venues of Influence: A New Theory of Political Control of the Bureaucracy." *Journal of Public Administration Research and Theory* 8: 13–38.

Weaver, Suzanne. 1977. *Decision to Prosecute: Organization and Public Policy in the Antitrust Division.* Cambridge, Mass.: MIT Press.

Weber, Max. 1946. *From Max Weber: Essays in Sociology.* Translated by H. H. Gerth and C. Wright Mills. New York: Oxford University Press.

Weingast, Barry R. 1981. "Regulation, Reregulation, and Deregulation: The Political Foundations of Agency-Clientele Relationships." *Law and Contemporary Problems* 44: 147–77.

———. 1984. "The Congressional Bureaucratic System: A Principal-Agent Perspective (with Applications to the SEC)." *Public Choice* 44: 147–91.

Weingast, Barry R., and Mark J. Moran. 1982. "The Myth of Runaway Bureaucracy: The Case of the FTC." *Regulation* 6 (May/June): 33–38.

———. 1983. "Bureaucratic Discretion or Congressional Control: Regulatory Policymaking by the Federal Trade Commission." *Journal of Political Economy* 91: 765–80.

West, William F., and Joseph Cooper. 1989–1990. "Legislative Influence Versus Presidential Dominance: Competing Models of Political Control." *Political Science Quarterly* 104: 581–606.

White, Halbert. 1980. "A Heteroskedastic-Consistent Covariance Matrix Estimator and a Direct Test for Heteroskedasticity." *Econometrica* 48: 817–38.

Wildavsky, Aaron. 1964. *The Politics of the Budgetary Process.* 1st edition. Boston: Little, Brown.

———. 1979. *The Politics of the Budgetary Process.* 2d edition. Boston: Little, Brown.

Williams, John T. 1993. "What Goes Around Comes Around: Unit Root Tests and Cointegration." *Political Analysis* 4: 229–36.

Williams, John T., and Michael D. McGinnis. 1988. "Reaction in a Rational Expectations Arms Race Model of U.S.-Soviet Rivalry." *American Journal of Political Science* 32: 968–95.

———. 1992. "Expectations and the Dynamics of U.S. Defense Budget Requests: A Critique of Organizational Reaction Models." In *The Political Economy of Military Spending in the United States,* ed. Alex Mintz, 282–304. New York: Harper-Collins.

Williamson, Oliver E. 1975. *Markets and Hierarchies: Analysis and Antitrust Implications.* New York: Free Press.

———. 1985. *The Economic Institutions of Capitalism: Firms, Markets, Relational Contracting.* New York: Free Press.

Wilson, James Q. 1980. *The Politics of Regulation.* New York: Free Press.

———. 1989. *Bureaucracy: What Government Agencies Do and Why They Do It.* New York: Basic Books.

Wilson, Woodrow. 1887. "The Study of Administration." *Political Science Quarterly* 2: 197–222.

Woll, Peter. 1963. *American Bureaucracy.* New York: Norton.

Wood, B. Dan. 1988. "Principals, Bureaucrats, and Responsiveness in Clean Air Enforcement." *American Political Science Review* 82: 213–34.

———. 1990. "Does Politics Make a Difference at the EEOC?" *American Journal of Political Science* 34: 503–30.

———. 1991. "Federalism and Policy Responsiveness: The Clean Air Case." *Journal of Politics* 53: 851–59.

————. 1992. "Modeling Federal Implementation as a System: The Clean Air Case." *American Journal of Political Science* 36: 40–67.

Wood, B. Dan, and James E. Anderson. 1992. "Bureaucratic Responsiveness and Administrative Design: The Independent Regulatory Commission Versus the Executive Bureau." Paper presented at the annual meetings of the Midwest Political Science Association, Chicago, Illinois. April.

————. 1993. "The Politics (or Non-Politics) of U.S. Antitrust Regulation." *American Journal of Political Science* 37: 1–40.

Wood, B. Dan, and Richard Waterman. 1991. "The Dynamics of Political Control of the Bureaucracy." *American Political Science Review* 85: 801–28.

————. 1993. "The Dynamics of Political-Bureaucratic Adaptation." *American Journal of Political Science* 37: 497–528.

————. 1994. *Bureaucratic Dynamics: The Role of a Bureaucracy in a Democracy.* Boulder, Colo.: Westview Press.

Woolley, John T. 1984. *Monetary Politics: The Federal Reserve and the Politics of Monetary Policy.* Cambridge, England: Cambridge University Press.

————. 1988. "Partisan Manipulation of the Economy: Another Look at Monetary Policy with Moving Regression." *Journal of Politics* 50: 334–60.

————. 1993. "Conflict Among Regulators and the Hypothesis of Congressional Dominance." *Journal of Politics* 55: 92–114.

Worsham, Jeff, Marc A. Eisner, and Evan J. Ringquist. 1997. "Assessing the Assumptions: A Critical Analysis of the Positive Theory of Political Control." *Administration and Society* 28: 419–40.

Yandle, Bruce. 1988. "Antitrust Actions and the Budgeting Process." *Public Choice* 59: 263–75.

Yates, Douglas. 1982. *Bureaucratic Democracy: The Search for Democracy and Efficiency in American Government.* Cambridge, Mass.: Harvard University Press.

Zellner, Arnold. 1971. *An Introduction to Bayesian Inference in Econometrics.* New York: John Wiley and Sons.

Index

Aberbach, Joel D., 2, 5

Addlyston Pipe and Steel Company v. U.S. (1899), 49

Administrative (agency) design, 4–42, 68, 88, 100–101, 109

Agency (administrative or bureaucratic) behavior, 3, 4, 6–15, 17–18, 35, 37; SEC enforcement behavior, 43–48, 67, 69, 73, 75; Antitrust Division enforcement behavior, 49–58; policy output, 59; political sensitivity to enforcement cases, 62, 66, 74, 84; Antitrust Division Enforcement Outputs, 86–88, 92, 98, 100, 101, 116, 129, 131–32

Agency budgets, 23

Akaike, H., 141

Allison, Graham, 32

Amacher, Ryan C., 87

Amemiya, Takeshi, 141

American Tobacco Corporation v. U.S. (1911), 50

Anderson, James E., 2, 8, 9, 12, 17, 18, 23, 30, 54, 57, 59, 62, 85, 87, 88, 102, 104, 113, 121, 132, 136

Anticipated (predictable) behavior, 31, 69, 82, 99, 105–06, 111, 118, 137

Antitrust Division (Department of Justice), 16, 25, 35, 38, structure and function, 39–42, Economic Policy Office (EPO), 52–54, 56, 87; changing regulatory priorities, 59; empirical application of dynamic systems model 84–99, 102–3, 105, 113; summary of empirical results, 114–17, 130

Antitrust regulation: policy background and history, 48–55; trusts, 49; Sherman Act, 49–50; Clayton Act, 50, 55; goals, 49; trustbusting, 49–50; rule of reason doctrine, 50; structure-conduct-performance (SCP),

50–53; Cellar-Kefauver Act, 51; Hart-Scott-Rodino Act, 52; Chicago school of economics, 52–56; Reagan's administrative strategy, 53–55; Merger Modification Act, 55; partisan differences, 59; determinants of, 85–88, 123, 130

Anderson, James E., 2, 8, 9, 12, 17, 18, 23, 30, 54, 57, 59, 62, 85, 87, 88, 102, 104, 113, 121, 132, 136

Arnold, Peri E., 8

Arnold, Thurman, 51

Arrow, Kenneth, 17

AT&T, 51

Austen-Smith, David, 14

Axelrod, Robert, 37, 92

Banks, Jeffrey, S., 6, 27, 32, 41, 60

Barnard, Chester I., 10, 15, 76, 100, 120, 121

Baruch, Hurd, 96

Baxter, William, 54

Beck, Nathaniel, 140

Bendor, Jonathan, 2, 3, 6, 9, 12, 14, 18, 23, 27, 32, 33, 41, 48, 60, 64, 66, 109, 111, 122, 146

Boender, C. Guus-E., 138

Bond, Jon R., 13, 62, 72

Bork, Robert H., 53

Bounded rationality, 32, 36, 65, 107

Breton, Albert, 7

Bryner, Gary C., 6, 74, 81

Budgetary behavior, 18, 48, 64, 67, 106, 118

Budgetary politics, 13, 62, 72

Budgetary signals, 14, 18, 48, 60, 62, 69-76, 78, 81–82, 84, 87–88, 90, 92–93, 95–100, 101–03, 106, 110, 113–15, 131

Bureaucracy, greater delegation of responsibility, 2

Bureaucratic autonomy, definition, 4; sources